WOMEN IN BRITISH PUBLIC LIFE, 1914–1950

University
Of Dundee
UNIVERSITY LIBRARY

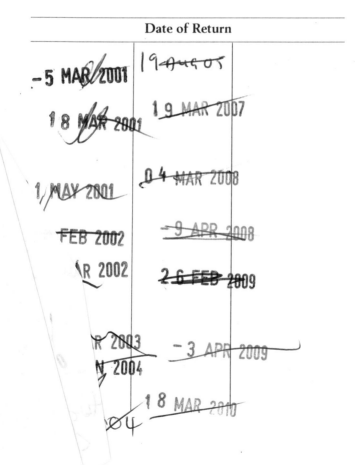

WOMEN AND MEN IN HISTORY

This series, published for students, scholars and interested general readers, will tackle themes in gender history from the early medieval period through to the present day. Gender issues are now an integral part of all history courses and yet many traditional texts do not reflect this change. Much exciting work is now being done to redress the gender imbalances of the past, and we hope that these books will make their own substantial contribution to that process. We hope that these will both synthesize and shape future developments in gender studies.

The General Editors of the series are *Patricia Skinner* (University of Southampton) for the medieval period; *Pamela Sharpe* (University of Bristol) for the early modern period; and *Penny Summerfield* (University of Lancaster) for the modern period. *Margaret Walsh* (University of Nottingham) was the Founding Editor of the series.

WOMEN IN BRITISH
PUBLIC LIFE, 1914–1950

Gender, Power and Social Policy

Helen Jones

Longman

An imprint of **Pearson Education**

Harlow, England · London · New York · Reading, Massachusetts · San Francisco
Toronto · Don Mills, Ontario · Sydney · Tokyo · Singapore · Hong Kong · Seoul
Taipei · Cape Town · Madrid · Mexico City · Amsterdam · Munich · Paris · Milan

Pearson Education Limited
Edinburgh Gate
Harlow
Essex CM20 2JE
England

and Associated Companies throughout the world

Visit us on the World Wide Web at:
http://www.pearsoneduc.com

First published 2000

ISBN 0 582 27731 0 PPR
       0 582 27732 9 CASED

British Library Cataloguing-in-Publication Data
A catalogue record for this book is available from the British Library

Library of Congress Cataloging-in-Publication Data
A catalog record for this book is available from the Library of Congress, USA

Set in 11/13pt Baskerville
Typeset by 35
Printed and bound in Great Britain by
T.J. International Ltd., Padstow, Cornwall

CONTENTS

CONTENTS

ACKNOWLEDGEMENTS

I am particularly grateful to Penny Summerfield, the series editor, as well as Jon Lawrence, Philippa Levine, John Macnicol, Alison Oram, Susan Pedersen and Ina Zweiniger-Bargielowska for their comments on various chapters.

For biographical details I have relied heavily on Olive Banks, *The Biographical Dictionary of British Feminists* vol. 1 (Brighton, 1985) and vol. 2 (1990).

Place of publication is London, unless otherwise stated.

PUBLISHER'S ACKNOWLEDGEMENTS

We are grateful to the following for permission to reproduce copyright material:

Plate 1 reprinted with permission from the Western Morning News Co Ltd; Plate 2 reprinted with permission from Save the Children; Plate 3 reprinted with permission from the Hulton Getty Picture Collection; Plate 4 reprinted with permission from the Hulton Getty Picture Collection; Plate 5 reprinted with permission from the Hulton Getty Picture Collection; Plate 6 reprinted with permission from Mary Evans Picture Library/Bruce Castle Museum; Plate 7 reprinted with permission from the Mary Evans Picture Library/ Fawcett Library; Plate 8 reprinted with permission from Lewisham Library.

AAM	Association of Assistant Mistresses
AHM	Association of Head Mistresses
ALP	Australian Labor Party
AMSH	Association for Moral and Social Hygiene
ATS	Auxiliary Territorial Service
BFBPW	British Federation of Business and Professional Women
BMA	British Medical Association
BDF	Bund Deutscher Frauenvereine (Federation of German Women's Associations)
CCG	Control Commission for Germany
CCWE	Central Committee on Women's Employment
CCWTE	Central Committee on Women's Training and Employment
CMC	Children's Minimum Council
COS	Charity Organisation Society
CWA	Country Women's Association
DBE	Dame of the British Empire
DFW	Deutsches Frauenwerk
DORA	Defence of the Realm Act
DP	displaced person
ECCC	Equal Compensation Campaign Committee
EPCC	Equal Pay Campaign Committee
ETS	Emergency Training Scheme
FANY	First Aid Nursing Yeomanry
FES	Family Endowment Society
FRG	Federal Republic of Germany
GDR	German Democratic Republic
GNC	General Nursing Council
GPO	General Post Office

HC Deb   Hansard Parliamentary debates
HMI   His Majesty's Inspector
HMWC   Health of Munition Workers' Committee

ICW   International Council of Women
ILP   Independent Labour Party
IMR   infant mortality rate
IRO   International Relief Organisation
IWM   Imperial War Museum

LCC   London County Council
LEA   Local Education Authority
LGB   Local Government Board

MMC   Maternal Mortality Committee
MMR   maternal mortality rate
MP   Member of Parliament
MWF   Medical Women's Federation

NBCA   National Birth Control Association
NCW   National Council of Women
NFWW   National Federation of Women Workers
NHS   National Health Service
NRF   National Relief Fund
NSA   Nursery Schools Association
NSA   National Sound Archive
NSD   National Service Department
NSF   Nationalsozialiste Frauenschaft (Nazi Women's Section)
NSPCC   National Society for the Prevention of Cruelty to Children
NUSEC   National Union of Societies for Equal Citizenship
NUWSS   National Union of Women's Suffrage Societies
NUT   National Union of Teachers
NUWT   National Union of Women Teachers
NYA   National Youth Administration

ODC   Open Door Council
ONMI   Opera Nazionale per la Maternità ed Infanzia (National Agency for Maternity and Infancy)

PBC   Pass the Bill Committee
PMB   private member's bill
POW   prisoner of war

PPS	parliamentary private secretary
PPU	Peace Pledge Union
PRO	Public Records Office
RAMC	Royal Army Medical Corps
RCN	Royal College of Nursing
SCF	Save the Children Fund
SF	Society of Friends
SSFA	Soldiers' and Sailors' Families Association
TG	Townswomen's Guild
TUC	Trades Union Congress
UAB	Unemployment Assistance Board
UAP	United Australia Party
UN	United Nations
UFCS	Union Féminine Civique et Sociale
UNRRA	United Nations Relief and Rehabilitation Administration
VAD	Voluntary Aid Detachment
VD	venereal disease
WAAC	Women's Auxiliary Army Corps
WCG	Women's Cooperative Guild
WFL	Women's Freedom League
WGPW	Women's Group on Public Welfare
WI	Women's Institute
WILPF	Women's International League for Peace and Freedom
WPC	Woman Power Committee
WPPA	Women's Publicity and Planning Association
WRAF	Women's Royal Air Force
WRC	War Relief Committee
WRNS	Women's Royal Naval Service
WSPU	Women's Social and Political Union
WTUL	Women's Trade Union League
WVS	Women's Voluntary Service
YWCA	Young Women's Christian Association

CHAPTER ONE

Introduction

The current position of women in politics

Twenty years after Britain's first woman Prime Minister took office senior women politicians are still hot news. In the mid-1990s women's role in national politics was again thrust centre stage with the controversy over women-only short lists for constituencies to select Labour Party candidates. Following the 1997 general election women MPs remained in the limelight. There were 120 women MPs elected of whom 101 were Labour, 14 Conservative and 6 from other parties. Women now comprised 18 per cent of MPs, a big leap up from the previous parliament. The dramatic increase in women MPs came largely on the Labour benches, due to Labour's women-only short lists, already outlawed by the time of the election, coupled with Labour's landslide victory.

As well as more women MPs, the number of women in government was greater than in the past, but not impressive. Tony Blair, the Prime Minister, appointed 5 women to his Cabinet; this figure, although not all the faces, remained unchanged after his first Cabinet reshuffle a year later. The arrival of increasing numbers of women in top jobs can be seen in many sections of society. In the professions women are catching up with men numerically but the more prestigious professions – and top positions within all professions – are systematically, although not exclusively, filled with men.

Following the 1997 general election serious analysis of Westminster gender politics was camouflaged under the popular press's image of 'Blair's babes'. There has been a mushrooming of press coverage of women in politics, but little reflective analysis. Newspaper articles in the broadsheets on women in politics still refer to the women's clothes and hair. The focus of media attention has been on the impact of more women MPs on the working of the House of Commons, and whether the structures are being put in place for more women-friendly policies to emerge across government. When in opposition, Labour had promised a Minister for Women with a seat in the Cabinet. In office, Blair tacked the responsibility on to another portfolio; it was an appendage to Harriet Harman's role as Secretary of State for Social Security, 1997–98, and then, after her sacking, to that of Baroness Jay, Leader of the House of Lords, who eschews the label 'feminist'. Blair also created a Women's Unit, serviced by a small team of civil servants, to coordinate and promote women-friendly policies across Whitehall. All policy proposals should now carry an explanation of their implications for women. The Women's Unit's launch and now its workings are much more low-key than the Social Exclusion Unit, established on the same principles.

Harriet Harman, in her first major speech after the 1997 general election, claimed that it had been a turning point in women's history. She went on to say that one of her principal concerns was to make sure that public policy recognised women's changing roles and particularly their need to combine work and home responsibilities. Later, in February 1998, while still in the Cabinet, she claimed that the government was committed to 'building and sustaining a new habit of governance that has women's voices and women's interests at its very 'heart'. A number of commentators have, however, asserted that gender politics are not fashionable under New Labour and that the coterie of ministers and advisors at the heart of government have created a 'laddish' culture. As a result of women's campaigns many women's issues have become mainstream, but in the process they have lost their radical edge and have been incorporated into a non-feminist agenda.

The question has been raised as to whether women MPs pursue women-friendly policies, as distinct from demanding more convenient working conditions for themselves. While the press has judged back-bench women largely by their commitment to women's issues, they judge women Cabinet ministers more on perceptions of their general competence. It is too soon to make assessments of the current clutch of women politicians, and generalisations about them and policies for women are fraught with difficulties. Clear differences between women MPs are obvious. Not only do policy differences and strategies vary between women in the different parties, but there are also differences between the attitudes and policies of backbenchers and ministers, and long-serving MPs and new ones. It is difficult, too, to demarcate particular policies as being 'women's policies'; what may be 'woman-friendly' for one woman or group of women, may not be so for other women.

These debates over women's role in national politics and policy making continue despite more than 70 years of women's enfranchisement, entry into

Parliament and presence in the civil service. Overcoming the enfranchisement hurdle (in part in 1918 and in full in 1928) was a huge achievement, but barriers to women's full and equal participation in national politics and policy making remained in place. The extent of their entrenchment is evidenced by women's continuing struggles at the turn of the twenty-first century. The main aim of this book is to examine women's social policy priorities and strategies in the first flush of enfranchisement and in a period of extensive restructuring and extension of state welfare. It analyses the role of women in policy making and the mechanisms of discrimination which operated against them. It is a study of gender, power and social policy making.

Definitions of gender, power and social policy making

Gender refers to the social construction of differences between women and men. As it is socially created it is possible to change it, and for it to change over time, both between and within societies.

Political scientists argue at length over definitions of *power*. In the context of social policy making it is the ability to make appointments and to determine aspects of policy. It involves having the right, and the resources, to take advantage of opportunities to participate in full in the decision-making process. Ham and Hill have emphasised the dynamic nature of decision making for policies. Thus, they have argued that *policy making* involves a course of action, or a web of decisions, rather than one single decision at one particular time. They argue that a decision network of great complexity may be involved over a long period. Policies can, of course, be as much about resisting as facilitating change.[1] As policy making is a process, often long-drawn-out, it was (and still is) important for women to be a part of the on-going process. It was (and is) not enough to offer opinions which may or may not be taken into account, or to be consulted on an arbitrary basis. It is important to be a consistent part, by right, of the policy process. One of the issues, therefore, with which this book is concerned is the role of women in policy making as politicians, civil servants or as experts in the fields of health and education.

It cannot be assumed that a member of any group, whether it be 'women' or civil servants, has a pre-determined set of attitudes and assumptions

---

1. Chris Ham and Michael Hill, *The Policy Process in the Modern Capitalist State*, 2nd edn. (Hemel Hempstead, 1993), p. 12.

which is brought to bear on policy making. It is necessary to tease these out. The *methodology* for investigating the ideas behind policies is not straightforward. This book draws on written sources, both unpublished and published. There is always a problem of how far those committing their views to paper are willing, or indeed able, to express them in writing, and how far the process of committing thoughts to paper actually changes them. Civil servants may be working in a shared political and cultural environment where it is not considered necessary or desirable to state explicitly their assumptions; thoughts committed to paper may be only the tip of the ideological iceberg, or expressed in a culturally coded language.

The debate

Historians' interest in governance during the period from 1914 to 1950 has focused on the way in which trade unions and employers' organisations arguably became part of the central government decision-making machinery. This shared decision making grew, according to Middlemas, from access for consultation during the First World War to full-blown shared responsibility for policy making in the Second World War.[2] Both Middlemas and his critics argue about the nature, speed and consistency of the process which he has identified. They do not attack the study for its lack of a gender analysis of policy making. Yet, employers' organisations and the labour movement were both male-dominated and largely reflected an industrial male power base. At a time when there was increased, albeit uneven, male pressure group influence on government, women's pressure group influence and role in policy making remained marginal.

Koven and Michel have shown how women, in a number of western countries, focused on influencing governments' maternal and child welfare policies. They rightly argue that maternalist policies were not only concerned with the welfare and rights of women and children, but also with critiquing the wider state and society. They claim that women transformed motherhood from women's primary private responsibility into public policy. While Koven and Michel maintain that women were a powerful influence in defining the needs of mothers and children, and in shaping institutions to meet these needs, a number of the chapters in their book consider the constraints on women in shaping policies and institutions. Although it is true, as Koven

---

2. Keith Middlemas, *Politics in Industrial Society: The Experience of the British System since 1911* (1979).

and Michel assert, that male bureaucracies, politicians and propaganda often encouraged women in their welfare work, nevertheless, they discouraged them when the women appeared to challenge either government policies or the processes and institutions which maintained male authority.[3]

A number of historians, who have looked at the influence of women on the emerging system of state welfare, have focused on the late nineteenth and early twentieth centuries. They argue that women had substantial influence on the development of the welfare state through voluntary organisations. Koven and Michel, Thane, Skocpol and Rutter, look at the late nineteenth and early twentieth centuries, yet it was in the 1940s that the main increases in state welfare took place.[4]

Here the focus is on the years of both world wars (1914–18 and 1939–45) and the years leading up to (1920s and 1930s), and including, the main period (1940s) of increased state welfare and restructuring of welfare provision. The aim is to provide an analysis of British women's direct role in central government social policy making in an era of major social upheaval and restructuring of welfare provision.

Themes and arguments

During the Victorian and Edwardian years women had challenged the educational, employment and welfare systems. They had operated, for the most part, around the periphery of state power. Women had exercised considerable power in local charitable work and in local government. Developments in welfare provision then shifted from the local to the national stage, and for this reason the focus here is on national politics.

As the new century dawned women had successfully opened up for themselves a role in public life and had organised numerous pressure groups which lobbied governments for change. For a number of years governments had offered women *ad hoc* appointments as civil servants or places on government enquiries. The limitations of a temporary, outsider's role in

---

3. Seth Koven and Sonya Michel, eds, *Mothers of a New World: Maternalist Politics and the Origins of Welfare States* (1993).
4. Pat Thane, 'Women in the British Labour Party and the construction of state welfare, 1906–1939', in Seth Koven and Sonya Michel, eds, *Mothers of a New World*; Theda Skocpol and Gretcher Ritter, 'Gender and the origins of modern social policies in Britain and the US', *Studies in American Political Development*, 5, 1991, pp. 36–93; Theda Skocpol, *Protecting Soldiers and Mothers: The Political Origins of Social Policy in the USA* (1992). For a review of, and contribution to, the debate see Jane Lewis, 'Gender, the family and women's agency in the building of "welfare states": the British case', *Social History*, 19, 1994, pp. 37–50.

policy making have already been mentioned. This book looks at the opportunities for, and barriers to, women taking a full role in policy making at a time when Britain was moving towards greater political rights through enfranchisement and more social rights through a state welfare system. It will be explained how and why, despite these developments, and women's manifest expertise and interest in social welfare, in areas such as health and education, women as a group were systematically discriminated against and excluded from the policy-making process. Women did not have the insiders' ability to network informally but had to rely on more cumbersome, formal and less effective lobbying. Women's role in policy making continued to be primarily as campaigners, not policy makers. Women's campaigns often ran counter to government economic policy and entrenched attitudes, hostile both to policies advocated by women's groups and to the women's groups themselves.

Women campaigners attempted to stamp their ideas on domestic social policy making and to inject a social policy dimension into international affairs. They tried to play a part in the policy-making process through the civil service; through Parliament; through lobbying government; through teaching, nursing, medicine and social work, and through promoting charitable services, which it was hoped government would imitate.

Government departments' targeting of resources and prioritising services often worked against women's demands. Women's whole approach was often more integrated and less compartmentalised than government organisation and attitudes could, or would, accommodate. Despite divisions between women, all the major welfare campaigns of the period recognised the unequal distribution of resources in families. The priority of women campaigners was poor working-class women and children in Britain, and middle-class women and children fallen on hard times on the Continent. From the First World War, British women were involved to an unprecedented extent with the welfare of continental Europeans. The gendered impact of poverty was the intellectual tree from which their campaigns and policies sprouted. The unemployment and fascism of the 1930s did not eclipse a gendered analysis of poverty, but contributed to one and gave it an added urgency.

The ability of women to contribute to policy in both world wars was strictly limited, even though they undertook responsible work in, and for, the government. Women were, for the most part, implementing decisions already taken. In both wars women were brought into government after certain key decisions affecting women had been reached. Women's role was, nevertheless, greater in war than in peace, and greater in the Second World War than in the First World War. Both wars created opportunities for women, but fewer for them than for men. In the Second World War, especially, the close relationship between women's organisations and government was vital to the effective pursuit of the war on the home front.

In both war and peace, few women played a direct part in policy making, and because there were so few women their work had no trickle-down effect on the power of women in general. There were too few well-placed women to create a network which could effectively challenge and dislodge structures and cultures which operated to women's disadvantage. In Parliament there were never more than 15 women at any one time, there were no women in the House of Lords and only a handful in the administrative grade of the civil service. Men, not women, had the power of appointment and promotion. Individual women exercised power, but not groups of women. As the numbers of women were small they were unrepresentative of the vast array of interests and circumstances of women, and this again limited the collective and feminist powers of women. Those women with influence, moreover, did not necessarily use it to enhance other women's policy-making powers.

Among women politicians, civil servants and women employed in health and education, their ability to exercise power related to the extent of the hierarchy in which they operated, the degree of flexibility and discipline, the homogeneity of the environment and the extent of an established male culture. Although there were women mounting attacks on governments across a range of domestic and foreign policy issues, and often linking the two through their analysis of welfare, there is little evidence that women in health and education, despite their expertise and experience, were able to contribute directly to decision making for welfare policies.

The most radical campaigns of women were not, moreover, wholeheartedly pursued by women through the political parties, which all sidelined women's issues. Women politicians displayed a mixed attitude towards women's specific needs. Not all women MPs believed in speaking on women's issues. They were, in any case, greatly constrained by the culture and practices of Parliament, and divided – like so many other women – over what they regarded as being in women's interests.

The effects of political culture permeated all areas, and its importance is underlined by reference to the fortunes of women in a number of other countries – France, Germany, Italy, Australia and the USA. When governments, whether in Britain or abroad, adopted policies advocated by women, it was to shore up existing gender relations, not to bring them tumbling down.[5]

---

5. It is recognised that there are certain differences in selection and presentation of the secondary comparative material which is utilised here but, at a general level, there is a value in this comparative enquiry.

Making the difference in Victorian and Edwardian Britain

During the first half of the twentieth century many changes sought by women in their lives depended on governmental social reforms. In the nineteenth century, starting from a lower base line, middle-class women were able to bring about changes in their lives without such heavy reliance on central government. Changes which women achieved in the nineteenth century in the fields of employment, local politics and education were the starting point and foundation for women's campaigns in the twentieth century.

In the early part of the nineteenth century most middle-class girls received their education at home; some attended private day schools. The aim of this education was to fit girls for their future role as wives and mothers, a role which middle-class convention dictated would exclude them from the paid labour force. When social disaster struck and young women failed to marry, male relatives were expected to look after them. Paid work for 'respectable' middle-class women was not an option. The hostility of male professionals, middle-class culture and the lack of suitable education all excluded women from training for professional employment. In the second half of the nineteenth century women began to provide suitable education by setting up girls' schools with academic curricula, and this in turn started to erode middle-class employment conventions. From the early 1870s the Girls' Public Day School Company (later Trust) established 38 schools; from the early 1880s the Church Schools Company opened 33 high schools. In the last three decades of the nineteenth century over 90 girls' grammar schools were founded.

The new girls' schools were not without their critics. Medical arguments were deployed against educating girls beyond puberty for fear of inducing insanity or diverting energy from the reproductive organs to the brain. Not all women approved of academically oriented schools, and the growing number of girls' schools consequently offered a diverse curriculum. Some women argued that schools should offer a curriculum designed to enhance girls' feminine qualities. Other women believed that girls should receive the same education as boys, so that girls would be equipped to compete in the boys' world.

Middle-class girls' education expanded to give an increasing number of young women the skills they required for economic independence, should a husband not materialise. The drive to raise academic standards and draw more girls into schools formed part of the overall strategy of those women who were trying to open up the public world to women. They perceived education as the *sine qua non* for wider opportunities. Women who ran schools with an academically challenging curriculum kept one eye on the labour market.

At the same time as women were establishing academic schools they were also campaigning for access to higher education. In the 1860s women gained admission to classes run by the university extension movement. In 1878 the University of London opened its doors to women on the same basis as men. It was followed in 1892 by Scottish universities, and in 1895 by the University of Durham. While women were gradually gaining entry to the universities, many had to run the gauntlet of prejudice from family, friends, and male members of the universities. Even so, by 1900 women comprised 16 per cent of university students. (The percentage of women students rose to 24 per cent in 1920, 27 per cent in 1930, dipping on the outbreak of the Second World War to 23 per cent.) Expanding educational opportunities meant greater employment opportunities, although it was not easy for women to step outside nineteenth-century middle-class culture with its artificially devised ideal public and paid world of men, and private and unpaid world of women.

Unpaid voluntary work with the local poor was an acceptable extension of middle-class women's home-based caring role. Voluntary work enabled women to contribute to the local community – usually poor women and children – through the skills they supposedly possessed as a result of their innate feminine qualities. When middle-class women broke into paid work it was a variation on the voluntary and caring theme. Teaching, nursing and social work all fitted the bill. There are no accurate figures for the number of women in paid work on the eve of the First World War. According to the 1911 census, which underestimated the number of women because some had refused to cooperate with it on account of their exclusion from the parliamentary franchise, there were 187,283 women teachers; 477 surgeons and general practitioners; 19,437 Poor Law, municipal, and parish officers and 31,538 civil servants.

By visiting the poor in their homes, workhouses and prisons, women gained a foothold in the running of local institutions dealing with the poor. This was all work, whether paid or unpaid, which was more or less respectable, reflecting the supposedly caring, sharing side of women's characters. In 1869 single, rate-paying women gained the municipal franchise; in 1870 they were permitted to sit on school boards; and in 1875 they could become Poor Law Guardians. In 1894 the same rights were extended to married women. By the dawn of the twentieth century there were roughly 1,000 Poor Law Guardians, 200 women members of school boards and 200 women parish councillors. Although there were relatively few women on school boards and women Poor Law Guardians, there were enough of them to influence local provision and policies. They could network effectively, and offer a distinctive contribution to the public, although still local, world.

Every step middle-class women took into the local public world of policy making and policy implementation was ideologically and organically linked to the previous one. As each step was justified and accepted with reference to the previous step, the process was slow and gradual. Not only was women's local public role portrayed as unconnected to national politics, but their role in local politics was also used as an additional justification for their exclusion from national politics. Anti-suffragists argued that women and men should play a complementary role in politics, as in other aspects of life; women had a place in local politics, while men ran the country and empire. Yet, throughout the nineteenth century, middle-class and working-class women had participated in national pressure group politics, such as the campaign against the 1834 Poor Law, Chartism, the Anti-Corn Law League, the temperance movement, divorce law reform, the campaign against slavery, the repeal of the Contagious Diseases Acts, changes to the Factory Acts, and access to educational and employment opportunities. The campaign for the suffrage, joined by women of all classes, is the best remembered of women's campaigns, and provided women with the opportunity to develop their powers of leadership and organisational skills. Women demonstrated their interest in national politics throughout the century, but there were serious social and economic constraints on their political leadership.

Women who before the First World War were cutting their teeth in local politics and women's campaigns, later took their place, by right, on the national stage. Eleanor Rathbone, Susan Lawrence, Marion Phillips and Ethel Bentham were all involved in local politics, and later entered Parliament. In the 1890s Margaret McMillan sat on a Bradford school board; by the First World War she was a national campaigner for nursery schools. These women were, however, the exception to the rule. It was difficult for women to obtain nomination to stand in local elections, and even more difficult to win them. Male party bosses regarded women as an electoral liability, and a waste of a seat because men often saw local politics as a stepping stone to national politics, from which women were banned. Until 1918 Westminster excluded women; a few were to be found in the corridors of Whitehall, but rarely behind desks where they could contribute to policy making.

By 1914 women had permeated many government departments outside Westminster, beginning with the General Post Office (GPO), where female telegraph operators were appointed in 1870. From the 1870s the GPO, and from 1899 the Board of Education, employed women as clerks. Other departments followed. The women were often better educated and from a higher class background than their male colleagues, from whom many received a good deal of hostility. Even women graduates found it extremely hard to gain government work of a senior or responsible nature.

Women who were appointed to senior posts were usually *ad hoc* appointments, so no precedent was set for employing other women. In 1873 Mrs Nassau Senior became a woman inspector at the Local Government Board (LGB) to inspect and advise on workhouse schools; in 1886 Miss M.H. Mason was appointed an inspector of boarded-out children. She was followed in 1898 and 1901 by two other women. In 1897 Miss Stansfield became an Assistant Poor Law Inspector along with four nurses who were appointed as inspectors at the LGB, but working as assistants to men. In 1883 the first woman was appointed as an inspector to the Board of Education, and other women followed. In 1893 the first two women Factory Inspectors were appointed; by 1914 their number had reached 21. In 1904 Mrs H.E. Harrison became an inspector of girls' reformatory and industrial schools, and in 1908 the first woman was appointed an inspector of prisons. Other breakthroughs came in 1891 when four women were appointed assistant commissioners to the Royal Commission on Labour and other university-educated women were appointed clerks to the Commission. In 1893 Clara Collet was appointed to the labour department of the Board of Trade. The first appointments of an administrative character came in 1910 when labour exchanges were set up around the country in which women, mainly graduates, were employed. The 1911 National Insurance Act involved the appointment of Insurance Commissioners to run the system. Four women Insurance Commissioners were appointed, along with women at all other grades.

On the eve of the First World War women's future in the civil service was unclear. For years women had campaigned for equal access to the civil service, but women were still banned from sitting the examinations for entry to the administrative grades. Evidence to the Royal Commission on the Civil Service, 1912–15, was generally favourable about women's past contribution, but witnesses were diffident and divided over women's future role.

By the First World War a number of factors facilitated women's participation in the public sphere and suggested that they were on the verge of a breakthrough in terms of national politics and social policy making. By the early twentieth century the dominant nineteenth-century ideology of separate spheres for women and men, and the accompanying assumption that women's proper place was in the home was no longer applied so vigorously to single women or to women without children. There was still a strong social expectation, however, that wives and mothers would be at home for their husbands and children.

The middle class increasingly limited the size of their families so that middle-class women were healthier, less worn down by childbearing, and with more time on their hands to devote to non-household matters. As middle-class women's reproductive role changed, there was the potential for their role in the family to change as well.

Women had demonstrated their competence in local government and women pioneers in education, the civil service and local politics had all displayed women's abilities and desire to contribute to politics and the policy process. The demands for replacement labour and the growth of government with its accompanying insatiable demand for labour in the First World War would suggest that women were well placed to exploit their education, experience and desire for a role in the governance of the country.

CHAPTER TWO

First World War

Introduction

Historians of the nineteenth century have pointed to women's efforts to expand their educational and employment opportunities. When we come to the First World War we find little attempt to assess the impact of well-educated women on the war effort. Historians have judged the extent to which social attitudes and gender divisions broke down by focusing on working-class women who took up industrial work.[1] Yet, these women were working-class, and thus unlikely to be in a position to make government policy decisions. In order to analyse the role of the war in enhancing women's policy-making power, it is important to consider those women, who although far fewer in number, were potentially well placed to take policy decisions themselves. While women entered a wide range of employment, very few stepped into senior management or advisory roles, even though government incorporated more men into such positions. Although women lacked the parliamentary franchise they had experience of local government, and central government had in the past used, and continued to use, a select number of women in quite senior and advisory roles. Why was the potential of educated and experienced women only partially realised?

Here it will be argued first, that weaknesses in the machinery of government (demonstrated by the National Service Department (NSD) and reconstruction planning) reduced both women's and men's influence; and second,

---

1. Angela Woollacott, *On Her Their Lives Depend: Munition Workers in the Great War* (Berkeley and Los Angeles CA, 1994); Gail Braybon, *Women Workers in the First World War: The British Experience* (1981).

that politicians and civil servants failed to appreciate the positive contribution women could make to policy decisions.

Middle-class women's authority over working-class women in the public arena was more a vicarious power of men operating through women than any real power among women. Women who lobbied government over infant welfare, suffrage, and venereal disease (VD) policies only obtained what they wanted when it accorded with government thinking. Those making the most immediate contribution to the war in the field, as nurses, doctors and in the auxiliary forces, were not taking policy decisions. Similar patterns of incorporation and exclusion of women can be found not only in Britain but also in other combatant nations.

General histories point to the wartime governments, especially under the influence of David Lloyd George, embracing businessmen and the labour movement, and incorporating women into the lower spheres of government as typists and clerical workers. Little mention is made of the virtual absence of women further up the hierarchy, and in a hierarchical institution, such as Whitehall, this is significant. As there were so few women taking decisions, the influence that individual women enjoyed did not have a knock-on effect on women in general. Women with decision-making powers, moreover, did not necessarily seek to use their position to facilitate other women's climb up the ladder. While individual women's direct input to policy decisions grew, this did not signal a greater decision-making role for women, or even for particular groups of women. Beyond Whitehall women were carving out powerful niches for themselves, but often this was in temporary, war-related activities, such as welfare work, and at the expense of working-class women's autonomy.

At a time when the parliamentary system of government still excluded women, the war provided some women with an opportunity to exercise influence in Whitehall, not informally through their male relatives and friends, but on account of the government work they themselves undertook. Women had sat on Royal Commissions and government committees before the war, and were already employed in parts of the civil service. On one Royal Commission appointed before war broke out women were able to contribute to recommendations even more pertinent in war than in peace. The 15-strong membership of the Royal Commission on Venereal Diseases, set up in 1913, included three women, a well-known gynaecologist, Mary Dacomb Scharlieb, 1845–1930; Louise Creighton, a social purity feminist and widow of the Bishop of London; and Elizabeth Miriam Burgwin, an Inspector of the Feeble-Minded. As 'loose' women were regarded as a menace, as carriers and spreaders of VD to men, it would have been appropriate to appoint many more 'respectable' women to the Royal Commission; there were, for instance, a number of women doctors who could have been approached. When the commission's report appeared in 1916 it linked deaths at the Front, the declining birth rate, the efficiency of the workforce and the scourge of VD.[2] The need to combat VD was seen as even more urgent than in peacetime. Its recommendation for the free diagnosis and treatment of VD was incorporated into the 1916 Public Health (Venereal Diseases) Regulation Act. Many feminists criticised the report for failing to recommend practical steps for the prevention of the disease, although it did lead to a network of clinics around the country offering a free and confidential service.[3]

Women were divided in their views over morality and women's culpability for the spread of VD and some certainly helped to whip up concern over the morality of (mainly young) working-class women. Defence of the Realm Act (DORA) regulations gave naval and military authorities the power to exclude from those areas where soldiers and sailors were stationed, any woman with a conviction for soliciting. Although the regulations proved impossible to enforce, in March 1918 a further DORA regulation 40D made it an offence for a woman with VD to have sex with a member of the Forces. This imposition on women was opposed by feminist groups, along with the Trades Union Council (TUC) and press, but remained in force until after the Armistice.[4]

Working in Whitehall

Martin Pugh has commented upon upper-class and middle-class women, already known in political circles, entering wartime government, but he does not explore the influence of their work either on policy or on other women's employment opportunities.[5] Government only tardily put women in positions of responsibility, when forced into it by a labour shortage caused by the call-up of men and the expansion of government activity. Women joined the civil service on a temporary basis, often on war-related work, and frequently on work well below their capabilities. Nevertheless,

---

2. PP 1916 vol XVI Royal Commission on Venereal Diseases Final Report.
3. Lucy Bland, ' "Cleansing the portals of life": the venereal disease campaign in the early twentieth century', in Mary Langan and Bill Schwarz, eds, *Crises in the British State, 1880–1930* (1985), pp. 201–6.
4. Lucy Bland, ' "Cleansing the portals of life" ', p. 205; D. Evans, 'Tackling the "Hideous Scourge": the creation of the Venereal Disease Treatment Centres in early twentieth-century Britain', *Social History of Medicine* 5 (1992), p. 432.
5. Martin Pugh, *Women and the Women's Movement in Britain 1914–1959* (1992), p. 8.

they did exercise responsibility, mainly in the new departments of state, but also in old ones such as the War Office and Ministry of Agriculture. In the War Office, according to Hilda Martindale, 1875–1952, civil servant and author of *Women Servants of the State*, women drafted letters, prepared decisions that would bind the department, and exercised their own judgement to a considerable extent. The evidence of women's capability for responsible work did not, however, dislodge deep-seated prejudices, as witnessed by the mixed reports of committees set up to report on the future of the civil service. While civil servants were willing to use women in war, to release men for service and to keep the wages bill down, they did not necessarily think women should be employed in peacetime. One civil servant could see no advantage – to whom he did not say – in putting women on the same footing as men after the war. Another civil servant thought the work in his division 'very unsuitable for women' as it dealt with convict petitions relating to subjects 'undesirable for women'.[6]

On the eve of the First World War, women Factory Inspectors were among the most powerful women civil servants. They had responsibilities equal to those of their male colleagues and in some ways were in greater demand, but their salaries remained lower and their promotion prospects to the highest echelons non-existent. The war did appear at first to enhance the role of women Factory Inspectors. Before the war it was relatively easy for women to inspect only factories and workshops where women worked, but the war made this division impossible to sustain. As women took on work hitherto confined to men, so women Inspectors broadened the scope of their work and gained technical experience previously denied them as they inspected women making fuses, shells and aircraft. Women Inspectors were involved in substitution of women for men workers, in assessing the need for General and Emergency Orders (involving a relaxation of the Factory Acts) and in encouraging welfare throughout industry. They undertook work for the Ministry of Munitions' Health of Munition Workers' Committee (HMWC), the Board of Trade, Labour Exchanges and the War Office.[7] Constance Smith, a woman Factory Inspector, believed that the male Inspectors still resisted sharing power. In 1917 she wrote, 'Our "hierarchy" goes on in its old way, &, though every man of capacity has been taken from the Department, seems determined not to give the most experienced

---

6. H. Martindale, *Women Servants of the State, 1870–1938: A History of Women in the Civil Service* (1938), pp. 75–86. On the outbreak of war there were about 65,000 women civil servants of whom 58,000 were in the Post Office; by July 1919 there were 170,000 women in the civil service employed across Whitehall. PRO HO 45/11527.
7. Helen Jones, 'Women health workers: the case of the first women factory inspectors', *Social History of Medicine* 1 (1988), p.175.

of the women a shred of power.'[8] During the war women Inspectors' work was less concerned with the protection of women workers than with ensuring that they worked efficiently for the war effort. This shift away from the specific health needs of women at work towards more general work was confirmed after the war when the women's and men's branches of the Inspectorate were fused, a move which was meant to enhance the promotion prospects of women Inspectors.

The war created opportunities for a few well-connected women to take up responsible posts in Whitehall. The two women who potentially held the greatest power in Whitehall were May Tennant and Violet Markham who, at the beginning of 1917, were appointed Director and Deputy Director of the Women's Section of the NSD. The experiment was not a happy one and ended in mud-slinging and bad feeling. Interdepartmental in-fighting meant that their power was strictly circumscribed and their work short-lived.

May Tennant, 1869–1946, had a long-standing knowledge of women's work. She had been treasurer of the Women's Trade Union League (WTUL) and secretary to Lady Emilia Dilke, 1840–1904, leader of the WTUL and suffragist. In 1891 she was appointed one of the four women assistant commissioners on the Royal Commission on Labour and in 1893 she became a Factory Inspector, resigning soon after her marriage in 1896 to the Liberal MP Harold John Tennant. With her husband she campaigned for factory reform and she supported the setting up of Trade Boards to set minimum wages in some of the worst-paid trades. During the war she sat on the Central Committee on Women's Employment (CCWE) – later known as the Central Committee on Women's Training and Employment (CCWTE) – which initially tried to find work for unemployed women with a grant from Queen Mary's Work for Women Fund. Tennant acted as chief advisor to the Ministry of Munitions on women's welfare. (After the war she continued to serve on the CCWTE. She was a strong supporter of protective legislation. In the late 1920s she and Gertrude Tuckwell launched a pressure group to try and bring down the high maternal mortality rate.) Tuckwell, 1861–1951, had supported women's suffrage before the war but had thrown her energies into campaigning through trade unions for improvements in working-class women's wages and working conditions. She had been active in, and held a number of posts in, the Women's Trade Union League (WTUL), Women's Industrial Council, National Federation of Women Workers, and the Anti-Sweating League. (After the war she was a JP and a founder member of the Magistrates' Association with a special

---

8.   Helen Jones, ed., *Duty and Citizenship: The Correspondence and Papers of Violet Markham, 1896–1953* (1994), p. 84.

interest in probation. She continued to display a concern for working-class women's working conditions, calling for equal pay although she took more of an interest in women as mothers than in the past. She demanded widows' pensions but did not press for family allowances because she feared they would depress wages. Above all, she fought for improvements in women's health.)

Violet Markham, 1872–1959, mixed easily with politicians and civil servants. Before the war she had come into contact with young working-class women through a Settlement she established.[9] The war gave her an insight into working-class women's paid work, and it led to her playing a part in drawing up policies for women's employment. She seized an early opportunity to work on the Executive Committee of the National Relief Fund (NRF) when she was recommended by Sir Robert Morant, a senior civil servant who, at the time, was chair of the National Insurance Commission. The committee included Pamela McKenna (wife of the Liberal Home Secretary and then Chancellor, Reginald McKenna), and Mary Macarthur, a leading trade unionist (see below). As various committee members gradually drifted away, Markham persevered, and other opportunities grew out of her work on the NRF. The NRF spawned the CCWE, with which Markham was involved for many years. Out of her war work Markham gained a permanent foothold in Whitehall, not as a career civil servant but with more power than many with a more orthodox career path. (After the war she sat on the CCWTE. In 1934 she became the statutory woman member of the Unemployment Assistance Board, and from 1937 its deputy chair.)

The war altered Markham's views, most significantly in favour of votes for women, although her attitude towards working-class women's paid work remained ambiguous. While calling for widening fields of employment and higher wages for working-class women, after the war she confined her promotion of paid work for working-class women to domestic service. Her desire for expanded opportunities for middle-class women was reflected in her demand for women in senior civil service posts and for the amalgamation of the women's and men's branches of the Factory Inspectorate, partly in the hope that this would improve the career opportunities of women Factory Inspectors. The government used Markham on an ad hoc basis in 1918, when it appointed a committee of five women with Mrs Deane

---

9. From the late nineteenth century to the early twentieth century numbers of middle-class women and men with an interest in social problems spent a period of time living together in 'Settlements' in working-class areas of cities in order to try and improve the social conditions of the local poor.

Streatfield, an ex-Factory Inspector as chair, and Violet Markham as honorary secretary, to investigate the morals of Women's Auxiliary Army Corps (WAACs) in France. The inquiry team found no evidence of depravity. The inquiry stands as an example of the way in which the cooperation of women with government could reinforce double moral standards, for there was no inquiry into the morals of soldiers.

When Lloyd George became Prime Minister in December 1916 and appointed Neville Chamberlain as Director of the newly created NSD, the initial aim was to bring together under one roof, and to coordinate, military and civilian recruitment for the war effort, which until then had been undertaken in an inefficient fashion by an array of departments. Civil servants and ministers in the various departments were unwilling to hand over their previous work and Chamberlain was unable to assert his authority in Whitehall. Lloyd George, whatever his initial intentions, came to see the department more as a symbol of coordination than one with real authority. So, the department got off to an inauspicious start and when Tennant and Markham arrived at the beginning of 1917, they felt that too much time had already dragged on without any proper coordination of women's work, and that further costly governmental bureaucracy at this stage in the war was going to be difficult. In order to avoid irritation and disappointment among women eager to do suitable work, Tennant and Markham were determined to get the organisation in place before making appeals to women to take up war work. Even so, they were inundated with a host of what Markham dismissively described as amateurs in voluntary organisations wishing to give service. Tennant and Markham had to cope with the jealousy of the Employment Department of the Ministry of Labour, which Markham believed to be 'disastrous' and 'contrary to the public spirit'. Matters came to a head in June 1917 when the NSD and War Office clashed head-on over which department should be in charge of recruitment to the WAACs. Particularly galling for the women was that Neville Chamberlain appeared to side with the War Office and thus contributed to the weak position of the Women's Section. May Tennant was away for most of the period so it was left to Markham to fight the Section's corner, and she ended her period at the NSD with great bitterness towards Chamberlain.[10]

Just as government incorporated male businessmen and trade unionists into the policy-making process, so too it brought in women from industry, albeit in much more limited numbers: there was no critical mass of women making policy decisions. In August 1914 Mary Macarthur was immediately

---

10. David Dilks, *Neville Chamberlain, Vol. One: Pioneering and Reform, 1869–1929* (Cambridge, 1984), pp. 200, 217.

appointed to the committee running the Queen Mary Work for Women Fund and, when that became redundant, she moved to the Labour Supply Committee. Macarthur, 1880–1921, a close friend of Gertrude Tuckwell and Margaret Bondfield, worked to improve the conditions of women workers through trade unions. In 1903 she had become secretary of the WTUL and in 1906 she founded the National Federation of Women Workers (NFWW). From 1911 she had fought to improve women's position in the National Health Insurance system. Her biographer wrote of Macarthur's influence in inflated and individualised tones, presenting her as a flawed heroine. This individualising of women's achievements is in one sense correct, for it was individual women who took decisions, not groups of women. The higher up the hierarchy the fewer the women, thus women munitions workers could quite correctly be presented in a group portrait, for it was their numbers, as much as what any individual was doing, which were significant. They did not, however, decide the policies which were directed at them. When recounting Macarthur's attempts to defend their interests, her biographer described her role with military metaphors, and Macarthur's discussions with Lloyd George even took on a cloak and dagger flavour: 'The full history of that struggle will never be known – a struggle carried on largely in the twilight of Government buildings and Trade Union offices – sometimes even in the sanctity of Ministers' rooms, when one is almost choked by a suffocating mist, which is known as the official atmosphere . . .'[11]

Macarthur was fighting a rearguard action, for the really significant decisions about women's pay and working conditions were made early on in the war, without any prior discussion with representatives of women trade unionists, and embodied in March 1915 in the first Treasury agreement with male trade unionists. While the WTUL and NFWW were still worrying about women's unemployment they had been overtaken by events.[12] Decisions taken in Whitehall could be circumvented by employers, for example, agreements to pay women and men the same rate could be avoided by employers making slight alterations to the work process. Thus the presence of Mary Macarthur on the Central Munitions Labour Supply Committee and on the HMWC did not necessarily bring gains for working-class women.[13]

During the war Macarthur also sat on the CCWE, along with Susan Lawrence, Margaret Bondfield, Dr Marion Phillips, and Mrs Gasson. Apart

---

11. Mary Agnes Hamilton, *Mary Macarthur: A Biographical Sketch* (1925), p. 156. See also pp. 133–4.
12. Sarah Boston, *Women Workers and the Trade Union Movement* (1980), Chapter 4 for a full discussion of the subject.
13. Sheila Rowbotham, *A Century of Women* (1997), pp. 77–8.

from a sprinkling of some of the obligatory upper-class ladies, all the women on the CCWE had a track record of defending working-class women's interests at work. Susan Lawrence, 1871–1947, from an upper-class background, had started life as a Conservative but a few years before the war had switched to Labour. Under Macarthur's influence she had joined the WTUL, and was also interested in working-class education. In 1917 she wrote *Women in the Engineering Trades* with Barbara Drake and in 1919 *Labour Women and International Legislation* with Tuckwell and Phillips. (After the war she was a Labour MP and briefly in 1924 Parliamentary Secretary to the President of the Board of Education.)

Margaret Bondfield, 1873–1953, began her career as a shop worker, became involved in the Shop Workers' Union, and between 1898 and 1908 served as its assistant secretary. In 1902 she gave evidence to the government's Select Committee on Shops and in 1907 to the Select Committee on Truck. In the years before the First World War she campaigned for a minimum wage, for improvements in the infant mortality rate (IMR) and child welfare, and for women's suffrage. She was a member of the Advisory Committee on the Health Insurance Bill, helping to ensure that maternity benefits, paid to the mother, were included. During the war she was heavily involved in the Federation of Women Workers. (In 1923 she entered Parliament, in 1924 was Parliamentary Secretary to the Minister of Labour, and from 1929 to 1931 Minister of Labour. Throughout the 1930s she worked for the trade union movement and during the Second World War was chair of the Women's Group on Public Welfare.)

Marion Phillips, 1881–1932, was born in Australia. In 1904 she came to London. She undertook research for Beatrice Webb, 1858–1943, the Fabian social investigator, who was sitting on the Royal Commission on the Poor Laws. She became the organising secretary to the WTUL and a member of the Women's Labour League. During the war she sat on the War Emergency Workers National Committee and the Queen's Work for Women Fund Committee. In 1917 she became secretary of the newly formed Standing Joint Committee of Industrial Women's Organisations. (After the war she undertook her best-known work as Chief Woman Organiser for the Labour Party; in 1929 she entered Parliament for a brief spell.)

The most public display of common aims between politicians and a leading woman campaigner came on 17 July 1915 when Lloyd George and Mrs Emmeline Pankhurst, 1858–1928, shared a platform at a rally organised by Mrs Pankhurst, but paid for by the government, to highlight the need for women in war work. On the outbreak of war, the militant suffragette organisation, the Women's Social and Political Union (WSPU), led by Mrs Pankhurst and one of her daughters, Christabel, postponed their suffrage campaigning – with its demonstrations, petitions, arson and subsequent imprisonment – for the duration. Instead of attacking government they turned their fervour into support for the war effort. Christabel Pankhurst justified her mother's decision, 'the country was our country. It belonged to us and not to the Government, and we had the right and privilege, as well as the duty, to serve and defend it.'[14] Whitehall's doors were firmly slammed on suffrage campaigners who went down the alternative path of pacifism.

Reconstruction

Over the course of the war, government set up a huge number of committees to draw up plans for the post-war world, with civil servants and outsiders sitting alongside one another. Of 87 main committees, 15 had women on them, 36 women altogether. Some women sat on more than one committee; Beatrice Webb sat on four. Beatrice Webb played a more prominent role than any other woman on reconstruction committees, sitting on the Local Government Committee, which accepted her recommendations for a break-up of Poor Law administration and redistribution of its functions to other ministries. Influence on the committee did not, however, mean success beyond the committee; its recommendations remained a dead letter.[15] This work, moreover, hardly offered Beatrice Webb greater influence than before the war when she had sat on the Royal Commission on the Poor Laws. If Webb's recommendations had been implemented, this would not have signified any growth of women's influence in policy making. Webb played a singular role in future thinking about governmental organisation and intervention.

The women were overwhelmingly outnumbered by men on reconstruction committees, although merely counting women's heads is not enough. First, we need to consider the attitudes of the women involved, very few of whom publicly defended or promoted the interests of other women. Second, we need to take account of women's position on the committees. No woman chaired a committee and those on which women sat tended to be either concerned specifically with women's, young people's or educational issues, or minor committees; indeed, many contemporaries might well have thought of women's issues as minor ones anyway. No women were involved in committees dealing with science, technology, trade, or aliens, although Mona Wilson, a National Health Insurance Commissioner, and Susan Lawrence both sat on a committee concerned with post-war

---

14. Christabel Pankhurst, *Unshackled: The Story of How We Won The Vote* (1959), p. 288.
15. Paul Barton Johnson, *Land Fit for Heroes* (Chicago, 1968), pp. 80, 99, 183–4.

industrial relations, and Beatrice Webb sat on the Machinery of Government Committee and the National Registration Committee.

Some of the women on reconstruction committees, such as Adelaide Anderson, Clara Collet and Frances Durham were civil servants and not playing a greater role in government than they had done previously. Adelaide Anderson, 1863–1936, was one of the best-informed people in the country on women's working conditions. She was born in Australia but came to England as a child. In 1889 she began lecturing to the Women's Cooperative Guild (WCG) and in 1892 was appointed clerk to the Royal Commission on Labour; two years later she became one of the first four women Factory Inspectors, and between 1897 and 1921 she headed the women's branch of the Factory Inspectorate.

Women, such as Mary (known as May) Paterson and Beatrice Webb, although not civil servants, had undertaken government work in the past. May Paterson, c.1861–1941, had a long-standing interest in industrial employment. In 1893 she was appointed one of the first women Factory Inspectors, a post she retained until 1912 when she became one of the first National Health Insurance Commissioners for Scotland. (After the war she threw herself enthusiastically into philanthropic and local civic activities.)

The motives behind the flurry of reconstruction plans were primarily to give the Liberals under Lloyd George some party political advantage, and to boost morale when enthusiasm for the war was in doubt. Government did not ask women to plan for the post-war world as a gesture of appreciation for their contribution to the war effort. Yet, reconstruction planning offered an ideal opportunity for including more women, many of whom were keen to make a useful contribution to society at this time of war.

From 1915 women's organisations pressed for an equal number of women and men on reconstruction committees.[16] Governments' failure to make more use of women in reconstruction planning reinforces the view that women were only brought in on sufferance and as a last resort when men could not be found, or when issues were seen as 'women's issues' and therefore requiring input from a woman (one was usually thought sufficient). Plenty of women who were not utilised had the requisite experience and skills. Women councillors, women Poor Law Guardians, women members of school boards, and suffragists had organisational skills and committee work experience. There were women with managerial experience in welfare work, and women in the labour movement, with a knowledge of the needs of the bulk of the population.

---

16. Cheryl Law, *Suffrage and Power: The Women's Movement 1918–1928* (1997), pp. 69–70.

Philip Abrams argued that the failure of social reform after the First World War was the result of administrative and ideological failures during the period of the war. He singled out the government's use of middle-aged, middle-class women for his harshest criticisms. First, Abrams claimed that Christopher Addison, Minister of Reconstruction, chose business leaders and active feminists, who were not representative of women as a whole, as advisors. On the one hand, he does not criticise the business leaders for not representing men as a whole, and on the other hand he provides no evidence to support his contentions that the women were active feminists and unrepresentative of women 'as a whole'. It is doubtful, anyway, whether a small group of women could ever represent 'women as a whole'. Second, he claims that the women were a distinct political interest in 1918, and the implication is that as such women should not be advisors to ministers. Yet, women were well known to be divided over many political issues, such as party allegiance and support for the war. Third, Abrams stated that it would not be surprising if the struggle for feminine rights had distracted the women from other issues of social policy. Abrams provides no evidence of this distraction, and, in any case, the distinction between feminist issues and social policy ones is artificial. Fourth, Abrams claimed that the priorities of reconstruction were limited by the social interests of the groups whom Addison relied upon for advice. Women, however, were not given the opportunity to display as wide a range of interests as they possessed; there were only a limited number of committees on which they sat, and often the remit of the committee was narrower than they wished. Finally, Abrams claimed that middle-aged, propertied women gained an extension of social and political 'privileges' and 'real access to the levels at which social policy was made'. In fact, some women did increase their political rights (not privileges), but they were prevented from exercising those rights to the full (as subsequent chapters will show). The failure of social reform cannot be explained by the presence of middle-aged, middle-class women, so much as by their limited access to ad hoc government committees, senior civil service posts and ministerial office.[17]

Although women sat on committees they could only make recommendations, which departments were at liberty to ignore. Few of the women were civil servants with an insider's ability to network informally for the adoption of policies. Post-war planning took place in committees with artificially hedged boundaries; policy proposals then had to be pressed on equally artificially created departmental boundaries. Neither the committee nor the departmental structures bore much relationship to the complex and

---

17. Philip Abrams, 'The failure of social reform: 1918–1920', *Past and Present* 24 (1963), pp. 43–64.

comprehensive approach of key women advisors. Initially this mismatch between proposals and departmental responsibilities led Whitehall to procrastinate. In the longer term, as wartime imperatives gave way to peacetime ones, dominated above all by financial stringency, Whitehall permanently shelved reconstruction proposals. Women advisors did not lack ideas or a vision of an integrated and comprehensive welfare system, premised first and foremost on the needs of women. The Women's Employment Committee demonstrates the problems faced by women on government committees.

In 1916 Asquith's Reconstruction Committee set up a sub-committee to study women's employment but, by 1917, now under the Ministry of Reconstruction, it was bogged down in a mire of quarrels with the demobilisation and war pledges committees. The Women's Employment Committee met, discussed and produced reports, but government took no action on them. In March 1917, at the request of the Women's Employment Committee, Adelaide Anderson wrote a wide-ranging and deeply knowledgeable report – for which she was able to draw on both her own extensive knowledge and that of other departments – on subsidiary health and related services for women; the report gathered dust for a few months until the end of the year, when she revised the figures. Nothing happened, and the following August, Anderson again revised the figures. A sub-committee on the entire subject was then created, comprising 15 members, of whom 13 were women, including Viscountess Rhondda, 1883–1958 (suffragette, after the war editor of *Time and Tide*, founder of Six Point Group and heavily involved with the Open Door Council), in the chair; two representatives of the WCG, Miss Enfield and Miss L. Harris; a representative from the College of Nursing, Miss L. Clark; a representative from the National Union of Trained Nurses, Miss Rimmer; Dr Janet Lane-Claypon from King's College for Women, and Elizabeth Macadam, a Liverpool social worker. At the end of 1918 the committee spawned various sub-committees of its own, which, in turn, brought in other women. In early 1919 it produced a report, based on evidence collected from a range of women, and a few men, representing mainly doctors and nurses, and informed by Anderson's memorandum, and there the matter rested.

Anderson's memorandum, and the following report which drew heavily on it, were comprehensive and inclusive documents. Anderson sketched out the possibilities for industrial women 'of a superior type' to work in health-related services. If her ideas had been implemented they would have created a wide-ranging welfare service for women – especially married women, who were those least likely to benefit from the existing national health insurance benefits and services – and a range of job opportunities for women, which would have included training programmes. She suggested more women should be trained as midwives, home helps, Sanitary Inspectors and health visitors, superintendents and forewomen in factories, care committee and boys' and girls' club organisers, policewomen and women patrols, probation officers and orderlies in hospitals; for work in infant welfare centres and schools for mothers, nursery schools and day nurseries, play centres and groups, public baths and laundries, and invalid kitchens. She also called for mothers' pensions, which would both reduce the number of women competing for jobs and enable mothers to provide personal care for young children.

The final report for the committee on Ancillary Health and Kindred Services, like Anderson's report, took a comprehensive and integrated view of women's health and welfare needs, and in some key respects foreshadowed later calls for a state welfare service to provide life-long and integrated protection. It was clearly written from the point of view of women. The report argued for coordinated and extended ancillary health services to provide for every stage of life and every locality; for the state to take responsibility for these health services; for training and qualifications for workers in these areas to be raised and standardised; for pay and conditions of work to be substantially improved to attract and keep the best workers, and for the scope of voluntary activity to be defined carefully. The range of services envisaged included: maternity, ante-natal and infant clinics; maternity hospital provision; clinics for children; school meals and milk; continuous health records; midwifery services; health visitors; home helps and domiciliary nursing.

Efforts to incorporate employment policies for women into social policy planning were hampered by government's failure to coordinate the work of various bodies with overlapping concerns. Thus, the sub-committee on welfare workers was told only to look at the health aspects of women's welfare work but the committee argued that this was superfluous as the HMWC had already done it, the new Industrial Fatigue Research Board was about to continue the HMWC's work, and the Factory Department of the Home Office was investigating the field.[18] Government failed to pull these different bodies' work together, and the all-inclusive vision of women was undermined.

In social policy planning for the post-war world, a field in which women were long recognised as having a particular interest and expertise, the number of women, and the type of women involved, does not suggest even a momentary gendered power shift. Reconstruction planning potentially offered women substantial influence, but because first the reconstruction committees and later the Ministry itself ultimately exercised little influence over post-war social policy, few of those involved in reconstruction saw their ideas put into practice.

---

18. Information on the above section comes from PRO MH 55/517 and MH 55/518.

Lobbying for change

Women who were not a part of the formal policy-making structures of government attempted to influence governments' thinking indirectly by lobbying and operating through informal contacts, as they did over both suffrage and the health of women and children. No women were directly involved in decision making in the area of electoral reform, and in particular the partial extension of the vote to women; the influence exerted by suffrage organisations on those men who were involved is a matter of dispute. Martin Pugh argues that women's influence was marginal: the key problem was the enfranchisement of the troops, out of which the total enfranchisement of men grew; the issue of enfranchising women was only a footnote to this concern. The suffrage societies, according to Pugh, did no more than remind the politicians that women were still capable of agitating for the vote.[19] Sandra Stanley Holton, in contrast, asserts that while suffrage groups were divided over their strategy, the idea of a Speaker's Conference to make recommendations to Parliament came from the United Suffragists, and those sympathetic to women's suffrage on the Speaker's Conference closely consulted suffrage organisations.[20]

Government, women's organisations and voluntary organisations (often with men in key positions) all made efforts to improve the health and welfare of babies. The response of governments to the welfare needs of infants was not solely a reaction to calls from women's organisations; indeed health policy was much narrower and less effective than women's groups would have liked.

Before the war, the WCG had placed mothers' health and wellbeing, as well as that of their babies, on the political agenda. The WCG had highlighted the way in which mothers' daily lives, their struggle with poverty and overcrowding, undermined their health. Margaret Llewelyn Davies, 1861–1944, educated at Girton College, Cambridge, was a voluntary social worker, Christian Socialist and leading member of the WCG. She campaigned before the war for a minimum wage, early closing of shops and better maternity care. In 1915, as part of the WCG's campaign for better maternity care, she edited *Maternity*, based on letters from working-class mothers. It drew public attention to the appalling lives of working-class mothers, and the need for change. (In the 1920s Margaret Llewelyn Davies

---

19. Martin Pugh, *Electoral Reform in War and Peace* (1978), pp. 62, 140.
20. Sandra Stanley Holton, *Suffrage Days: Stories from the Women's Suffrage Movement* (1996), pp. 225–6.

devoted most of her time to pacifist and pro-Russia activities and in 1931 she edited *Life As We Have Known It*.)

The WCG had demanded maternity benefits, which Lloyd George incorporated into the 1911 National Insurance Act, although it took an amendment in 1913, again pressed for by the WCG, before they were paid direct to the mother. During the war the WCG continued to send deputations to Whitehall, drafted circulars for the Local Government Board (LGB) to use, put pressure on local authorities, organised lectures, meetings and relief work such as dinners, milk and home helps for pregnant and nursing mothers.[21] The WCG campaign was part of women in the labour movement's calls for municipal health centres, health education, home helps and health visitors. Llewelyn Davies kept up remorseless pressure on the LGB. Her class and educational background meant that she was able to deal with civil servants on equal social terms, and her experience (during the First World War she was in her fifties) all helped her to capture the attention of civil servants. The LGB responded sympathetically to Llewelyn Davies, and government policies reflected WCG demands.

Concern over population replacement was nothing new, but the war acted as a spur to existing plans for a larger and healthier nation, and reinforced the traditional emphasis on a woman's role as wife and mother. This destiny for women was supported by a wide range of official and feminist opinion. Action came from both government and voluntary bodies. On the outbreak of war a number of well-to-do women in London distributed pure milk to families who could prove their poverty.[22] Millicent Fawcett, 1847–1929, President of the National Union of Women's Suffrage Societies (NUWSS), and campaigner for women's education; and Selina Cooper, 1864–1946, a working-class member of the NUWSS and WCG, and one of Eleanor Rathbone's first supporters for family allowances, opened a maternity centre. Women's trade unions, the Labour Party leadership and the WCG all enthusiastically embraced the campaign to reduce the death rate among babies.[23] In 1917 the National Baby Week Council (the top posts of which were all occupied by men) launched the highly popular Baby Week, a vehicle for the display of yet more patriotic fervour. The Babies of the Empire Society called for more nurseries, breast-feeding and better baby care.[24] In 1918 when

---

21. Imperial War Museum (IWM). Welfare 1/10 M Llewelyn Davies 9 June 1915.
22. IWM. Welfare 5/5 Report and appeal of the National Milk Hostels Committee. N.D.
23. Martin Pugh, *Women and the Women's Movement in Britain*, p. 17; Gail Braybon, *Women Workers in the First World War*, p. 123.
24. Jay Winter, *The Great War and the British People* (1986), p. 192; Martin Pugh, *Women and the Women's Movement in Britain*, p. 17; Margaret Llewelyn Davies, ed., *Maternity: Letters from Working-Women* (1978). First published 1915.

Hayes Fisher, President of the Local Board, introduced the Maternal and Child Health Bill he tapped into wartime sentiment by claiming that its provisions would help repair wartime ravages to the manpower of the country.[25]

An improvement in infant health fitted with the broader interests of various members of the government. Herbert Samuel, President of the LGB when war broke out, had a general interest in public health and the Poor Law. Lloyd George and RB Haldane, Lord Chancellor from 1912 to 1915, were both keen to build up the Local Government Board into a health department, and Beatrice Webb was continually pressing Lloyd George and Samuel to overhaul the Poor Law and health services together. Public health officials were keen to develop the LGB into a health department, and civil servants are never averse to a higher profile and status for their own department. Although government was unwilling to offer medical treatment or financial support to mothers, which would have improved their standard of living, it was willing to support infant welfare clinics which were educational advice centres for working-class mothers. From 1915 the LGB obliged parents and medical attendants to notify local authorities of a birth in order that a health visitor could visit the baby and try to persuade the mother to attend an infant welfare centre. The LGB provided local authorities with subsidies to open more infant welfare centres and extend their work to ante-natal care and to children between the ages of one year and five years. During the war LGB circulars to local authorities emphasised the importance of these facilities. Not all local authorities responded, as some disapproved of the measures in principle, fearing that they might undermine individual responsibility among the working class, who, they claimed (often rightly), did not want health visitors entering their homes. Some local authorities simply did not want to make a financial contribution.

Ellen Ross is correct in stating that the 1918 Maternity and Child Welfare Act, which offered central government money to local authorities for providing a series of maternal and infant welfare services, was the product of major campaigning by feminist and suffrage organisations, yet it is also the case that the development of local authority maternity and infant welfare services served the differing interests of various groups of civil servants and politicians, and fitted well with a wartime desire to replace the population lost on the battlefields. In contrast, women's organisations, such as the WCG, were primarily concerned with tackling the underlying problem of women's poverty and lack of money.[26]

---

25. HC Deb. vol. 107 24 June 1918 col. 803 Hayes Fisher.
26. PRO MH 55/543; Ellen Ross, *Love and Toil: Motherhood in Outcast London, 1870–1918* (1993), p. 201.

Power in the country

Welfare work in industry

Numerous examples exist of individual women increasing their personal powers in a public setting when they undertook governments' bidding. Women welfare officers in industries employing large numbers of women gained influence, although not necessarily within government. Lilian Barker, 1874–1955, was the best known and least typical welfare supervisor. Barker's father was a tobacconist in London. She trained as a teacher at Whitelands College, Chelsea and then taught in an elementary school. In 1913 the London County Council (LCC) appointed her Principal of its Women's Institute. In 1915 she became the first Commandant of the Women's Legion cookery section, training cooks for the army. A few months later she was appointed Lady Superintendent at Woolwich Arsenal, where she set up canteens, cloakrooms, rest rooms and first aid posts for the women munitions workers. She organised recreational activities outside the factory and holiday homes. She visited ill workers and arranged for unmarried mothers and their babies to be looked after. Barker was popular with the women munitions workers at the Arsenal, perhaps because they shared a common class background. (After the war she joined the training department of the Ministry of Labour and in 1920 became an executive officer of the CCWTE. In 1923 she became governor of the Borstal Institution for Girls at Aylesbury and in 1935 she was appointed the first woman assistant commissioner for prisons, a post she held until 1943 when she retired.)

In her popularity, as in her working-class origins, Barker was unusual among the mainly middle-class women brought into industry during the war as welfare supervisors. Most welfare supervisors were middle-class while most female munitions workers were working-class. There is evidence of tensions between middle-class welfare supervisors and working-class munitions workers, as well as between the few middle-class munitions workers and the bulk of working-class ones.[27] Under the direction of the Ministry of Munitions, welfare provision and welfare supervisors were introduced to boost productivity. Welfare supervisors exercised enormous control over the women workers, both inside and outside the factory, with powers ranging from hiring and firing to ensuring the provision of sanitary and recreational facilities, a power which was as much resented for its controlling motives and effects as it was appreciated for improving working conditions.

---

27. Gail Braybon, *Women Workers in the First World War*, pp. 162–3.

The root of the welfare supervisors' power lay in the control they exercised over women munitions workers, a power which was, however, strictly controlled by government; welfare supervisors were introduced at the bidding of government and removed at the end of the war when the government no longer required them. Welfare supervisors implemented government policy, they did not help to make it.[28]

Social work

Despite the increased suffering in the community caused by the war, it was in industry that trained social workers found employment. The Ministry of Munitions, as part of its attempt to boost productivity, made efforts to attract trained social workers into munitions factories. Just as the demand for trained social workers increased, so their numbers dried up as women found alternative wartime employment. In an effort to attract women into social work, the Welfare Department of the Ministry of Munitions helped universities to mount short intensive courses, and the Ministry provided student grants. In an attempt to standardise the quality of courses a Joint Social Studies Committee was established, and as a result of conferences hosted by the Home Office (responsible for working conditions other than in munition factories) a Joint University Council for Social Studies, to coordinate and develop the work of social studies departments, was established.[29] One long-term effect of the war, therefore, was an umbrella organisation to control social work training. The short-term effect was a temporary increase in demand for trained and paid industrial social workers, but this did not extend to social work in general. Women social workers were shifting the justification for their activities from female moral authority to non-gendered competence and expertise. Gaining a recognition of the need for training and pay were a part of the process. In the long term this change helped to ensure the survival of social work and the state's increasing employment of social workers. Women police and patrols were also walking a tightrope in developing a career based less on moral and more on legal authority.[30]

---

28. For an excellent discussion of welfare supervisors see Angela Woollacott, *On Her Their Lives Depend*, pp. 71–5, 137, 167–70.
29. Ronald G. Walton, *Women in Social Work* (1975), pp. 91–4.
30. Angela Woollacott, 'From moral to professional authority: secularism, social work, and middle-class women's self-construction in World War I Britain', *Journal of Women's History* 10 (1998), pp. 85–111.

Women patrols and police

Two distinct groups of women police emerged in the war, the Women Police Service, which aimed to extend its work into traditional areas of policing, and women patrols who trudged the streets in order to keep a watchful eye on working-class women's behaviour and morals in public places. The former had their uses for working-class women, but the latter were no more than a nuisance. Woollacott has argued that whereas these two groups had differing attitudes towards double moral standards, the roots of both groups lay in pre-war suffrage. Levine is more sceptical of this link, arguing that while the organisers may have had links with the suffrage campaign, there is no way of knowing the attitudes of the bulk of the women towards women's suffrage. Certainly, policewomen, unlike feminist groups, did not challenge double moral standards as embodied in the DORA regulations 40D. Earlier links with feminist organisations may have remained strong in the minds of those senior policemen who wanted no truck with ex-suffragettes, but policewomen themselves quickly shook off their personal identity with feminist organisations in their attempt to fit into the culture of policing. Whether the protection or the control aspects of policing were uppermost is a contentious and unresolved issue, but the women's identification with the latter in the war meant that ultimately their work in wartime played an important part in the slowly established career of policing for women.[31] At first women patrols and police (unlike their male counterparts) were more likely to be middle class than working class. Women patrols laid the basis for the later development of women police and thus they played a role in opening up working-class women's opportunities, but at the same time they helped to reinforce double moral standards for women. They do not appear to have influenced government thinking over issues of sexuality, which were closely tied to policies on VD.

Women police gained employment in munitions factories to discipline and control women workers. While employers used women police partly to protect women, they were primarily engaged to promote the smooth running of the factory. They were also part of a project to establish women policing as a career, and so the more effectively they could control the women workers, and thus fulfil the requirements of productivity, the more they strengthened the case for women police. While some women were able to use the war situation to develop their careers, others undertook more voluntary work.

---

31. See Philippa Levine, '"Walking the streets in a way no decent woman should": women police in World War I', *Journal of Modern History* 66 (1994), pp. 34–78 for an excellent and full discussion.

Welfare work in the community

Following the declaration of war, men volunteered in their droves, leaving many wives and families with no financial support until the government extended the armed forces' separation allowances scheme to them. In the meantime charities, old and new, attempted to help poor mothers and their families. In the East End of London, better-off suffragists made contributions to those women hardest hit by the upheaval of war, for instance, by running an employment bureau and a communal restaurant. Ray Strachey threw herself into the work of the Women's Service Bureau, set up by the London Society, to find women to replace men who had joined up.[32] Ray Strachey, 1887–1940, a leading member of the NUWSS, fought for better working conditions and equal pay for women. She was highly critical of women's unpaid charitable work in wartime. In 1917 she was involved in backroom negotiations, along with Pippa Strachey and Millicent Fawcett, over women's enfranchisement. (After the war she acted as Parliamentary Secretary to Nancy Astor, Conservative MP, 1919–45. Astor, an American married to Waldorf Astor, stood in his Plymouth constituency in 1919 when he was elevated to the peerage on the death of his father. She became the first woman to take her seat in the House of Commons. Astor had not been active in the suffrage movement before the war, but she subsequently took up a number of employment and family issues, over which women's organisations campaigned. Although some found her irritating, she did have friends from across the political spectrum, including Ellen Wilkinson. Strachey provided Astor with briefs on numerous subjects. In 1935 she took a job with the Women's Employment Federation which sought better jobs for women, and in 1939 she was involved in a campaign among women MPs to deal with the problem of unemployment among professional women.)

On 6 August 1914 the Prince of Wales launched the National Relief Fund (NRF) and Queen Alexandra appealed for contributions to the Soldiers' and Sailors' Families Association (SSFA); on 11 August the two funds merged. Pedersen has pointed out that women qualified for separation allowances solely on the basis of their relationship with a man. It was a soldier's or sailor's right to have his wife supported. The idea of a male breadwinner and dependent wife underpinned the system. The women had no automatic right to the payment, and indeed 16,000 women, about two per cent of claimants, had their allowance withdrawn, on the grounds of their allegedly immoral behaviour.

---

32. Sylvia Pankhurst, *The Home Front: A Mirror to life in England During the First World War* (1987), pp. 21, 22, 43. First published 1932.

A huge team of SSFA middle-class women volunteers (50,000 by 1915) visited working-class women receiving separation allowances to offer guidance on household management and to observe the women's behaviour. Pedersen has described how volunteers investigated claims and helped women clear up muddles. They visited women in their homes in order to make assessments, a throwback to women's charitable work in the nineteenth century and a clear indication of the way in which nineteenth-century private, charitable ways of operating melted into twentieth-century state professional work. The motives of the volunteers were not so different from their nineteenth-century mothers either: a sense of public service heightened by the war; Christian duty; and a desire to offer advice to less fortunate women. From 1915 the administration of separation allowances was taken away from the volunteers amid a barrage of criticism from the labour movement and Parliament. They criticised SSFA for its allegedly inefficient, parsimonious and prying methods. There was some truth in the criticisms, but politicians and the male-dominated labour movement wanted to wrench control from independent middle-class women and bring them under the aegis of the state. Government brought SSFA under its control and the surveillance continued. Attempts were made to police the women receiving separation allowances, although the police force itself shrank back from undertaking the task when requested to do so by the War Office.[33]

Control over working-class women remained contested territory, both between women and between women and male-dominated government departments of state. Sylvia Pankhurst's East London Federation of Suffragettes and Charlotte Despard's Women's Freedom League demonstrated unsuccessfully against the state's surveillance of soldiers' wives. Charlotte Despard, 1844–1939, was a socialist and philanthropist who, although rich herself, chose to live among the London poor, so she saw at first hand the effects of the war on poor women's lives. She was also a pacifist, which reinforced her sympathy for poor women adversely affected by war. Sylvia Pankhurst, 1882–1960, one of Mrs Pankhurst's daughters, who had broken away from the WSPU before the war, and unlike her mother, Emmeline, and her sister, Christabel, remained a committed socialist, called for a negotiated peace settlement. Sylvia devoted her energies to the needs of working-class women in the East End of London. (After the war she focused her campaigning on the needs of refugees from, and victims of, fascism.)

The government set up Local Representation Committees to coordinate the relief work of state and voluntary bodies, the numbers of which soared

---

33. Susan Pedersen, 'Gender, welfare and citizenship in Britain during the Great War', *American Historical Review* 95 (1990), pp. 983–1006.

during the war. Johanna Alberti has provided a review of the way in which those women who had been campaigning for the vote before the war turned their organisations and individual effort to relief work. The Active Service League was the focus of relief work; similar organisations grew out of the WSPU. Mary Sheepshanks, 1872–1958, suffragist, pacifist, socialist, active in women's international issues, used the International Women's Suffrage Alliance offices to help German women stranded in Britain when the war broke out; after the fall of Belgium, Sheepshanks, along with Chrystal Macmillan, 1872–1937, suffragist, pacifist and member of the NUWSS executive, went off to Flushing in Belgium with the first food convoys. (After the war she was one of the first women barristers, she helped to form the Open Door Council, was a member of the National Union of Societies for Equal Citizenship and the Association for Moral and Social Hygiene; she also campaigned for women who married a foreigner to retain their own nationality.) They put pressure on the government to help refugees, and indeed many suffragists helped refugees.[34] Women's desire to make an immediate contribution to the war was thereby met, but their influence over the nature of relief work and government policy was strictly circumscribed.

Upper-class and middle-class women took the lead in organising help for Belgian refugees who fled Belgium when the German army arrived. Here was an opportunity for women to give a practical and positive expression to their patriotism. Dame Flora Lugard, the wife of an ex-colonial administrator, and a former correspondent for *The Times*, quickly gained the support of those well placed in London political circles for a War Relief Committee (WRC). Dame Muriel Talbot, who had launched the Victoria League a few years earlier, immediately used the League to help refugees. Voluntary Aid Detachments (VADs) initially worked in WRC hostels and undertook administrative work for the relief operation. The main work involved placing refugees with families, and when the supply of private homes dried up, organising accommodation in hostels. Women in a range of organisations, from NUWSS to the Union of Jewish Women all helped in the day-to-day work. Men often played a role as figureheads of relief committees and organisations, just as they had done in nineteenth-century charities.

Apart from the involvement of women, which was only to be expected as relief work was presumed to require caring qualities which women supposedly enjoyed in far greater abundance than men, the other striking feature of Belgian relief was the strong and explicit way that upper-class and middle-class women saw it as a means of helping their own class. The relief workers operated the system to the explicit advantage of the better-off Belgians, who

---

34. Johanna Alberti, *Beyond Suffrage: Feminists in War and Peace, 1914–1928* (1989), p. 39.

at least initially formed the bulk of refugees. (Presumably better-off Belgians had more resources to organise their flight and potentially had much to lose in material terms from a German invasion.) British women relief workers attempted to put refugees in families with a similar class background. If refugees entered hostels they were divided along class lines. Local refugee committees often specified that they only wanted to help 'better-class' refugees and some hostels advertised their priorities by their name, for example, the Hostel for First Class Belgians in Chelsea and the Duchess of Somerset's Homes for Better Class Belgian Refugees. The Union of Jewish Women also offered help to better-off refugees. Professional groups of doctors, lawyers and architects also helped their Belgian counterparts. In contrast, trade unionists viewed the refugees with suspicion and were loath to offer assistance.[35] As we will see in a later chapter, middle-class and upper-class empathy with foreigners of a similar class continued after the war when women were at the forefront of efforts to help the defeated enemy.

Nursing, medicine and relief work

The initiative for women to play a paramilitary role came from, and was opposed by, both women and men. In 1907 upper-class women organised themselves into the First Aid Nursing Yeomanry (FANY), supplying their own horses and uniform, with the idea of riding onto the battlefield to rescue wounded soldiers and then nurse them. In 1910 Mabel St Clair Stobart founded the Women's Convoy Corps to demonstrate to government women's potential role in war at a time when suffragists were countering the anti-suffragists claim that women should not have the parliamentary vote because they did not defend their country and should not therefore have a say in governments making war and peace. Opponents of women's paramilitary organisations based their hostility on a number of grounds. Some felt that it flew in the face of women's natural role, and others, especially a number of feminists, argued that women should not be aping men with military-style uniforms and activities. Some argued that women would never be able to cope with the horrors of war, while others asked who men were meant to be fighting to protect if not women. Women, it was claimed, had a complementary role to play in war, that of repopulating the nation. Despite the hostility, women organised themselves for work abroad.

---

35. Peter Cahalan, *Belgian Refugee Relief in England During the Great War* (New York, 1982).

In order to exert more control over women's paramilitary activities and out of a desperation to meet manpower demands, the armed forces and the War Office reluctantly agreed to Katharine Furse's suggestion for a women's auxiliary corps. In 1909 Furse, 1875–1952, joined the newly formed Red Cross VADs attached to the Territorial Army. In 1914 she became head of the first VAD unit to go to France. She soon returned to Britain – to be replaced in France by her friend Rachel Crowdy – where she helped develop the VADs until 1917 when she resigned along with some of her colleagues in frustration at the constraints on her power. Furse wanted women to be trained in leadership and to be given real responsibility in war. In 1917 she got her way when she became Director of the new Women's Royal Naval Service (WRNS). (After the war she worked for a travel company and became one of the leaders of the Girl Guides.) Rachel Crowdy, 1884–1964, had also joined the VADs before the war. (In 1919 she was created a Dame of the British Empire (DBE) and began her work in charge of social questions and the control of opium traffic at the League of Nations where she gained an international reputation. In the 1930s she sat on various national and international bodies, including royal commissions. From 1939 to 1946 she was an advisor to the Ministry of Information.) In 1917 the WAAC was also formed and in 1918 the Women's Royal Air Force (WRAF) briefly came into being until the end of the war when all three women's auxiliary services were disbanded. Government listened to women's views, but sparse attention was paid to them.[36] There was no question of women contributing to strategy or establishing a permanent professional niche in naval and military circles.

Women who went abroad during the war in a nursing or medical capacity, with the FANYs, VAD and medical units, were inspired by a mixture of motives, which included proving women's powers of leadership in war. Their work may have had an indirect influence on changing attitudes towards women in the public sphere. Nurses grew in numbers and esteem during the war, the latter reinforced by government propaganda, although the government's use of angelic images of nurses to create an idealised and pure image of a British woman – as opposed to the cruel and brutal picture of German women, which the government projected – was an attempt to reinforce gender divisions. How far these images played any part in shaping society's views of women is, however, impossible to judge.

---

36. Jenny Gould, 'Women's military services in First World War Britain, in Margaret Randolph Higonnet, Jane Jenson, Sonya Michel and Margaret Collins Weitz, eds, *Behind The Lines: Gender and the Two World Wars* (New Haven, CT, 1987), pp. 115–24.

It is hard to detect any direct or substantial occupational gains for women as a result of women's work in war zones. There is no evidence, for instance, that as a result of the war nurses enhanced their status, pay, working conditions or influence over the development of nursing. Nurses continued to be organisationally weak and divided. Before the war, the main division was between Poor Law and voluntary hospital nurses. The arrival of VADs, often unpaid, with only three to four months' training and typically from a higher social class than career nurses, often increased the divisions between nurses. Career nurses feared that women undertaking nursing duties with only a few months' training would downgrade an already weak occupation for women and, since numbers of VADs were unpaid, possibly drive down the already low wages. The government's creation at the end of the war of a General Nursing Council (GNC) which standardised nursing qualifications is not seen by historians of nursing as a sign of the growing strength of nursing. Instead, it is argued that the Ministry of Health manipulated the GNC to keep it weak and under government control. After the war nurses remained divided and their numbers dropped dramatically.[37]

War casualties created a demand for more doctors. In December 1914 Mary Scharlieb published a letter in *The Times* encouraging more women to enter medicine; an editorial backed up her letter. Those medical schools and hospitals which had so long spurned women now reluctantly accepted them. Between 1914 and 1921 the number of women doctors doubled.

Women doctors took the initiative in offering their services to the armed forces and, when rebuffed, turned to Allied governments, who accepted the women. In some cases women doctors set up their own medical units where they had autonomy and independence. The best known of these initiatives was that of Dr Elsie Inglis, an active suffragist, who was keen to provide a high-profile example of women's medical abilities, normally hidden by prejudice. With the assistance of the Scottish Federation of Women's Suffrage Societies she had founded the Scottish Women's Hospitals. On the outbreak of war she offered their services to the War Office, and when it turned down her offer, she organised women's medical and nursing units to assist the Allies. Women doctors worked in every type of hospital and in a range of capacities. As male doctors joined the Royal Army Medical Corps (RAMC), women filled the posts they had vacated. Louisa Garrett Anderson and Flora Murray, both doctors, organised the female staffing of hospitals in France and Britain.

---

37. Robert Dingwall, Anne Marie Rafferty and Charles Webster, *An Introduction to the Social History of Nursing* (1988), pp. 72–89.

In 1916 the War Office asked women to volunteer for service with the armed forces. When the British army was forced by the shortage of doctors to use women, it treated them as inferior to the men. The women worked as auxiliaries to the RAMC without commissions or honorary rank. In military hospitals women doctors were always kept in a subordinate position to even the most inexperienced men doctors; women were not allowed to have men working under them. In 1917 Dr Jane Turnbull was appointed to the War Office as an advisor on medical matters relating to women. A corps of medical women was then created to serve with the WAAC and the following year with the WRAF. These women enjoyed better working conditions than those working in military hospitals.

In 1917 a group of women doctors founded the Medical Women's Federation, which immediately took up the issue of medical women working under the War Office. In February 1918 officers of the Federation met Sir Alfred Keogh, the Director General of Medical Services, and General Goodwin, who was soon to replace him. The War Office responded in part to women's request for uniform and military rank by issuing an order the following month that all medical women on annual contracts should wear a uniform. Along with the British Medical Association, the Federation fought cases of unequal pay. The Federation also took up general health issues, for instance by organising a conference on the establishment of a Ministry of Health and discussing the DORA regulation 40D concerning the arrest and forced examination of women suspected of suffering from VD and soliciting or having sex with members of the armed forces. On both issues the women were divided.[38]

Women doctors' contribution to the medical needs of the armed forces received wide and favourable press coverage. They were praised for their skills and fortitude which directly affected the ability of the British to continue the war. In reality, the greater women doctors' independence from the hierarchy and prejudices of male doctors in the armed forces and men in the War Office, the greater women's scope for making a medical contribution. What best served women's interests also best served the interests of the war effort.

While official government propaganda was projecting images of nurses as angelic and passive, women wrote about their contribution to the medical and nursing needs of the war in much more dramatic tones which challenged gender stereotypes. Women described specific cases of individual women demonstrating an ability to organise and lead, and to endure hardships and

---

38. Wellcome Institute for the History of Medicine, Contemporary Medical Archives Centre, Medical Women's Federation. First Annual Report, 1918.

privations, but the implication of these accounts was that other women also had these capabilities. In describing women's contribution to the immediate needs of the war they were also pointing to women's potential in peacetime.

During the First World War, and after the Second World War, women's relief work meshed with government policies, but the experience of organising various ad hoc relief schemes during the war fed into the post-war relief work of British women on the Continent, undertaken in the face of government hostility. Although the women's relief work in the war received governmental support, the women's motives were not necessarily in accord with official thinking. Suffragists wanted to prove a point about women's role in war, and pacifist Quakers wanted to mitigate the effects of governments going to war.

Quaker women in France worked with civilians running maternity and out-patient clinics, and they helped with sanitation in the Marne and Meuse areas of northeast France. Often the Quakers' outlook was very different from the people with whom they worked. Edith Pye wrote of French women referring to their baby boys as 'mon petit soldat', not an appealing term of endearment to a pacifist. Descriptions sent back to Britain of the appalling conditions of refugees were also an implicit criticism of war. Kathleen Courtney wrote a number of letters home from Salonika, where she was engaged in relief work, which also point to the cultural differences between herself and the refugees, and between herself and the French management of refugee camps. Kathleen Courtney, 1878–1974, was a leading member of the NUWSS before the war and in 1912 she helped to secure Labour Party support for women's enfranchisement in return for a NUWSS fighting fund for Labour candidates. Her wartime pacifism led her out of the NUWSS and into the Women's International League for Peace and Freedom (WILPF). (After the war she continued to focus on pacifism and foreign affairs although in the Second World War her opposition to fascism outweighed her opposition to war and she actually spoke in the USA on behalf of the Ministry of Information.)

British women's experiences in a wider context

Despite the varied circumstances of women in warring nations, a number of broadly similar trends can be identified. Governments, initially dismissive of women's participation in anything other than their traditional wartime role, gradually accepted women's demand to play a bigger part. Over the course of the war the relationship of women's organisations with governments changed, although because this change was war-related it did not survive the Armistice.

At the instigation of women – most often those who had campaigned for the vote – formal links were established between governments and women's organisations. Just as in Britain the overwhelming bulk of women and feminist organisations – most notably suffragists and suffragettes – threw themselves into the war effort, so too on the Continent did the Associazione per la Donna in Italy, the Conseil National des Femmes Françaises in France and the Vaterländischer Frauenverein in Germany.[39] In Germany women's organisations banded together to form a central coordinating body, the Nationaler Frauendienst (National Women's Service), which as well as disseminating propaganda for the war effort, worked closely with local authorities and welfare agencies. The respect government accorded these women, in particular women in the Social Democratic Party (SPD), was something quite new.[40] For the duration, women were incorporated into the governance of the country, although always off-centre from the real locus of decision making.

In turning their organisational skills over to the war effort, suffrage campaigners lost the momentum of the immediate pre-war days when they were on the verge of success. The vibrant pre-war suffrage campaign in France ground to a halt just at the moment when it appeared it might achieve its goal; although women reactivated the campaign in 1917 it never regained its pre-war momentum. Women diversified their campaigning: some went off to join the communists, others turned their attention to the war debt, reparations, pacifism, or the League of Nations. Those interested specifically in women's issues concentrated on welfare measures for women and their families.[41]

Women's willingness to turn their efforts to the war did not involve a quid pro quo with government over suffrage. Many women did assume, however, that they would be rewarded, although it seems that in those countries, such as France and Italy, where women's hopes were highest, they gained least. While women may not have gained the vote from their participation in the war, they did gain other more personal 'rewards', by fulfilling a sense of duty to participate for patriotic reasons. Some women were able to grasp some of the excitement and adventure of war, and to exercise authority over others.

---

39. Mabel Potter Daggett, *Women Wanted: The Story Written in Blood Red Letters on the Horizon of the Great World War* (1918), p. 77.

40. Ute Frevert, *Women in German History: From Bourgeois Emancipation to Sexual Liberation* (Oxford, 1993), pp. 160–1.

41. Steven Hause with Anne Kenney, *Women's Suffrage and Social Politics in the Third Republic* (Princeton, NJ, 1984), pp. 191–5, 202–6.

The French government rejected – on the grounds that they strayed too far from women's traditional role – both Marguerite Durand's suggestion that women should serve as auxiliaries in the military, undertaking non-combative duties such as cooking, and Mme Jack de Bussy's attempts to organise a Ligue des Enrolées (League of Women Volunteers). Instead, the government encouraged women in Red Cross, and other charitable, work. Women who worked with the Red Cross were unpaid, but the war did highlight the need for more properly trained nurses working in better conditions. Women had been heavily involved in philanthropy before 1914, and the war prompted a tidal wave of volunteering among middle-class women in the cities. Middle-class women established a range of organisations, often headed by a man, which supported women and the war effort. For example, one supported battered women while another organised middle-class women to replace working-class women voluntarily one day a week in factories. The tone of most of the charities was a morally uplifting one, expressing concern over prostitution, alcoholism, and upholding the family.

The American army turned down offers of medical and nursing help from suffragists, who established the American Women's Hospitals in Europe. Other Americans channelled their aid overseas, for instance, Anne Morgan and Mrs Murray Dilke founded the American Committee for Devastated Regions. It may be that the further they were from home, the greater the autonomy women enjoyed.

In the USA women had to press their services on the government and while the Women's Committee was established in April 1916 in response to women's organisations' offers to serve their country, it failed to influence policy decisions. Later, in 1918 women's organisations succeeded in persuading the government to set up federal agencies to facilitate women's employment. The women involved, such as Mary Van Kleeck and Mary Anderson, prioritised women's training and protection at work. In April 1918 when the National War Labor Board was established to arbitrate in industrial disputes it was committed to equal pay for equal work, and to a minimum wage set at a level that would ensure an acceptable standard of living.

In Germany the government incorporated women into official welfare agencies and consultative bodies dealing specifically with women's concerns. The government assumed that women would have to be used to encourage other women to take up industrial work. So, they put Marie-Elisabeth Lüders, one of the leaders of the Federation of German Women's Associations (Bund Deutscher Frauenvereine, the BDF), in charge of employment exchanges, and nearly 1,000 women were drafted into factories to undertake welfare work among the new female recruits to industry.[42] The ability of women to exercise any real influence on government policies, especially in those areas which most intimately affected women, remained strictly limited. Women's views rarely figured in official reports, and indeed women ridiculed the government's attempts to fashion pronatalist policies without consulting women or bringing them into the policy-making process.[43] Women's views and actions were only welcome when they were controlling other women on behalf of government.

In France, men incorporated women to a limited extent into government. In April 1916 the Ministry of Armaments established a Board of Female Labour (Commission du Travail Féminin) comprising 45 members, of whom 10 were women, which looked into women's wages and working conditions; it was only moderately successful in bringing about change. In some villages women served as mayors but, according to Hause, such appointments only occurred as an extreme measure where there were no educated men left, and women only exercised very limited powers. Some women may have had the opportunity to take decisions when they were given official papers to sign, although their signatures may have been rubber stamps for decisions already taken by men. Elsewhere in France women sat on municipal councils but without voting rights. In 1915 the government gave women parental authority for the duration, but only in urgent cases and with judicial approval, a move not prompted by feminism but by a need for businesses to keep going.[44]

Most of the activities in which women exercised initiative and leadership were in the welfare field, although this did cover a wide range of work. Italian women ran hospitals and soldiers' canteens; they organised assistance for veterans, widows and orphans, and campaigned against luxury expenditure. German women formed the Women's Relief Force, which acted as a bridge between government agencies and women suffering hardships. In France women assisted refugees from northeast France and Belgium, helped reunite families, and cared for the sick and wounded.

---

42. Ute Frevert, *Women in German History*, p. 160.
43. Cornelie Usborne, '"Pregnancy is the women's active service": pronatalism in Germany during the First World War', in Richard Wall and Jay Winter, eds, *The Upheaval of War: Family, Work and Welfare in Europe, 1914–1918* (Cambridge, 1988), pp. 389–416.
44. Steven Hause, 'More Minerva than Mars: The French Women's Rights Campaign and the First World War', in Margaret Higonnet et al. *Behind The Lines*, pp. 99, 107; S. Hause, *Women's Suffrage and Social Politics in the Third French Republic* (Princeton, NJ, 1984), pp. 193–4; Mathilde Dubesset, Françoise Thébaud, Catherine Vincent, 'The female munition workers of the Seine', in Patrick Fridenson, ed., *The French Home Front, 1914–1918* (Oxford, 1992), p. 187.

They campaigned for more state aid for large families, support for pregnant women and measures to reduce alcoholism, all of which would, it was hoped, reduce the infant mortality rate and boost the birth rate, a goal in which they were in close accord with the government and society as a whole. The war strengthened France's pronatalist obsession, which in turn reinforced women's role in the family. French women's war-related activities were lauded in print, but wartime heroines were expected to be peacetime mothers.[45]

German women, for the most part, supported the pronatalism of the government in principle, although in practice they opposed government attempts to reduce the availability of contraceptives, to make abortions more difficult and to act in a more intrusive fashion in women's lives. The widespread support for pronatalism had the effect of reinforcing both double standards and the assumption that women's role in society was a procreative one.

In Germany large numbers of women undertook voluntary social work, organising soup kitchens and clothing supplies, working with refugees and helping poorer women eke out an existence with extra home-made food.[46] Christoph Sachße has pointed out that the rapid expansion of war relief created a demand for voluntary assistance which the women's movement provided. A number of trained social workers, and others with organisational experience in the BDF, publicly proved their usefulness to the Fatherland. Local sections of the Nationaler Frauendienst (NFD), started by Gertrud Bäumer, chair of the BDF, sprang up around the country. They worked closely with local municipal agencies in war relief work. Sachße goes on to argue that it gave thousands of women responsibilities and influence in the public sphere, but as the war continued the women's autonomy decreased and the BDF became subordinated to war needs. It also led to the growing influence of conservative women leaders. Women's social work became less a tool of social criticism and women's emancipation, and more supportive of existing society and politics. It led away from, rather than towards, feminist cultures.[47]

The impact of the war on Australian women was less than in many other countries; Australia was geographically far removed from the fighting and the economic and social impact of the war on Australia was weaker than elsewhere. Even so, there is evidence that double moral standards were

---

45. Françoise Thébaud, *La Femme au Temps de la Guerre de 14* (Paris, 1986).
46. Ute Frevert, *Women in German History*, p. 160.
47. Christoph Sachße, 'Social mothers: the bourgeois women's movement and German welfare-state formation, 1890–1929', in Seth Koven and Sonya Michel, eds, *Mothers of a New World: Maternalist Politics and the Origins of Welfare States* (1993), pp. 150–51.

reinforced in wartime, with police crackdowns on women in prostitution, which continued after the war rather than diminishing as in some other countries. Women in the labour movement led the campaign for the federal government to open up all public and professional employment to women. In 1918 the combination of legislation, along with changing attitudes towards the employment of unmarried women, contributed to the growing number of women in clerical, retailing, professional and administrative work.[48] While women were interested in widening employment opportunities, they continued to display an interest in education, infant welfare and working conditions.[49] Divisions between women remained strong, and while women's attitudes towards their own role in society may have been changing, suspicious attitudes persisted among women voluntary workers towards women applying for charitable support.[50]

Conclusions

Similar patterns of experience can be identified among middle-class women in a number of countries. British women were not unique either in their attempts to share in government policy decisions, or in the barriers they faced. War made it harder for women to improve their position because war so distorted reality. Apparent gains at the time turned out to be illusory. Angela Woollacott has argued that in Britain during the war middle-class and upper-class women dramatically pushed forward the process of women entering the professions and in so doing they transformed the nature of middle-class power over the working class, from power based on moral authority to power based on education and expertise.[51] Yet, many of the apparent advances in middle-class women's control over the working class were for the duration only. Often the power these women exercised over working-class women was not derived from their own powerful class position but from the powerful class position of men who 'allowed' women

48. Chris McConville, 'The location of Melbourne's prostitutes 1870–1920', *Historical Studies* 19 (1981), pp. 86–97; Raelene Davidson, '"As good a bloody woman as any other bloody woman . . ." Prostitutes in Western Australia 1895–1939', in Patricia Crawford, ed., *Exploring Women's Past: Essays in Social History* (1983); W.A. Sinclair, 'Women and economic change in Melbourne', *Historical Studies* 20 (1982), pp. 278–91.
49. South Australia State Library Adelaide SRG 116/1/1 Minutes of Women's Political Association of South Australia 1918.
50. The State Library of Victoria, Melbourne. Melbourne Ladies Benevolent Society Annual report 1916–1917.
51. Angela Woollacott, *On Her Their Lives Depend*, pp. 163–4.

to exert control. From the point of view of working-class women at the time, the lack of autonomy imposed on them by the middle class was real enough, it is only with hindsight that the fragility of middle-class women's power, both in relation to the working class and in relation to middle-class men, is apparent. Moreover, the fact that middle-class women may have been able to influence working-class women's public behaviour, in the street or factory, during the war does not mean that they influenced their attitudes or beliefs: working-class women may have adapted their behaviour in the factories to suit the factory culture, but this does not mean that they allowed their culture outside the factory to be undermined. Historians have tended to focus on the power of middle-class women over working-class women during the war, but when middle-class women's power vis-à-vis those men making policy is also considered, the weakness of women becomes more obvious. The continuing tensions between middle-class women and those men with policy-making powers is apparent in the following chapters, when middle-class women take up the cudgels of working-class women's interests. The experience of the war may have further separated rather than brought together women of different classes; it is ironical therefore that after the war middle-class women's campaigns were overwhelmingly driven by a desire to improve the conditions of working-class women. The war highlighted some of the barriers which would remain in place once women were partially, and then wholly, enfranchised, and just how far women still had to go in storming the citadels of Westminster and Whitehall power bases.

CHAPTER THREE

Working in Education, Health and Welfare

Introduction

This chapter discusses the constraints on, and opportunities for, women's work in teaching, nursing, medicine and social work, and offers an integrated overview of developments in these areas. Women's subordinate position to men in all four occupations, and women's limited autonomy, reflected and contributed to the long-standing sexual division of labour and women's subordinate position in the labour force.

A substantial body of literature offers a range of explanations for gendered employment patterns, encompassing biological differences, socialisation, domestic ideology and male work culture, which includes the active exclusion of women and the artificial creation of gender boundaries. Most of the research on which these arguments are based relates to working-class, manual occupations, or women's contemporary position in the labour market. There is a need, therefore, to look at the specific experience during the inter-war years of women in education, nursing, medicine and social work.

Women both challenged and reinforced the sexual division of labour and domestic ideology, and, as a group, displayed a contradictory and ambivalent attitude towards employment. On the one hand, many young women were attracted to those occupations requiring supposedly 'feminine' qualities and some women campaigned against the employment of married women. On the other hand, women attempted to open girls' eyes to a range of career openings, and campaigned for equal opportunities within the professions.

There is nothing remarkable about women holding different views on their personal career plans or on the appropriate place for women in the labour market. What needs to be explained is first, why certain groups of women challenged the dominant view of women's paid work as a stop-gap before marriage and instead argued that women should have the choice of pursuing an interesting career with good prospects; and second, why women were more successful in some careers than in others.

A wide range of factors shaped a woman's view of her work. The most important common influences on a woman's attitude towards her work reflected her private relationships – in particular, whether she married or not – and also a more public relationship with her work. Four key aspects of this public relationship were especially important: the career's hierarchy, discipline, unity and extent of male domination. The more hierarchical, disciplined and fragmented the career, the more difficult women found it to assert themselves within it. For this reason women's views, and career advancement, frequently divided along occupational lines.

Teaching, nursing, medicine and social work operated within the context of the inter-war political culture, apparent in government policies, in particular the marriage bar. They were influenced by domestic ideology, demonstrated here through careers advice, the marriage bar and perceived economic self-interest.

Education and careers advice between the wars

Most girls attended an elementary school from the age of five to 14, when they left with no paper qualifications. Roughly 14 per cent of children transferred to an academically oriented secondary school (normally known as grammar or high school) at the age of 11. Of these children half had passed a scholarship examination which entitled them to a free place. Most children left secondary school at the age of 15, or 16 after taking the School Certificate. A minority stayed on until the age of 18, when they took the Higher School Certificate. The number of grammar and high schools varied between local education authorities, but invariably there were fewer places for girls than for boys.

Feminists made efforts, both directly and indirectly, to counter the largely negative influences of government policies and the wider society on women's careers. Long-standing attempts by women to facilitate other women's employment continued. In the 1930s the National Union of Societies for Equal Citizenship (NUSEC), under the direction of Ray Strachey, concentrated on widening women's career options. One serious hurdle for girls was the lack of careers information. The Central Employment Bureau and Students' Careers Association, founded in 1898, believed that a lack of information about how and where girls could train and a lack of knowledge about career openings were the main difficulties in women's search for employment, so it periodically published a volume of information, and helped educated women and girls search for paid work. An appointments department helped already qualified women, and there was also a loan fund for women who could not afford to equip themselves for work.[1]

There was a need to fill a gap in girls' knowledge and to counter much careers advice which reinforced gender, class and racial stereotypes. How far careers books were available to girls, or consulted by them, is not known, so an analysis of these books is only suggestive of the type of literature girls or their parents may have picked up. In one careers guidance book the secretary to an editor of a leading London newspaper wrote that only a small percentage of women had executive ability; the majority were better suited to work as secretaries, complementing a master brain, rather than being the brain that directed.[2] Leonora Eyles, a journalist who wrote in Lansbury's *Labour Weekly* about baby clothes and feeding, and later worked on *Woman's Own*, warned that women flouted their bodily functions too much, and that it was a recognised scientific fact that women of the south were more languid because much of their bodily energy went into the process of pigmentation of the skin. Women should not take on trades or professions which 'common sense' tells us are naturally more suited to the 'stronger and less handicapped sex'. Yet, in the same book Eyles complained about newspapers which hailed the woman barrister for her charm and her clear ringing voice, and the woman MP for her Paris frocks. She further complained that women had to fight male jealousy and entrenchment hallowed by custom, the conservatism of women and men, and masculine sentiment which wanted to 'smooth' things for women.[3] The authors of another *Careers for Girls* not only reinforced stereotypes about women's reproductive functions and their suitability for certain kinds of work, and the different mental characteristics of women and men, but also offered quite gratuitous comments on race as well as gender, cautioning against women missionaries as the 'coloured races seem to exercise an uncanny influence over many young women'. They claimed that such unions were almost always tragic, and that even inter-marriage among white 'races' was 'seldom successful', for there was generally something 'abnormal or precocious' about the children.[4]

1. Central Employment Bureau for Women and Careers Association, *Careers and Professional Training: A Guide to Professions and Occupations of Educated Women and Girls* (1931 and various other editions).
2. J.A.R. Cairns, *Careers for Girls* (1928), p. 28.
3. Leonora Eyles, *Careers for Women* (1930), pp. 25–6, 16–17.
4. L. Bamberg and Charles Platt, *Careers for Girls* (1933), pp. 1, 10–18.

It was hardly surprising that, with such explicit attempts to reinforce stereotypes and with government-sponsored training schemes limited to domestic service, many girls entered retail and office work.[5] Lower-grade work, moreover, offered the prospect of more secure employment than a job with a career structure which had a marriage bar.

Government policies

The shifting political culture and its interaction with domestic ideology can be seen in the gendered labour market policies of inter-war governments. In 1919 Parliament passed the Sex Disqualification (Removal) Act which opened all occupations to women, but with important exceptions, the armed forces, the Church, the Stock Exchange, and most significantly, government employment: governments never set an example of best employment practice. The Act, while removing formal barriers to women's employment in professions such as law and accountancy, did nothing to remove other barriers in order to facilitate women's arrival in significant numbers as barristers and accountants. As Ray Strachey argued at the time, the effects of the Act were felt lower down the employment scale as women entered occupations allied to high-flying professions, such as clerical and secretarial work, with lower pay and status and fewer prospects.[6] Instead of pulling down barriers to women's employment, government actually reinforced them by excluding its own employees from the law, by upholding the marriage bar, by only operating training schemes for domestic service, and by its gendered operation of national unemployment and health insurance legislation.

Governments ran the National Insurance and National Health Insurance systems to women's disadvantage. Under the 1931 Anomalies Act a married woman had to satisfy a more stringent test than a man or single woman. In the first year of the Act's operation 179,888 married women were unable to qualify for benefits from an insurance scheme to which they had paid compulsory contributions.

Margaret Bondfield, as Minister of Labour, successfully defended the Act against the ire of Eleanor Rathbone, an Independent MP for the Combined Universities, 1929–46, and a number of Labour MPs including Jennie Lee,

---

5. Gregory Anderson, ed., *The White-Blouse Revolution* (Manchester, 1988), pp. 12, 13; Jane Lewis, 'Women clerical workers in the late nineteenth and early twentieth centuries', in Gregory Anderson, ed., *The White-Blouse Revolution*, p. 40.
6. Ray Strachey, *Careers and Openings for Women: A Survey of Women's Employment and a Guide for Those Seeking Work* (1937), pp. 44–6.

MP, 1929–31 and 1945–70; Cynthia Mosley, MP, 1929–31, and wife of Oswald, the fascist leader in Britain; Marion Phillips, MP, 1929–31, and Ellen Wilkinson. Wilkinson was a suffragist, trade unionist and Labour MP, 1924–31, and 1935–47. She worked closely with the National Union of Societies for Equal Citizenship (NUSEC) and campaigned for women's pensions, for women to keep their nationality on marriage to a foreigner, for maternity services, for free milk for children, for equal pay and for an end to the marriage bar in the civil service. Between 1929 and 1931 she was Parliamentary Secretary to Susan Lawrence at the Ministry of Health (from 1940 to 1945 Parliamentary Secretary to Herbert Morrison at the Home Office and from 1945 to 1947 Minister of Education with a place in the Cabinet).

In 1932 women MPs of all parties united with the Labour Party to defeat the National Government's attempt to require women, but not men, to requalify as new entrants on marriage. Under the 1933 National Health Insurance Act married women's benefits were reduced. Women were segregated and penalised for their higher health insurance claims than men, yet for unemployment insurance purposes they were grouped with men, even though men made more claims on the unemployment system than women; women's 'surplus' was put in the common fund. As the majority of women were not in pension schemes they were also financially worse off than men when they retired.

Those women who opposed protective legislation – that is, legislation which regulated the hours and conditions in which women and children, but not men, could work – saw it as another means by which governments hindered women's advancement. Women were divided over the issue of protective legislation, and although it was only one issue among many to interest women in the employment field it has received a good deal of attention as the occasion for a split in the women's movement. It is misleading, however, to focus too much attention on it, for protective legislation was only one small constraint on women's career advancement, and working-class women's issues were seen overwhelmingly from the point of view of working-class mothers in the home; it was their domestic work, not their work in the paid labour force, which was the focus of women's campaigns.

Immediately after the war the government did open windows of opportunity for a few women by sponsoring training schemes for women under the auspices of the Central Committee on Women's Training and Employment (CCWTE). Initially there were grants (to cover fees, and in some cases maintenance), for women to train as teachers, massagers, nursery nurses, midwives, and cooks, but from early 1922 the CCWTE limited its support to domestic training, the one area of employment girls and women aspired to avoid. No longer was government willing to help young women train for a real career and enter a job with some interest.[7] For most girls social mobility would continue to depend on finding a husband rather than a career with prospects.

Paid work and marriage

Throughout the inter-war years, women's organisations attacked the marriage bar. In the 1930s they gave greater prominence to attacking unequal pay, focusing on government policy towards civil servants and teachers in their campaigns (see Chapter Six).

The bulk of women in the professions were single, which reflected specific government policies and domestic ideology. The number of married women in paid work was relatively small; in the 1931 census seven out of eight married women were housewives. It was not until after the Second World War that married women increasingly went out to work. A number of factors held back married women from pursuing a career. It was relatively unattractive to be saddled with the double burden of work in the home and work outside the home, especially when most of one's married friends would not have been in paid work, and there was a strong belief – which permeated all sections of society – that married women should be at home, looking after husbands and children. Ray Strachey believed that in professional and well-paid work women would gain from having more interests and contacts as well as their family, but for the majority of women in badly paid industrial work, life was hard and wearing.[8]

For many women who might have chosen to continue in a career once married, there was no choice because of a marriage bar. In some occupations it operated throughout the 1920s and 1930s, in others it was only introduced in the 1930s. Some local education authorities (LEAs) introduced a marriage bar for teachers in the early 1920s, but there was no extension of marriage bars by LEAs in the early 1930s, and in the late 1930s some LEAs raised them because of political pressure and staff shortages. The BBC, without the custom and practice of excluding or subordinating women, pursued equal opportunities in the 1920s, but in 1932 it introduced a marriage bar on the grounds that married women were taking jobs away from single women who had no other means of support.

---

7. Ministry of Labour, *Gazette*, September 1923, pp. 317–18. The only help the government gave women after 1922 was the production of careers leaflets.
8. Ray Strachey, *Careers and Openings for Women*, pp. 63–4.

The 1919 Sex Disqualification (Removal) Act laid down that a person should not be dismissed from employment or disqualified on grounds of her or his marital status, with the exception of those in central and local government. In practice, because of the way in which the courts interpreted the law, it failed to protect married women's right to work. The explicit exclusion of government employment from the Act was challenged in 1927 by Sir Robert Newman's Private Member's Bill. In favour of removing the marriage bar it was argued that if a woman was old enough to decide whether to marry or not she was old enough to decide whether or not to pursue paid employment; there was no evidence to support the claim that women became less efficient when they married; married women who worked did so for various reasons, including economic necessity; it was economically inefficient to invest money in training women and then lose their services when they married; if married women were excluded from the employment pool the choice before society was more limited, and no-one suggested that married women in low-paid jobs should be sacked. Examples were given of married women in public life with successful careers, for instance, Harley Street specialists or actresses, such as Sybil Thorndike. Nancy Astor, a Conservative MP, sharp-tongued as ever, criticised the Bill's opponents, which included the government, '. . . when I listen to the opponents of the Bill, I feel that I know women who could have twins every year and still be more efficient than some Members of Parliament. . . . It is not really a question for the Government as to whether women are married or single. Their primary concern is efficiency. . . . But we have to fight a long-standing enemy, and that enemy is that a man should judge where a woman should be.'[9]

The government opposed the Bill, which was of little interest to MPs and it was defeated by 83 votes to 63. The arguments which won the day included: if a married woman was employed she would sooner or later become pregnant and would either have to be sacked then or would have a long absence from work; if a woman remained in post after marriage she would discuss her work with her husband and confidentiality would end; when a woman married her heart was in the home and a marriage would be a failure if this was not so; working married women would keep the birth rate down, and this was especially undesirable among civil servants and teachers, whom it was hoped would produce more, not fewer, children. One opponent of married women's employment claimed that the grievance was a limited one 'like many of the grievances put forward by the leaders of

---

9. HC Deb. vol. 205 col. 1198, 1199. Nancy Astor.

the women's movement'.[10] Such comments, even if unsupported, could undermine the arguments of women, who were grossly underrepresented in Parliament and were therefore unable to defend their position effectively.

The divided opinions over the desirability of married women's employment were grounded in perceived economic interests, and in notions of respectability and domestic ideology. Married women in the workforce were seen as taking jobs away from men and bringing wages down because of the assumption that a married woman was only earning 'pin' money while a man had to earn a family wage, that is, enough to keep himself, wife and children. Boston has argued that the male-dominated labour movement was equivocal towards the employment of married women. In 1922 the Labour Party and TUC jointly published a pamphlet which expressed outrage at the dismissal of highly skilled women, such as doctors, but it made no mention of the less skilled. They did not object to the marriage bar in principle, but they thought it difficult for it to operate fairly. There was confusion, too, over the issue of equal pay. A man's wage was regarded as a 'family' wage, which justified the fact that women were paid less, but women's low wages were also seen as leading to a general lowering of wages.[11]

The needs of the economy were frequently cited as a reason for excluding married women from the labour market. It was argued that high unemployment meant that there were not enough jobs for all who wanted them, and if married women were not in the labour market there would be more jobs for those who actually needed them. This was a politically acceptable argument because it fitted in with the ideology supported by many women, as well as men, that a woman's place was first and foremost at home looking after her husband and children. It was, however, a doubtful economic solution, resting on the assumption that married women did not need the money; it was an easy policy option to solve a complex problem and did not tackle the underlying causes of unemployment. In many minds it was linked with politically objectionable fascist policies on the Continent.

By supporting a marriage bar governments gave the appearance of doing something for the family when in reality it was a sham. Although the marriage bar seemed to be prioritising the needs of the family man it actually made no distinction between married and single men. The idea that governments were greatly concerned with the needs of unemployed

---

10. HC Deb. vol. 205 29 April 1927 cols 1176–1196, 1201, 1204. Quotation from Freddy Macquisten col. 1200.
11. Sarah Boston, *Women Workers and the Trade Unions* (1987), pp. 141–2, 145.

men and their families, moreover, ring hollow in the context of the limited steps taken by governments during the depression to create work for men or to alleviate the poor health of working-class women.

It is too simplistic to see the disagreements over married women's work in terms of a female/male divide, for numerous women went out of their way to prevent married women working outside the home. Women clerks in banking and insurance supported the widespread marriage bar in the belief that it would help to maintain wage levels. One of the arguments in favour of equal pay was that single women had family responsibilities, and it was felt that this argument was weakened when married women, with husbands to contribute to household expenses, entered the labour force.[12] In 1924 Lettice Fisher, the wife of H.A.L. Fisher, the Liberal politician, endorsed married women remaining at home when she argued in a public lecture that a woman who earned always did at least some of the house-keeping, with the result that in trying to do two jobs she did neither well; a married working woman's efficiency as a worker suffered; and this attempt to have the best of both worlds inevitably affected her earning power.[13] Yet, there is also evidence that some single women, most notably those in the National Union of Women Teachers (NUWT), did support the right of married women to paid work. The National Union of Teachers (NUT) also supported the right of married women to work in theory although it did not put much weight behind its views, except when it financially supported a couple of test cases of married women teachers.

Many young women viewed employment as a stop-gap, an attitude which lowered women's expectations about pay and conditions, and this worked to the detriment of all women in work, whether married or single. Strachey emphasised that girls were handicapped by their own attitudes; most as-sumed that paid work would be temporary so that poor working conditions and low pay seemed more acceptable than they might have done if women thought their career was for life. (Ghastly working conditions in turn made marriage a more attractive alternative.)

It was widely assumed that an unmarried woman's work should be sub-ordinated to the needs of her immediate family, and that married women should prioritise unpaid work in the home over paid work. One of the means by which women attempted to circumvent domestic constraints and pursue a career was by employing a domestic servant. Middle-class women

---

12. Sheila Lewenhak, *Women and Trade Unions: An Outline History of Women in the British Trade Union Movement* (1977), pp. 225–6.
13. Mrs H.A.L. Fisher, 'The economic position of the married woman', The Stansfeld Trust Lecture, University of London, 1924.

could never find enough domestic servants, and the job remained unpopular. Government efforts focused on training more girls, but despite the early post-war recommendations of a Ministry of Reconstruction committee on domestic service and a later Ministry of Labour report, government did nothing to make the work more attractive by regulating the pay and conditions of service. In the 1930s the government was presented with an easy way out when it allowed limited numbers of refugees from Nazi Germany into the country to work as domestic servants (see Chapter Five).

While private strategies for coping with the domestic ideology and domestic division of labour, without actually challenging them, involved employing a domestic servant, public campaigns for expanding all women's employment opportunities challenged the ideology which shored up the division of labour. These campaigns were frequently conducted by women within particular occupations.

Teaching

Teachers divided along the lines of the type of school, nursery (working-class children up to age 5), elementary (working-class children aged 5 to 14) or grammar school (predominantly middle-class children aged 11 to 16 or 18), in which they worked. There was a clear pecking order between schools which reflected the schools' resources, the age and social class of pupils, and the level of the teachers' education and qualifications. From the early 1920s most LEAs imposed a marriage bar on women but not on men. Women in elementary schools were divided between membership of the NUT and NUWT. Those in the latter enjoyed a strong sense of camaraderie which went beyond blackboard and chalk. Secondary teachers joined the Association of Assistant Mistresses (AAM) and heads joined the Association of Head Mistresses (AHM). The Association of Teachers of Domestic Science promoted a higher status for themselves and for domestic science for girls in elementary schools. The bulk of teachers worked in elementary schools following a two-year training course. Teachers in grammar schools possessed a degree, and were not required to undertake a teacher-training course. A very small number of teachers worked in nursery schools, a role for which women were developing training courses.

Teaching was one of the longest-established occupations for women, and the one which women had done most to expand over the previous generation. Women teachers temporarily gained greater employment opportunities as a result of the war; they took over posts in boys' schools vacated by male teachers, who left in their droves to join the forces. (By 1915 half of male teachers had joined up.) Women teachers exerted authority over their boy pupils, and married women were able to return to teaching because of the desperate teaching shortage. Nevertheless, boys' schools and the higher pay and promotion afforded men remained contested territory, with male teachers fighting a rearguard action to prevent women permanently benefiting from the men's temporary absence. Women's pay remained lower than that of their male colleagues.[14]

The individual personality of teachers was important, and all teachers had some degree of autonomy in the way they taught their class. Teachers in elementary schools were able to be more flexible in the curriculum they followed, although most would have emphasised the three Rs and domestic science for girls, teaching in an authoritarian and formal manner. Grammar school teachers, despite enjoying a higher status, had less scope for varying the curriculum. Domestic science would not have loomed so large as middle-class girls were not assumed to need as much training to be good mothers; for them it supposedly came more naturally. It is unlikely that any girl would have been taught domestic science by a teacher who was herself a mother. As in elementary schools, grammar school teachers tried to inculcate respect for authority.

While the Board of Education and the NUT accepted the assumption that teaching was especially suited to women's supposed characteristics, and women's maternal instincts could be used in working with children, research into women's motives for going into teaching showed that they were similar to those of men. Both women and men were attracted to teaching as a profession with reasonable pay, status, security and job satisfaction.

Most teachers in grammar schools required a degree; in elementary schools they required a teacher's certificate. Teacher-training colleges tended to benefit students academically and culturally as individuals, but they did not foster a collective view of the world; indeed, many operated a system of socialisation and social control, trying to replicate the culture of the middle-class home. How far these attitudes stayed with the bulk of women teachers is hard to gauge, for the most interesting work on women teachers, notably by Alison Oram, has focused on their collective pursuit of feminist goals through the NUWT.[15]

---

14. See Dina M. Copelman, *London's Women Teachers: Gender, Class and Feminism, 1870–1930* (1996), pp. 228–9; Alison Oram, *Women Teachers and Feminist Politics, 1900–1939* (Manchester, 1996), p. 75.
15. Elizabeth Edwards, 'The culture of femininity in women's teacher training colleges, 1900–1950', *History of Education* 22 (1993), pp. 277–88; Alison Oram, 'Inequalities in the teaching profession: the effect on teachers and pupils, 1910–1939', in Felicity Hunt, ed., *Lessons for Life: The Schooling of Girls and Women, 1850–1950* (Oxford, 1987), p. 122; Alison Oram, 'A master should not serve under a mistress: women and men teachers, 1900–1970', in Sandra Acker, *Teachers, Gender and Careers* (1989), p. 22.

Few nursery schools which opened in the nineteenth century were able to survive, due to lack of funds, but by the early twentieth century a small number of nursery schools were established in working-class urban areas. The Froebel movement trained a few nursery teachers and during the inter-war years a six-month Montessori course was offered in alternate years in London. Before the First World War, Margaret McMillan, the most prominent advocate of training for nursery teachers, opened a training centre attached to her nursery school in Deptford, which in 1919 gained Board of Education recognition. Some students, who were already trained as teachers, followed a ten-month course dedicated to nursery teaching; others, with no previous teacher-training, followed a three-year course, while a few upper-middle class young women followed the course as an alternative to more traditional charitable work with the urban poor. In 1930 the training expanded when the Rachel McMillan (named after Margaret McMillan's dead sister) Training College opened with money largely put up by Nancy Astor.

Most women elementary teachers were members of the NUT although in 1920 many of them broke away to form the NUWT because of the NUT's lack of active support for equal pay, despite the fact that this had been official union policy since 1919. Feminist teachers' key demands were for equal pay and scrapping the marriage bar (widely introduced between 1921 and 1923, when LEAs sacked thousands of women teachers as an economy measure). According to Oram, married women teachers were portrayed as greedy, unfeminine and neglectful of home and family. On this, and other, occasions male teachers' and governments' interests coincided.[16]

Women in both the NUT and NUWT took up issues beyond their sectional interests and networked with other women's organisations. In the 1920s the Ladies' Committee of the NUT was actively involved with the League of Nations, and in 1927 it supported the Peace Pilgrimage organised by the Women's International League for Peace and Freedom; it called for more women police; it was part of a deputation to the Home Secretary calling for the raising of the age of marriage to 16, and it took an interest in the treatment of young offenders, children's rescue work, maternal mortality, the status of Indian women and the need for more women magistrates. In the early 1930s the women's voice virtually ceased to be heard in the NUT, although the NUWT was as active as ever. The NUWT pursued an explicitly feminist agenda. Its critique of society went beyond policies towards teaching, but saw education as a key to breaking the

---

16.   Alison Oram, 'A master should not serve under a mistress', pp. 24, 32.

mould of an unequally gendered society. Whereas the NUT's support for equal opportunities was unreliable, the NUWT adamantly supported equal opportunities in education; it campaigned for changes in the curriculum, and in their lifestyles many of the women attempted to create a less gendered society. They also set specific attacks on women teachers in a wider context of attacks on all women workers. The NUWT was more than a body for promoting the professional interests of women teachers; it acted as a social club with a specific political outlook, and as a means of networking with women in other organisations. The NUWT's feminism did not stop at the school gates, which was important when teachers had a high public profile as wielders of power and authority over children, and as figures of standing in the local community. The NUWT linked up with other women's organisations in campaigns for equal moral standards, equal sentencing procedures by courts, and equal franchise.[17]

As well as demanding equal pay and an end to the marriage bar, women teachers were constantly disgruntled over their promotion prospects in relation to men. On the one hand, the sexual division of labour intensified in these years as women were increasingly employed to teach younger children, and men the older ones, but on the other hand, women and men teachers were increasingly employed together in mixed schools.[18]

In the 1930s women linked gender inequalities in teaching with wider, sinister political developments: fascism and anti-feminism were seen as two sides of the one bad pfennig. In 1938 the NUT published a series of articles on equal pay as a challenge to the views of the National Association of Schoolmasters, which upheld unequal pay. The articles' authors argued inter alia that those men who opposed equal pay were toying with a fascist mode of thought and arousing occupational prejudice against women, much as Hitler was doing so expertly. It was argued that it was dangerous to stir up sex antagonism, for a civilisation based on it could not escape 'sadistic debauchery'. On this point the NUT and NUWT were at one, for the NUWT also feared that a heavy emphasis on masculinity led to fascism and militarism. It cited events in Germany where women were muscled out of the professions and stripped of any meaningful power in public life.[19]

17. NUT *Report* 1920–1939; Alison Oram, '"Embittered, sexless or homosexual" attacks on spinster teachers, 1918–1939', in Arina Angerman, Geerte Binnema, Annemieke Keunen, Vefie Poels, Jacqueline Zirkzee, eds, *Current Issues in Women's History* (1989), p. 183; Alison Oram, 'Inequalities in the teaching profession', p. 110; Hilda Kean, *Deeds not Words: The Lives of Suffragette Teachers* (1990).
18. Alison Oram, 'A master should not serve under a mistress', p. 25.
19. NUT, *Equal Pay in the Teaching Profession* (1938); Alison Oram, 'Inequalities in the teaching profession', p. 110.

Teachers' unions represented the interests of their members over pay and conditions, and expressed their views to the Board of Education on issues such as the structure of schools, the age range of pupils and the curriculum. The range of teachers' unions, their meetings, resolutions and correspondence with the Board of Education are all testimony to their concern and activities over education policy. According to Hunt, teachers' unions were in broad agreement over key educational issues, although they differed over specifics. The NUWT, for instance, called for single-sex schools, and women's unions did not agree over the place of domestic science in the curriculum. All the teachers' unions put their views to the Board of Education in an attempt to influence curriculum and examination policies. None of them made much headway. The Association of Head Mistresses had some success in securing changes to the School Certificate examination but it was a slow process. Why were teachers, and women teachers in particular, unable to influence the Board?

According to Hunt, Board of Education civil servants held rather negative views – based on class, sex and intellectual snobbery – of those outside the Board. They were dismissive of teachers and, in particular, women teachers. The Board took no notice of the NUWT, wrongly assuming that its views were being put by the NUT, so the most radical women teachers were excluded completely from consultation. Board civil servants did not think that girls' education was unimportant, but they operated with assumptions about girls' education which they were not willing to question, and they listened to views which accorded with their own. Those within the Board seemed to be of one mind about girls' education.[20]

While alternative views may have been forthcoming from women HMIs (His Majesty's Inspectors), unlike their male colleagues, they were not automatically included in policy discussions at the Board. Although they exercised a good deal of responsibility and authority when undertaking their inspection duties, on substantial policy and spending issues it was explicit Board policy that women should defer to their senior male District Inspector colleagues. While women HMIs inspected girls' schools and joined inspection teams in mixed schools, and had responsibility for particular issues affecting the life of the girls' schools they inspected, general policy issues had to be passed on to the male District Inspector.[21]

In 1931 the Board responded to the growth in nursery schools and nursery classes by incorporating nursery provision into the remit of one woman

20. Felicity Hunt, *Gender and Policy in English Education: Schooling for Girls 1902–44* (Hemel Hempstead, 1991).
21. PRO ED 22/138 25 March 1934 and memorandum revised June 1929.

HMI in each of the country's nine divisions. Women were at the fore-front of the campaign to develop nursery provision, they worked in nursery education and the care and education of young children was seen as women's special responsibility. Although educationalists and Whitehall broadly accepted the case put – largely by women – for nursery education, its position was precarious. It was the newest and least developed of all stages of education; it was not a statutory requirement of LEAs to provide nursery education, and it therefore had a low priority in the pecking order of educational provision. Women were left an almost free hand by men uninterested in controlling such a low-status branch of education. Women HMIs inspected nursery schools once they were approved, but they could not grant the initial 'recognition' (government approval) to nursery schools alone, but only in consultation with male District Inspectors.[22]

The Royal Commission on the civil service, 1929–31, (Tomlin Commission) recommended that the women's and men's inspection sections should amalgamate, in stages, beginning immediately. Amalgamation was neither swift nor smooth. There was widespread unease among the women who felt that there was neither plan nor principle behind the amalgamation. They thought that there were women who were quite capable of doing the work of a District Inspector but the women were kept on the old unaggregated pay scale, while other women were given the aggregated pay but not the responsibility, due, the Board argued, to the fact that there were too few jobs to go around. The women disliked the method by which aggregation was implemented, without regular meetings to discuss it, and while in theory women could be promoted to any post, the fact that a salary scale was not given for a woman Chief Inspector was interpreted by the women as meaning that the Board had no intention of promoting a woman to the level of Chief Inspector.[23]

Thus, while women teachers pressed their views on the Board of Education, it chose not to take any real notice of them. Within the Board, women HMIs, who may have offered alternative views on girls' education, were treated with less respect than their male colleagues (often excluded from policy discussions and decisions, and paid less), although their advice within schools was not necessarily any less welcomed or acted upon than that of the men.

---

22. PRO ED 22/106 The Inspection and Recognition of Nursery Schools.
23. PRO ED 23/713 Statement by the women members of the executive committee of the Inspectors' Association ND. 1936? Bosworth–Smith, Board of Education to J.H. McCraig, Treasury 12 January 1937; and report of meeting 4 May 1938 between Bosworth–Smith and Miss Ibberson.

Nursing

From limited evidence it would seem that women often went into nursing with little or no support from their families, who were unenthusiastic about girls entering nursing for various reasons: the work was hard, the girls had to live at the hospital, and some parents thought it was a waste of an education for their daughters to enter nursing. Girls took up nursing for a variety of reasons. Some had contact with nurses either when they were patients or through relatives; some wanted a lifelong source of income (as an insurance against not marrying), albeit a low one; while for others, more likely middle-class, the experience of working as a VAD in the war led naturally into nursing. What is striking from these nurses' accounts is that none seem to have entered with any romantic notions about nursing. The failure of nurses to mount effective collective campaigns cannot, therefore, be explained in terms of nurses' angelic devotion to a vocation. Rather, various aspects of nursing made it very difficult to organise for change. Probationers found that nursing virtually took over one's life, with the system of living in the nurses' home, strict discipline, long hours and little social life. Those probationers who failed to finish the course usually dropped out because the work was too physically demanding or they could not abide the regulations which ruled their lives. The standard of training varied enormously but everywhere it emphasised hygiene and cleanliness, which in an age before antibiotics could mean the difference between life and death.

Nurses always called each other by their surnames, but between nurses of the same grade there seems to have been a strong sense of comradeship, whatever their background. Barriers existed between different grades of nurse, between nurses and doctors, between nurses in different types of hospitals, and between nurses in different branches of nursing, whether hospital, health visiting or midwifery. Hierarchy was strictly maintained, with rules such as a ban on junior nurses overtaking more senior ones in the corridor. For most nurses the matron was a remote figure who was unlikely to have acted as a role model for young nurses. As well as a hierarchy within hospitals there was also a pecking order between them, with voluntary hospitals enjoying a higher status than Poor Law Infirmaries (after 1929 known as local authority hospitals). Standards for both patients and nurses were regarded as higher in voluntary hospitals, and accommodation for nurses was usually more comfortable. As well as nurses in hospitals for physical ailments, there was a separate branch of mental health nurses – both women and men – working in large mental health institutions.

Outside hospitals health visitors worked in the community, mainly with working-class mothers, as part of the campaign to reduce the infant mortality rate. Health visitors undertook a range of duties, depending on the requirements of the local authority for which they worked. The backgrounds of health visitors varied: some, but not all, had undertaken nursing training; increasingly, health visitors were trained nurses. Likewise, not all midwives were trained nurses, and indeed even in the 1930s a small number of midwives possessed no formal midwifery or nursing qualification. As a result of the various hierarchies and different branches of nursing, nurses were divided across and within institutions, which meant that it was hard to foster a sense of a common identity.

The College of Nursing confined full membership to registered general nurses, so creating a further barrier between nurses, and indeed it made a point of drawing a distinction between its members and other nurses. It supported the low wages of nurses during training in the hope of attracting women with families rich enough to support them. In an effort to establish the 'professional' credentials of nursing it opposed nurses' incorporation into the National Insurance Scheme. It did, however, demand higher wages, with little success, and a superannuation scheme, which was eventually introduced.[24]

In the 1930s general and white-collar unions successfully recruited nurses, especially those in public health departments and local authority hospitals, although as the unions competed with each other and with the College of Nursing, membership was diffused and nurses were not well served. In the late 1930s the TUC attempted to draw all unionised nurses together. It formed the National Advisory Committee which issued a Nurse's Charter relating to training, pay and conditions. Although the College of Nursing tried to discredit the campaign, it received widespread support from nurses and the general public and extensive press coverage. Alarmed at the sympathy nurses were whipping up, the Ministry of Health set up a wide-ranging committee, chaired by the Earl of Athlone, to inquire into recruitment, training, registration and conditions of service for nurses and to make recommendations for hospital and domiciliary nurses. From the Ministry's point of view this committee had the twin virtues of making the government look as if it was taking action while at the same time delaying it.[25]

The poor wages and working conditions, especially for young nurses, contributed to the chronic shortage of nurses. This was aggravated by first, the living-in system which in practice excluded married and older women;

24. Robert Dingwall, Anne Marie Rafferty and Charles Webster, *An Introduction to the Social History of Medicine* (1988), p. 100.
25. Dingwall, Rafferty and Webster, *An Introduction to the Social History of Nursing*, pp. 101–3.

second, the growth in demand for trained nurses (health visitors, midwives, industrial nurses) and third, the shortening of hours. Instead of improving pay and conditions, in the 1930s local authorities employed more non-certified nurses, a move which outraged nurses' organisations. Despite the almost universal dissatisfaction over pay and conditions and the shortage of nurses which put them at a premium, nurses were prevented from effect-ive bargaining. In 1919 the government had established the General Nurs-ing Council (GNC) and with it the registration of nurses. The government, however, built a basic weakness into the GNC, for it was unable to take any unilateral steps which carried financial implications for training schools.[26] It thus lacked the autonomy which professional bodies usually enjoy.

Although nurses were active, hard-working and tough in their ability to cope with the discipline and demands of the work, governments helped to keep nurses collectively weak. The difficulties nurses faced in mobilising for change were the result of four related factors. First, there was moral pressure on nurses to live up to an angelic image of nursing carefully fos-tered by the government during the war. Second, their employment was hierarchical, disciplined and diffuse. Third, government purposefully cre-ated the GNC in order to make it difficult for nurses to act in a strong and active fashion in their dealings with employers and government. Fourth, trade unions offered nurses a poor service through their competition for members, which further divided nurses. When the TUC provided nurses with a vehicle for strong and collective action they responded.[27]

Doctors of medicine

Over the previous half-century, unlike women in nursing, teaching and social work, women doctors had formed only a small proportion of medical practitioners. Girls' education had provided relatively few women with the appropriate qualifications for medical schools. Those who were qualified encountered fierce opposition from male doctors and students, and, once trained, women doctors faced discrimination in appointments and promo-tion. During the war, attitudes towards women applicants to medical school

---

26. National Sound Archives c545 RCN History Group Interviews; The College of Nursing *Bulletin* 1920–1926; Dingwall, Rafferty and Webster, *An Introduction to the Social History of Nursing*.

27. The above two paragraphs are based on Dingwall, Rafferty and Webster, *An Introduction to the Social History of Nursing*.

and medical posts had softened, partly as a result of the drastic increase in the need for doctors, and partly as a result of the way women doctors publicly proved their competence. Attitudes which had gradually shifted during the war rapidly moved back into place at the war's end. Arguments against women doctors were expressed less in terms of what women could not do than in terms of what they should not do. Women publicised their medical war work so effectively that it was no longer possible to argue with any credence that women were not capable of the work, but the argument that women should prioritise home and family gained a new lease of life. Old arguments about decency also resurfaced. Discussion in the press about mixed classes of female and male medical students prompted St Clair Thomson of King's College Medical School to defend the practice; the students knew nothing of the 'coarseness, immodisty and indelicacy' referred to by some correspondents to *The Times*.[28]

After the war access to training was again made difficult. The London medical schools, apart from the Royal Free, slammed their doors in the face of women. (University College Hospital accepted ten women annually on higher entrance requirements than men.) Scotland and the English provinces continued to accept women and indeed, over the course of the interwar years, the number of women medical graduates increased noticeably. The barriers to access which medical schools erected against women was due in part to their fear of flooding a post-war contracting market for doctors. Why sift out the women rather than take the best-qualified candidates? Carol Dyhouse has suggested that at this time the concept of male professionalism in medicine took shape and hardened. The war had proved the competence of women doctors and some of the men felt threatened; the easiest way of beating the threat was by removing it, and by letting old prejudices ride to the surface. Louisa Martindale, 1873–1966, a suffragist and sister of Hilda Martindale, who qualified as a doctor in 1899, practised as a GP and then became a leading gynaecologist, commented on the jealousy and rivalry of some men towards women, which she believed was fuelled unconsciously by their wives (who presumably saw women doctors as a financial threat to their husbands' income and a threat to their status as wives and mothers). Martindale commented that there were eminent and distinguished surgeons and doctors who were 'great' enough and 'keen' enough on their work to solicit and welcome the opinions of women doctors. Thus, opposition may well have been strongest from those doctors who suspected that they were not as good as the women (which in many cases was

---

28. *The Times*, 15 March 1922.

probably a true reflection of their skills, given that the women doctors had qualified despite having the odds stacked against them).

During the war women had been attracted into medicine, but the long training and the apparent uncertainty of gaining work was thought at the time to have discouraged more girls than boys from applying to medical school. In the 1920s the uncertainty was more apparent than real. In 1926, of 216 women graduates from the Royal Free between 1923 and 1925, ten had given up work because of marriage and 13 could not find medical work, but the rest were all in medical posts.

The small number of women doctors meant that many worked in isolation from each other. Women doctors continued to work in general practice, sometimes with another woman, which was one way around the difficulty of finding public health or hospital posts, but it did mean that they were isolated from other doctors. While the British Medical Association (BMA) now admitted women, there were so few women members that their chances of being elected to the Council were slim.

Women responded to their professional isolation by working through the BMA, and in 1917 by setting up their own organisation, the Medical Women's Federation (MWF), which provided a means of expressing their collective voice, and a means of communication between women doctors in Britain and abroad.

The Federation provided a channel for the Ministry of Health to contact and work with women doctors. When the Ministry was first formed it invited the Federation to nominate one member to sit on a panel to guide the Minister in choosing a Consultative Council to advise him on medical and allied services. The Federation nominated Dr F.H. Ives, who went on to sit on the Consultative Council along with Dr Janet Lane-Claypon. Dr Laura Sandeman was also nominated to sit on the Scottish Board of Health Consultative Council.

The Federation gave expert advice to government on matters relating to women's and children's health, sometimes at the request of government, for instance, in the mid-1920s for an enquiry into assaults on young people, and a few years later for plans for a national maternity scheme, and for information relating to maternal mortality. On occasion, the Federation lobbied government. It repeatedly demanded that a woman should sit on the Board of Control, which dealt with mental hospitals, particularly as more women than men were in-patients, and this request was accepted. In the mid-1930s the Federation, along with other bodies, lobbied successfully for the Ministry of Health to set up an enquiry into abortion.

The Federation defended women doctors' employment conditions, standing firm with the BMA against local or central government paying women less than the men in the same post, a ploy which some local authorities tried unsuccessfully when looking to fill public health posts. Both organisations also tried to expand the fields in which women could work, and to improve the promotion prospects of women. Neither the BMA nor the Federation could prevent central and local government promoting men rather than women and thus paying the men more. Local authorities were loath to appoint women doctors to senior posts, although by the 1930s both Stepney in London and the City of York had appointed women Medical Officers of Health. Medical women were excluded from public health posts (except maternity and child welfare work, and school medical work) which carried administrative responsibilities. As a result of this policy, women were re-stricted to junior posts in public health and barred from promotion, partly because they could not gain the appropriate experience. Women were also rarely appointed to tuberculosis posts, which were often seen as stepping stones to higher administrative posts, so again women's chances of promo-tion were reduced. The Federation campaigned to break down prejudices against employing and promoting women doctors. It had some limited success in fighting a marriage bar which some hospitals and local author-ities imposed on women.[29] The most senior woman doctor in government employment was Janet Campbell. Before the war she had worked for the Board of Education; on the creation of the Ministry of Health in 1919 she became head of its Maternity and Child Welfare Department with a staff of six women doctors (see Chapter Six).

Social work

Like nursing, teaching and medicine, social work was disunited and male-controlled, but at least it was less hierarchical. The term 'social work' cov-ered a wide range of activities, which included working in clubs, Settlements, police court missions and rescue work; with the unemployed, infants and mothers, and handicapped children; as well as for the Charity Organisation Society and charities for the blind. House property managers and almoners were also part of social work. Charities, hospitals and, to a limited extent, local authorities all employed social workers. This range of activities mili-tated against a common work experience and common identity, but in most

---

29. All information relating to the Medical Women's Federation is culled from the Annual Reports of the MWF, Wellcome Institute for the History of Medicine London, Contemporary Medical Archives Centre.

cases social work was not as hierarchical as nursing. Despite its broad scope, its attractiveness to middle-class girls was waning as they gradually opened wider the doors of other paid employment with the potential for improved prospects. The main alternatives to social work were teaching, especially for graduates, and nursing. (Social work may superficially appear to share the characteristics of women's work but in fact there was a far higher proportion – 46 per cent – of men in social work than in teaching or nursing.)

Ronald Walton, the main historian of women social workers, argued that men dominated social work, despite its being seen as women's province. Throughout the period there were only ever male secretaries of the Charity Organisation Society. Almoners were all women but they struggled with male-dominated hospital boards, which saw almoners' role as assessing and collecting hospital fees. Almoners, in contrast, perceived their role as a medico-social one. There were very few almoners, so they were isolated, and they did not campaign to have their definition of their role accepted by hospitals. Both women and men worked as probation officers but despite the fact that the men were usually less well educated and qualified than the women, they dominated probation work, both in their numbers and status.[30]

Women's motives for entering social work were mixed: they often assumed that it was not a career. Social work training courses were offered around the country, notably in London at Bedford and Westfield Colleges, and the London School of Economics. Barbara Wootton later reflected that few of the students she had taught at Westfield College were training to be paid social workers as most of them were young women of means and leisure who wished to engage in various charitable activities. Indeed, this comment reflects the continued mixture of paid and unpaid, trained and untrained social workers. The bulk of social workers were voluntary; even among the paid ones most were not trained. Those who had a social science qualification and social work training tended to work in London and the south. Trained workers went into both voluntary and statutory agencies as either paid or voluntary workers. Since there were few financial rewards, Ray Strachey believed that most entered social work in a vocational spirit. There was little incentive to organise for change and with such a disparate range of activities, little sense of common purpose. There was no single body representing social workers, and the different branches of social work developed independently of each other. Women's control over their work was most easily achieved in new openings,

30.   R.G. Walton, *Women in Social Work* (1975), pp. 115–24.

such as house property management, where there was no male culture or traditional practices.

House property management

House property management grew out of women's philanthropic activities and the work of Octavia Hill; in 1916 the Association of Women House Property Managers was founded with the aim of bringing together all those involved in the work, to arrange for training and to promote knowledge of the fledgling career. Here was one area of social work composed entirely of women. It immediately fed into post-war reconstruction plans, with members sitting on reconstruction committees. Most workers came from a social work background, but one of the first women surveyors, Irene Barclay, also undertook house property management. In partnership with Evelyn Perry she made surveys of housing conditions in various London boroughs and in other towns, worked for private clients converting houses into flats, valued houses and building sites and reported on houses for intending purchasers. They collected data for housing reports and publicised this new field of work for women by lecturing and writing. The bulk of their time was taken up by property management.

The majority of posts for women with the House Property Managers' certificate was on local authority estates. The new estates, created in the 1930s as slum clearance programmes took off, led to their own problems as families found them lonely and expensive. The amount of control given the women by local authorities varied. A typical day involved dealing with letters containing rent or explaining why the rent could not be sent; letters from people living in damp basements or threatened with eviction for overcrowding who were asking for accommodation; and enquiries from other boroughs or social workers requesting to see an estate or nursery. House property managers scrutinised accounts, and dealt with plans and reports from architects, along with personal callers with various housing problems. They went out collecting rents, noting repairs to be undertaken and inspecting the progress of ones already under way. There might be a meeting with a district surveyor or sanitary inspector.[31] Here was a new occupation for women, which offered a real career with job satisfaction, but the openings were relatively few, and although publicised by a number of successful women, house property management remained a small opening.

---

31.   J.M. Upcott, 'Women house property managers', *The Building News* (1925), pp. 34–6; Irene Barclay, 'Property management', in Margaret Cole, ed., *The Road to Success: Twenty Essays on the Choice of Career for Women* (1936), pp. 144–54.

Protecting women's sexual morals

More women continued to be engaged in the traditional social work activity of the moral regulation and protection of working-class women and girls than in the new and small opening of house property management. After the First World War moral welfare work was given a new lease of life. In 1920 the Josephine Butler House opened in Liverpool with the aim of training educated women for 'preventative' work. The Association for Moral and Social Hygiene's (AMSH) commitment to equal moral standards for women and men, and to a strong Christian ethos, dominated the training. The significance of the Josephine Butler House was threefold. First, it was part of the continuing movement towards the trained social worker. Second, it reflected a desire for women's welfare work to have an impact on the entire nation: work in one area would hopefully have a knock-on effect. In practice its influence was very limited. It could never have done much to change public attitudes; over a twenty-year period it trained under 200 women, and they dispersed to work in a wide range of settings, such as refuges, clubs, settlements, hostels, and homes for unmarried mothers. Some went abroad.[32]

Third, rescue work continued to regulate the sexual morals of working-class girls and women rather than men. The justification for working with girls and women was that the social consequences for women of sex outside marriage, if it led to pregnancy or allegations of prostitution, were momentous. The bulk of the work involved finding places in mother and baby homes for unmarried pregnant women, helping to get an affiliation order, and arranging for the women to receive domestic training. Some societies worked with children who had been sexually abused, others 'protected' the 'mentally deficient' or those with VD. The language used by rescue workers was 'protection' 'special friend and advisor' of those who had 'misunderstood sex; overstimulated, misused or perverted it; blindly, weakly or deliberately followed the sex impulse in the face of social convention, of law and of religion and who have to pay the price'. Notwithstanding the decline in organised religion, rescue work was organised overwhelmingly through denominational societies so that the Church continued to exercise influence and control.[33]

---

32. Josephine Butler Memorial House, *Annual Report* (1938), pp. 12–15, University of Liverpool.
33. Hilda Morris, 'Southwark Diocesan Association for Preventive and Rescue Work', in Women's Employment Publishing, *Careers After the War*, 5th ed. (1919), pp. 125–7.

Conclusions

Many women were socialised into a culture in which women were responsible for home making and caring, and paid work was secondary for them. The male work culture, moreover, deterred many women from applying for certain jobs. Not all women accepted this culture. Those women not tied down by family commitments were increasingly able to pursue a career and their ability to follow it depended more on the career than on the women's commitment or personality. Hierarchical, fragmented and strictly disciplined occupations, such as nursing, worked against women's career advancement; in occupations such as teaching and the civil service (see Chapter Six) which were also hierarchical and fragmented but less disciplined, women enjoyed some limited success. Women had greatest autonomy and scope in those branches of occupations, such as house property management, which were not hierarchical or strictly disciplined, although their small size limited the opportunity for women to enjoy the career.

The potential or limitations of any career for women has to be placed in the context of the political culture of the day. The way in which the political culture of Britain restricted women can be seen most clearly in legislation which explicitly denied women opportunities.

Women in teaching, nursing, medicine and social work were, through their training and work, among those most likely to have informed views on the various ways in which welfare policies might be developed and delivered to large sections of the population, yet governments largely ignored their views. A previous generation had used charitable work to carve out public space and influence. During the inter-war years social work diversified, but trained and paid social workers failed to influence government policies for their clients, the poor. A previous generation of educators had opened and run girls' schools and pressed successfully for women's access to higher education. Only in nursery education, as the next chapter will show, did inter-war women educationalists make political waves. Campaigners in the NUWT were overshadowed by the NUT, and the Board of Education paid scant attention to the views of women teachers. Women in the past had influenced the development of nursing, but in the inter-war years it remained weak and divided. The factors which weakened women's position in these occupations – disunity through diffuse employment, hierarchy, a strong emphasis on discipline and a dominant male culture – were the same factors which worked against women in these occupations contributing to welfare policies.

Other calls for changes in welfare policies came from women who were, on the whole, not educated and trained in education or health work and had no formal expertise in their areas of interest, but who worked through common networks and organisations to express their views on welfare policies. The following chapters analyse the reasons for their successes and failures.

CHAPTER FOUR

Campaigning against the Gendered Impact of Poverty

Introduction

This chapter examines the main campaigns undertaken by politically active and reform-minded women to improve welfare and health services for the mass of women. It provides cameo biographies of four exemplary women, Eglantyne Jebb, Margaret McMillan, Eleanor Rathbone and Marie Stopes. They all believed that poverty was gendered in its impact: it affected women and men differently, and within families women typically bore the brunt of poverty. Jebb, McMillan, Rathbone and Stopes attempted to alleviate women's poverty in their complementary campaigns.

Historians have painted a multi-layered picture of industrial discord, cultural clashes and political disagreements between an industrial male working class and inter-war governments. For many years the role played by women was barely thought worth a footnote.[1] In recent years historians have shown that the role of women in the labour movement involved more than envelope-licking and tea-making.[2] In contrast, women outside the labour movement who challenged governments' policies, with the exception of pacifist women, have received little collective attention. Historians who have looked at women's campaigns have focused on women's organisations and their split in the late 1920s, and engaged in a debate over the use of labels such as 'welfare' and 'equality' feminists but this misses much of the most interesting analyses and campaigning of women, and focuses too much

---

1. For example Keith Burgess, *The Challenge of Labour: Shaping British Society, 1850–1930* (1980).
2. Pamela Graves, *Labour Women: Women in British Working-Class Politics, 1918–1939* (Cambridge, 1994).

on the 1920s at the expense of the 1930s when women's organisations were weak.[3]

Organised groups of women, and individual women, mounted attacks on governments across a whole range of foreign (see Chapter Five) and domestic policy issues, including poverty and unemployment, nursery schools, family allowances, birth control and double moral standards. Historians have usually analysed these campaigns separately, although in truth they overlapped in terms of political analysis, cross-institutional and professional involvement, and individual personalities. The campaigns often encompassed a broad spectrum of party political support; the leading lights frequently held strong, and different, party political commitments. The campaigns were also all-embracing in that, although dominated by women, they did not exclude men. Women forged the way ahead in their calls for family allowances, nursery schools and wider access to birth control, issues which most immediately affected working-class married women and their young children but, the campaigners argued, potentially influenced the whole of society.

The historiography of twentieth-century poverty studies has assumed that an analysis of the distribution of power and resources in a family is a feature of late-twentieth-century studies. In recent years there has been a 'rediscovery' of women's poverty and an emphasis on analysing the distribution of resources within a family. This focus is nothing new. Throughout the twentieth century various campaigners and welfare workers recognised the different and unequal resources of women and men within families. Women campaigners certainly recognised it, and they wanted policies which took it into account.

Susan Kent has lambasted inter-war 'welfare' feminists for what she sees as their acceptance of the dominant discourses on sexuality, which meant that they were trapped in a concept of women in domestic and maternal roles and unable to advocate equality and justice. According to Kent, the potential for 'welfare' feminists to be radical and to draw in working-class women was undermined by the arguments put forward to shore up their demands. She goes on to argue that by emphasising the needs of women as mothers rather than women's rights and by making demands based on women's tradition of special needs and functions, they ceased to challenge the dominant discourses on sexuality, and their ideology was often confused with that of anti-feminists.[4] In contrast to Kent, Koven and Michel claim that those who promoted maternalist policies may have evoked traditional

3. Olive Banks, *Faces of Feminism: A Study of Feminism as a Social Movement* (1981).
4. Susan Kingsley Kent, *Making Peace: The Reconstruction of Gender in Interwar Britain* (Princeton, New Jersey, 1993), pp. 6–7, 118.

images of 'womanliness' and extolled the virtues of domesticity but, at the same time, they were challenging the boundaries between the private and the public, women and men, and state and civil society.[5] This chapter will likewise emphasise the genuinely radical nature of the policies discussed.

Throughout the 1920s and 1930s, among a group of women not personally affected by economic misfortune, there was a strong culture of alternative thinking and action in which the gendered impact of poverty was the intellectual tree from which all other policies and projects branched. A gendered analysis of society was explicit in the work of Margaret McMillan, Eleanor Rathbone and Marie Stopes; and implicit in the work of Eglantyne Jebb and Save the Children Fund (SCF). These related campaigns aimed to improve the quality of life for women and children within working-class families. Taken together, the implications of the women's proposals were far-reaching, for their successful implementation would have not only raised the standard of living for working-class women, but also, in the process, rearranged the existing pattern of gender relations in the home. Nowhere during the inter-war years did women succeed in doing this, although in some countries governments adopted similar policies to those advocated by women, not to alter social relations but to shore up existing ones. British governments subsequently adopted most of these policies, but again not normally for the reasons women had campaigned for them.

The majority of the campaigners called for more intervention by the state. There is already a lively debate, as mentioned in Chapter One, on the extent of women's influence on the development of state welfare in the twentieth century, although it tends to focus on evidence from the late nineteenth century and early twentieth century, which is a whole generation before the main provision of British state welfare. One of the aims of this chapter is to examine the relationship between women's welfare campaigning and the state in the years leading up to the main extension of state social welfare. As many of the campaigns were only partially successful, or did not bear fruit until later years, we are analysing ideas and a culture of protest rather than major policy changes.

While historians have analysed and described the relationship between middle-class women and the urban poor of Victorian and Edwardian Britain, they have paid less attention to the way in which that relationship was fostered anew in the middle of the twentieth century. Middle-class women were building on a long tradition, but fashioning it afresh as they gradually professionalised their work, and aimed to have a national rather than local

---

5.   Seth Koven and Sonya Michel, eds, *Mothers of a New World: Maternalist Policies and The Origins of Welfare States* (1993).

impact, although a limited, local impact was what they often achieved. In the 1920s and 1930s the public lives of middle-class women intersected with the private worlds of working-class women, not by 'home'/'slum' visiting as in the nineteenth century and Edwardian years, but by the public campaigning of middle-class women over private and intimate daily aspects of working-class mothers' lives. The First World War was a bridge rather than a watershed in this changing relationship. The women at the forefront of campaigns gained their knowledge of working-class lives and formulated their political ideas in the years before the war, and the war added an additional layer to their experiences and ideas, which fed into campaigns in the inter-war years.

Women such as Jebb, McMillan, Rathbone and Stopes shared a common aim in wanting to improve the standard of living of working-class married women and their young children. They believed that the needs of poor mothers and children should be tackled together. Linking women and children was not an insult to the women, but a recognition of the interdependence of mothers and children. The campaigners shared a common assumption that what was first and foremost in the interests of working-class mothers would work in the interests of all women and, ultimately, of the whole of society. Whereas in the nineteenth century campaigners linked women and children in the context of the labour market and protective legislation, now campaigners linked them in the context of state intervention in the domestic sphere.

As well as women talking to other women about the things that were within their power to alter, they concurrently made efforts to change government policies in order that the circumstances in which poor mothers and children struggled would be made easier. They put pressure on governments both directly through campaigns and petitions, and indirectly by taking action which they hoped governments would imitate, for instance, through the opening of birth control clinics, or nursery schools in deprived areas.

Facilities specifically aimed at women were few and far between. In any discussion of services for mothers it is essential to include provision for children because women were, and were expected to be, responsible for their children's health and wellbeing. Most women were excluded from national unemployment and national health insurance, and those who were covered paid in less and received less than men. After the First World War local authorities increasingly provided infant and maternal welfare centres, which had been started originally by voluntary groups. Local authorities also employed health visitors. From 1930 married women who already had children and for whom further pregnancies posed a medical threat could be given birth control information in local authority clinics. As infant and maternal welfare services were local but not national they depended on local authority resources, so that provision was often poorest in poor areas or in areas where local politicians or medical officers of health did not approve of such services. By the 1930s most local authorities provided milk and other nutritional supplements for pregnant and nursing mothers, and for children up to at least the age of one and sometimes the age of three. A number of local authorities provided free school meals. Nursery school provision was patchy and relied on a mixture of charitable and local authority support. It was not until the end of the Second World War that government introduced family allowances.

Marie Stopes and the birth control movement

Marie Stopes, 1880–1958, an eminent scientist who, before the war, supported women's suffrage, in the 1920s was the leading figure in a campaign to encourage the use of contraception by the working class. She was a controversial figure among contemporaries – she did not work well even with those who shared her aims – and she has remained so among historians. Stopes publicised birth control through her writings, campaigning and opening birth control clinics. In March 1921 she established the first birth control clinic where consultations were free and contraceptives were sold at cost price, unless the women could not afford them, in which case they were free. Stopes subordinated her eugenicist and political aims to the health and happiness of individual women, whatever their class. Jane Lewis depicts a complex character, who campaigned for birth control information to be made freely available, out of a concern both for individual mothers and for the future of the race. As Lewis points out, Stopes deployed the two arguments in conjunction, not in contradiction. She was the first British birth controller to make the connection between birth control as a means of improving the health of women and improving the health of the race at the same time.[6] In this ability to mesh the two aims she was typical of many women at the time; it is only a later generation of historians who find this problematic; it was not so for contemporaries.

Women birth controllers based their demands on the connection they made between the health and wellbeing of working-class mothers and the health of the children they bore; in turn the health of the children was

---

6. Marie Stopes, *Wise Parenthood* (1918); Deborah Cohen, 'Private lives in public spaces: Marie Stopes, the mothers' clinics and the practice of contraception', *History Workshop Journal* 35 (1993), p. 97; Jane Lewis, *The Politics of Motherhood: Child and Maternal Welfare in England, 1900–1939* (1980).

linked to the health of the whole nation. (This analysis, which moved out from mother and baby to the entire nation, was paralleled in other campaigns.) Many supporters, most notably Mary Stocks, of the birth control movement also supported other campaigns, such as the one for family allowances. The birth controllers adopted two linked strategies. First, they opened birth control clinics, which they hoped governments would imitate; second, they called on governments to make birth control information available to mothers at maternal and child welfare clinics. The sacks of letters Stopes received from working-class women and the interest of rank and file women in the Labour Party are testimony to many women's desire to limit the size of their families. Many women activists saw birth control as an integral part of their social welfare strategy for alleviating working-class poverty. In 1923 the Women's Cooperative Guild (WCG), having campaigned since before the war over maternity issues, came out in favour of birth control information being made widely available to women, and it was followed in 1925 by the National Union of Societies for Equal Citizenship (NUSEC), in 1927 by the Women's Liberal Association and 1929 by the National Council of Women (NCW). Between 1924 and 1927 the Labour Party's Women's Conference passed resolutions in favour of working-class women having access to birth control information, and in 1924 formed the campaigning Birth Control Group. In the 1930s these organisations kept up their pressure on governments. (More unusually, in 1924 the WCG, and in 1936 NUSEC, called for abortion to be legalised.) One of the arguments deployed by women's organisations in favour of birth control was that it prevented abortions.

In the 1920s Marie Stopes spearheaded the birth control movement, in the 1930s the National Birth Control Association (NBCA) kept the issue alive although there was no single figurehead as well known as Stopes. Lady Denman chaired the NBCA, providing it with financial support as it opened clinics and coordinated the work of various birth control organisations. 'Trudie' Denman, 1884-1954, had supported the dissemination of information about birth control in the decade before she became chair of the new organisation, arguing that poor women should have access to the same information and support as better-off women. She was well connected (before the war her husband had been Governor-General of Australia) and during the First World War she had chaired a committee which, at the government's behest, established Women's Institutes (WIs) around the country. She continued to be involved with the WI for many years. (She helped to set up the Women's Land Army and throughout the Second World War championed better pay and conditions; after the war, when ex-Land Army women were not accorded the same benefits as civil defence workers, she resigned, which had the effect of prising some concessions

from the government.) Despite the NBCA benefiting from Denman's lobbying skills and connections, and receiving women's cross-party support,
it never achieved much success with governments.

Whitehall civil servants and ministers were sympathetic to the argument
that contraception could help improve the 'standard' of the British population by cutting down on the number of children born in poor and less
healthy families. As a result, in 1930 the Labour government made one
concession by agreeing that a nursing or pregnant mother could be offered
contraceptive advice at a maternal and child welfare centre, or gynaecolo-
gical clinic, if further pregnancies would endanger her health. In 1934 the
National Government extended the provision to include women suffering
from TB, heart disease, diabetes and chronic nephritis. These gestures were
typical of governments during these years: they took small steps but without
the vision or all-encompassing strategy of many of the women campaigners.
The measures fell far short of those demanded by women's organisations
and the NBCA. Why?

Governments, reflecting widespread public concern, wanted to do nothing
which might adversely affect the birth rate. The overarching concern of
governments in this context was to maintain and increase the population.
While many health officials recognised that there was a link between a high
maternal mortality rate (MMR) and a high birth rate, they preferred not to
interfere directly with the birth rate but to rely on other measures to bring
down the infant mortality rate (IMR). The medical profession, moreover, was
divided in its attitude towards birth control.[7] Some of the leading women
doctors, such as Scharlieb (a Roman Catholic) and Louisa Martindale,
opposed artificial contraception. The overwhelming hostility of the medical
profession in the nineteenth century to contraception had modified but the
government now received conflicting messages from the medical world and
this, along with the low priority accorded women's health in Whitehall,
meant that governments tiptoed around the issue.

Eglantyne Jebb and Save the Children Fund

In contrast to governments, SCF's support for a range of welfare initiatives
exemplifies the broad imagination of women campaigners such as SCF's
founder, Eglantyne Jebb, 1876–1928. In 1876 Jebb was born into a landed
Shropshire family. She was educated at home where she learnt French and
German, skills which would stand her in good stead in later years; in 1895

---

7. Jane Lewis, *The Politics of Motherhood*, Chapter 7.

she went up to Lady Margaret Hall at the University of Oxford where she read history. Her family background not only provided money and facilitated connections and an ability to deal with the good and the great (her brother-in-law was a Liberal MP) but it also influenced her outlook on life. Her mother had brought her up with a strong sense of duty towards the local poor and had started an arts and crafts movement among the local working class. Liberal middle-class culture at this time emphasised a girl's duty not only in the home but also in the wider community. Young women and men frequently undertook a spell of charitable work, often in a Settlement. Jebb appears to have been motivated by a deep, almost mystical, religious zeal, a sense of duty and, later during the war, by pacifism. With family wealth behind her she did not need to worry about paid employment; she was free to put into practice her personal sense of public duty.

Jebb's first foray into 'good works' was not the predictable one of charitable social work, but of teaching when she signed on for a teacher-training course at Stockwell Training College. Her decision to teach rather than enter social work reflected her special interest in children. Stockwell Training College was one of the most advanced of its day, influenced by Froebel methods of child-centred learning. Whatever Jebb's qualities as a teacher she was racked by self-doubt and ill-health, and after one year of teaching at an elementary school in Marlborough she abandoned teaching, disheartened and depressed. Brief though her teaching career proved to be, it gave her the opportunity to work with children and to work to a strict routine. It also brought her into a professional, rather than charitable, relationship with the working class.

Jebb moved to Cambridge where in 1902 she threw herself into work with the Charity Organisation Society (COS) for six years, and sat on the Cambridge Education Committee, thus continuing her contacts with the working class, and children. She ran a register for boys' employment and a Social Training Union to interest girls in questions of citizenship. Her work in Cambridge for the COS, and particularly her research for *Cambridge: A Brief Study in Social Questions*, which she published in 1906, led Jebb to believe in the 'scientific' approach to social problems, and a systematic approach to poverty and charity. In *Cambridge* she spelt out ideas which were later to become an integral part of SCF philosophy, in particular, the importance of coordination, of collecting detailed information, and of seeing charity not as a gift but as a mutual relationship.[8]

---

8. Kathleen Freeman, *If Any Man Builds: The History of Save the Children Fund* (1965), pp. 17–18; Eglantyne Jebb, *Cambridge: A Brief Study in Social Questions* (Cambridge, 1906) looked at Cambridge's history, and current social issues.

In 1913 Jebb travelled to Macedonia to undertake relief work with those caught up in the second Balkans war. This experience of seeing people suffering under the privations of war meant that when the First World War broke out she could vividly visualise the sufferings of combatants, whether ally or enemy, and this must have strengthened her pacifist convictions. During the war Jebb, her sister, Dorothy Buxton, and friends scanned and translated the foreign press for evidence of conditions in war-torn Europe. This information was supplemented by material supplied by the International Red Cross in Vienna. They published their findings in the pacifist *Cambridge Magazine* and attempted to arouse concern about conditions on the Continent through informal talks.

In 1919 Eglantyne Jebb founded SCF to raise money for starving children in Austria and Germany (see Chapter Five). In 1921 SCF established a separate fund for poor children in Britain. The name 'Save the *Children* Fund' is indicative of the priority accorded children in much inter-war relief work. Why were children prioritised when it might have been thought that men home from the trenches had suffered most at the sharp end of the war, and when, for the many pacifists involved in relief work, helping ex-enemy combatants might have seemed just as symbolically appropriate as helping children? Culture and individual preferences explain why organisations, such as SCF, prioritised children. The importance accorded children in relief work is a reflection of western culture where the suffering of children arouses special sympathy and children are seen as being in need of special protection. They are the 'innocent' victims of war, whereas adults may be considered culpable. Women were viewed as 'natural' protectors of children. Eglantyne Jebb, moreover, had a special interest in children. She was not only the driving force behind the foundation of SCF, but she also stamped her philosophy on the organisation and determined the way it was to develop even after her untimely death in 1928 at the age of 52.

In 1919 and 1920 criticisms were levelled at SCF for only helping children in ex-enemy countries, but SCF's launch in 1921 of a home-based fund brought forth a torrent of abuse, privately from the Archbishop of Canterbury, who did not think that SCF should have suggested in its publicity that British children were starving, and publicly from certain sections of the press and from the COS. The criticisms were two-pronged. It was claimed that SCF exaggerated and sensationalised the plight of British children, and the COS in particular argued that government and philanthropic schemes absolved SCF of the need to assist children. The COS claimed that SCF was ignorant of existing charitable work with children. Part of the explanation for COS hostility lay in the fact that it was no longer the dominant charity and felt threatened by competition from other voluntary organisations. SCF defended its publicity on the grounds that the public only opened its purse in response to emotional campaigns.[9]

For all the fuss over SCF's campaigning – and indeed it did pioneer high-spending publicity campaigns in order to raise big sums – the nature of the work was not pioneering: it did not at first run any schemes itself, but funded those already operated by existing organisations. SCF targeted children, although it also helped mothers. In the 1920s SCF mainly subsidised meals for poor pregnant nursing women and young children. It made small grants for day nurseries and creches, and experimental artificial light treatment, and in 1926 it opened its own open-air school by the sea for 'delicate' children.[10]

While women, such as McMillan, Rathbone and Jebb, campaigned throughout the inter-war years to improve the lives of working-class women, one key moment, the mining dispute of 1926, harnessed their joint efforts. Charities and professionals joined together to tackle the dire poverty of mothers and their young children.

The 1926 General Strike and industrial dispute

The General Strike lasted from 4 May to 12 May, but the miners' dispute dragged on until the end of November. Some strikers' families received grants or loans from local Poor Law Guardians, some Guardians even gave relief to strikers themselves. The government recommended not more than 12s 0d for wives and 4s 0d for each dependent child. Poor Law Guardians' policies varied over whether they would give loans towards rent. Strike pay from trade unions varied, although smaller unions often gave nothing or only support in kind. Most miners received very little strike pay. The hardship and distress in the coalfields was recorded and condemned by various independent bodies, although never accepted by the government. Many in the population at large, in particular women, rustled up support for miners' families.

Eglantyne Jebb was closely involved in SCF's policy making and visited mining areas to see conditions for herself. On 2 June a letter appeared in *The Times*, signed by Nancy Astor; Margaret Wintringham, 1879–1955, a Liberal MP, 1921–24, who campaigned on a wide range of women's issues,

---

9. SCF *Annual Report* 1921; SCF archives 22/3 September 1920, 2 May 1921; 22/4 Eglantyne Jebb papers; 22/3 3 May 1921.
10. SCF *Annual Report* 1923, 1924, 1925, 1926.

including suffrage, women police, nationality of married women and equal pay; Lady Clarendon; and Mrs Edith Lyttelton, a writer (and widow of Alfred) on behalf of SCF. SCF investigated conditions among children in mining areas where it found evidence of undernourishment but not of children starving to death. It launched an emergency fund for the relief of children under school age and for nursing and pregnant women. A broadcast appeal on 26 June by Astor on behalf of SCF infuriated some of the women on the labour movement's Committee for the Relief of Miners' Wives and Children because Astor said that she had not seen or heard of starvation, although she did go on to say that undernourishment and real suffering would occur soon. The appeal raised over £9,000, which was spent largely on milk. In addition, the National Union of Teachers (NUT) raised £5,000, which SCF spent mainly on boots for children. SCF used teachers working in areas affected by the industrial dispute to pinpoint those children in greatest need.[11]

On 20 May the labour movement's Women's Committee for the Relief of Miners' Wives and Children met and agreed to raise money in order to distribute food and other basic necessities. On 22 May 1926 it launched an appeal with a letter to the press signed by a number of women active in national and local politics, with Ellen Wilkinson in the chair.

Other women who signed the letter included Susan Lawrence MP; Marjorie Slesser JP as treasurer; Margaret Bondfield; Lilian Dawson JP, and Madeleine Symons JP; Edith Picton-Turbervill; Margaret Llewelyn Davies; Ethel Bentham JP; and Eleanor Barton JP. Three days later the actress, Sybil Thorndike, issued an appeal for the committee. Edith Picton-Turbervill, 1872–1960, had a concern for women and girls both at home and abroad which was motivated by a strong religious and moral imperative. Before the war she undertook missionary work in India, and worked for the Young Women's Christian Association in India and then in Britain. A suffragist, she was especially concerned with 'moral' welfare issues, and campaigned against state-regulated brothels and the selling of child brides. Along with Nancy Astor she called for more women police for the protection of women. She was also a member of the Labour Party, and between 1929 and 1931 she sat in Parliament.

Other leading labour women such as Marion Phillips and Barbara Ayrton Gould were also involved, and 60–70 women gave their services at the Committee's London headquarters. Ayrton Gould, 1886–1950, had been a suffragette although she broke away from the Pankhursts to form the United Suffragists, who continued campaigning throughout the war. After the war

---

11. SCF *Annual Report* 1927; SCF M1/4; *Labour Woman*, 1 June 1926.

Ayrton Gould displayed a new-found interest in foreign affairs, and linked foreign and domestic issues such as the nationality of married women. She was a Labour activist, briefly Chief Woman Organiser and editor of *Labour Woman*, and involved in the Joint Committee of Industrial Women's Organisations. From 1929 to 1931 she sat on the Royal Commission on the Civil Service and advocated equal pay. She also took an interest in women in the context of their families. She was particularly concerned about the impact of unemployment on the family, supporting family allowances and later in the 1930s the Children's Minimum Council (CMC). As almost a postscript to her long years of campaigning, between 1945 and 1950 she sat in Parliament.

It was the mass of ordinary Labour Party women who ensured the committee's success. On 30 May a rally at the Albert Hall raised £1,000. Women demonstrated their support for the miners and their families by serving on strike committees; they raised money for miners' families and took miners' children into their own homes.[12] They participated in 'Lamp Days' (flag days when people wore images of a miner's lamp), house-to-house collections, jumble sales, auctions, and sales of postcards. They attended concerts, dances and whist drives.[13] This action was typical of the attitude of many women in the labour movement towards offering formal welfare outside their local community: they responded with generosity when their welfare work tied in with their political sympathies. They tended not to mobilise to help others outside their community if there was not a clear political and class imperative. Given their daily informal welfare work for their families and friends, this was a rational (whether conscious or not) apportioning of their efforts. A similar mobilisation occurred during the Spanish civil war (see Chapter Five). This link between a commitment to the labour movement and the welfare of women and children was also explicit in the work of Margaret McMillan.

Margaret McMillan and the campaign for nursery schools

Margaret McMillan, 1860–1931, grew up in a lower-middle-class family in Scotland. She was a socialist, member of the ILP, journalist and propagandist. In 1893 she moved to Bradford and joined the local Independent

---

12. Pamela Graves, *Labour Women* (1994), p. 92.
13. *Labour Woman*, 1 July 1926.

Labour Party (ILP). From 1894 to 1902 she sat on the Bradford school board, pressing in particular for meals and medical inspections for school-children. In 1902 she moved to London with her sister Rachel, 1859–1917. They opened clinics for young children and then founded an open-air treatment centre and nursery school in Deptford, south London. Her socialism and educational philosophy were integral. According to Carolyn Steedman, McMillan publicised 'a coherent theory of childhood and socialism, with a regenerated working-class childhood proclaiming the path to new social relations'.[14]

Margaret McMillan portrayed an essentially romantic image of the working class, and yet she was highly practical in her approach. Through her writings, lectures, presidency of the Nursery School Association (NSA), formed in 1923 to promote nursery schools along McMillan's lines, and the opening in 1930 of the Rachel McMillan Training College – named after her sister – she aimed to transform the public's view of the importance of nursery education and to spread a particular type of nursery school.

McMillan wrote about the 'intrinsic beauty and heroism' of the 'common man'.[15] She believed that slum children should be able to play in a green environment. Nursery schools should be surrounded by gardens: 'The garden is the essential matter. Not the lessons, or the pictures, or the talk.' In the garden the child's senses and spirit could awake.[16] Playing, especially in a garden, was all-important. Partly because of the emphasis she placed on the importance of play, she opposed nursery classes being tacked on to infant classes. She believed that play should take place in an environment where the child was surrounded by nature and where s/he could learn the importance of cleanliness and thus develop health-enhancing life skills. All three: play, cleanliness and good health could be promoted by baths for children at the nursery school.

In view of the environment in which slum children lived, McMillan advocated a long nursery school day of nine hours. She underlined that this did not reduce the responsibility of the mothers but gave them new power and knowledge. This impact on the mothers was vital for McMillan, who wanted the influence of the nursery school to extend into the local community. Mothers were encouraged, therefore, to become an integral part of the school; token gestures of inviting them in for the odd show days and fetes were simply not good enough. McMillan practised what she

---

14. Carolyn Steedman, *Childhood, Culture and Class in Britain: Margaret McMillan 1860–1931* (1990), pp. 3–4.
15. Margaret McMillan, *Education Through the Imagination* (1923), p. 7. First published 1904.
16. Margaret McMillan, *The Nursery School* (1930), pp. 1, 2. First published 1919.

preached; at her nursery school in Deptford there was a weekly club for the mothers.[17]

McMillan was not alone in her belief in the potential impact of nursery schools. Katharine Bruce Glasier was a socialist writer and campaigner, and, like McMillan, linked nursery schools to her socialist aims. Carolyn Steedman drew attention to Bruce Glasier's view that hopes for a better world rested on nursery schools, for 'nursery school bairns will not tolerate slums when they grow up!'[18] During the 1930s and 1940s Susan Isaacs, 1885–1948, undertook research into child development and published evidence that nursery schools assisted intellectual development.

In many ways, despite her socialist motivation, McMillan's views were far more acceptable to governments than those of Marie Stopes, Eglantyne Jebb, or Eleanor Rathbone. She was no lone voice crying in an educational wilderness. Despite some scepticism from the teaching profession, women – such as Mrs Evelegh, chair of the Jellicoe nursery school, Miss Owen, Principal of Mather Training College, Elsie Murray of Maria Grey Training College and Lillian de Lissa of Gipsy Hill Training College – all reinforced McMillan's high-profile campaigning.

Government supported nursery education in principle, but always had reasons for not supporting it in practice. McMillan's belief in the importance of fresh air and cleanliness accorded with the views of Sir George Newman and Sir Arthur McNalty, successive Chief Medical Officers of Health. During the First World War nursery schools fitted in with government concern over child health. A government commitment to nursery education existed on paper from 1918 when the Education Act authorised local education authorities (LEAs) to supply or aid nursery schools for children whose attendance was necessary for their physical and mental development. The Board of Education was empowered to pay grants in aid of nursery schools. As the Act was only advisory, not mandatory, it was virtually a dead letter. In the early 1920s the Board of Education rejected proposals for new nursery schools on the grounds of cost; from the mid-1920s the Board did not reject them out of hand, but regarded them as relatively costly because, in order to be near young children's homes, they tended to be small. Trained teachers in nursery schools were also seen as an unnecessary luxury by the Board and Ministry of Health, and discussions took place between the two departments' civil servants over the possibility of making nursery provision at low cost by using untrained staff – 'a few sensible and motherly people rather than a technical, certified and expensive

17.   Margaret McMillan, *The Nursery School*, pp. 12, 38, 39, 133.
18.   Carolyn Steedman, *Childhood, Culture and Class in Britain*, pp. 59–60.

teaching staff'. This would have been anathema to McMillan and the NSA who argued for high-quality nursery education. At the end of the decade when the Ministry of Health wanted to urge LEAs to make nursery provision, the Board procrastinated because it wanted first to pursue with LEAs the question of raising the school leaving age.[19]

The 1933 Hadow Report on infant and nursery schools, set up under the auspices of the Board of Education, lauded McMillan as a 'great exemplar of nursery education in England' and reiterated her emphasis on the importance of nursery education; it recommended that every LEA should survey the needs of its area and take steps to meet these needs. The paucity of nursery schools was of 'grave significance'. The report also endorsed McMillan's methods by arguing that young children should spend time in the open air, with trees, plants, animals, pools to paddle in and sand pits to dig in; objects and materials in the nursery school should stimulate their senses; training at the nursery school should aid 'natural growth', and there should be active cooperation with parents in order that training in the school would spill over into the home. In practice the Board was only interested in nursery schools in slum areas. It opposed the NSA's call for nursery schools on new housing estates where families moved as a result of slum clearance. While the NSA argued that rents were higher on new estates, often forcing mothers to go out to work, that the new homes and gardens were often small, and that nursery schools could help children and their parents adapt to the new environment, the Board maintained that nursery schools could never be universal, presumably because of the costs, and should only be provided where economic conditions were below average, and that was in the slums.[20]

The political parties supported the expansion of nursery schools in principle; in 1925 the Labour Party and TUC issued a joint statement in favour of the expansion of nursery schools and nursery classes, but MPs of all parties, with certain honourable exceptions such as Nancy Astor and Margaret Wintringham, remained apathetic. From the moment Astor and McMillan met in mid-1926 until McMillan's death in 1931 they remained close friends. Astor was immediately converted to McMillan's campaign for nursery schools and gave money and influence to the cause. Waldorf Astor, Nancy's husband, bought the land in Deptford for the Rachel McMillan Training Centre to be expanded into a college and Nancy raised £20,000

---

19. Elizabeth Bradburn, *Margaret McMillan: Portrait of a Pioneer* (1989), pp. 162–3. PRO ED 102/1, ED 102/2, ED 102/3 and ED 102/4.
20. Board of Education, *Report of the Consultative Committee on Infant and Nursery schools* (Hadow Report) (HMSO, 1933), pp. xv, xix, 179, 182–3, 188.

for it. A nursery school was opened in Astor's constituency in Plymouth, and, despite her socialist credentials, McMillan actually spoke on behalf of Astor during the 1929 general election campaign when Astor won the seat by the narrowest of margins.

As well as undertaking research and putting pressure on governments, women attempted to right the wrongs highlighted in surveys and reports. In February 1933 SCF launched a special committee, the Emergency Open-Air Nursery Committee, to oversee the establishment of nursery schools in the distressed areas at a time when the government was stonewalling grants for nursery schools. SCF operated in conjunction with Unemployment Centres. Initially the National Council of Social Services and the Pilgrim Trust made grants and Nancy Astor provided £1,500 towards superintendents' (equivalent to headteachers) salaries. Later, the Commissioner for the Special Areas gave building grants.[21]

SCF identified poverty and undernourishment (and occasionally neglect) as the root cause of physical problems – such as sores, verminous heads, running eyes and boils – of the little children in its nursery schools. SCF claimed that after a few months of attending nursery school these problems usually cleared up, and the children's behaviour and outlook improved; no doubt this was true, but SCF does not appear to have monitored the children in detail. The nursery schools aimed to help poor children's overall wellbeing, not just their physical health. SCF's emphasis on health and cleanliness echoed the philosophy of Margaret McMillan, as did its hope for influencing the children's mothers, and thereby the entire population around the schools. In 1936 SCF prided itself that its nursery schools stimulated the mothers to adopt nursery school standards in their own homes, thus acting as a beacon of hope in the distressed areas.[22]

In national terms, however, the nursery schools had a meagre impact. Initially, in the early 1930s SCF launched four schools; by 1937 the government recognised 78 nursery schools for the purposes of grants, of which SCF had started ten. (Others involved in opening nursery schools included Margaret McMillan and the LEAs.) The numbers were low, but SCF was trying to open nurseries at a time when governmental social and economic policy worked in the opposite direction. In the early 1930s many LEAs held up plans for new nursery schools, some nursery schools were closed, others had their staff numbers slashed, some were forced to merge with local infant schools and supplies of milk decreased.[23]

---

21. SCF *Annual Report*, 1932–33, 1937.
22. SCF *Annual Report*, 1936.
23. SCF *Annual Report*, 1932.

The NSA did not mince its words when it railed against the government's 'reactionary policy' and pointed to the vast number of unemployed parents who had too little food to put on children's plates. In the mid-1930s the Board of Education's cold attitude began to thaw, and the NSA renewed its pressure on LEAs to open nursery schools. As legislation was only permissive rather than obligatory, the NSA aimed to change the climate of opinion so that nursery schools would be seen as a desirable investment of scarce resources. As well as pressure from female-dominated organisations, such as SCF and the NSA, individual women, such as Nancy Astor, Katharine Bruce Glasier and Margaret Wintringham all campaigned for more nursery schools.[24]

The Board of Education accepted the case for nursery schools but at a time when LEAs' budgets were under pressure it was easy for central and local government not to act. Even if financial restraint had not worked to limit the number of nursery schools, those within government who had the greatest interest and knowledge of nursery education were sidelined. Women inspectors of schools, as we saw in Chapter Three, were marginalised in the policy decision-making process.

Eleanor Rathbone and family allowances

Middle-class women, many of whom had been active in the suffrage campaign and who were involved in a range of women's causes, were the driving force within SCF and the Family Endowment Society (FES). Men were involved in both campaigns but women took the initiative and undertook the day-to-day running of the Society.

The FES grew out of a meeting held in 1917 to discuss family allowances. The Society's leaders were Eleanor Rathbone, 1872–1946, Independent MP for the Combined English Universities, 1929–46, Eva Hubback and Mary Stocks, all of whom had been involved in the pre-war suffrage campaign and deployed the same tactics in both campaigns. Eleanor Rathbone, Kathleen Courtney, Maude Royden and Mary Stocks were all active in the National Union of Women's Suffrage Societies (NUWSS) while other supporters were more closely aligned to socialism than feminism. Marjorie Green, 1905–1978, had been an active member of the Liberal Party in Scotland before becoming the secretary of the FES, as well as secretary in the 1930s of NUSEC and the CMC.

Eva Hubback, 1886–1949, was a social worker and Poor Law Guardian before the war, supporting women's suffrage and social reform. From 1920

---

24. Nursery Schools Association, *Annual Report*, 1932, 1933, 1938.

to 1927 she undertook paid work for NUSEC, working closely with Rathbone, Elizabeth Macadam (warden of the Victoria Women's Settlement in Liverpool and Rathbone's companion) and Stocks, while networking around Westminster in order to promote legislation for NUSEC's policies on equal pay; equal moral standards in divorce and prostitution; equal franchise; equal guardianship of children, and widows' pensions. In the late 1920s she was instrumental in setting up the Townswomen's Guild, modelled on the Women's Institutes, for women living in urban areas. She always supported Rathbone's campaign for family allowances (although her motives shifted from a desire for women's independence to pronatalism) and she was a founding member of the CMC.

Mary Stocks, 1891–1975, was active in the NUWSS before the war. She supported family allowances from the outset. In the 1920s she lectured on birth control, and in 1925 opened a birth control clinic in Manchester. She also spoke out against the problems faced by professional women, such as doctors and teachers. She sat on numerous government committees and commissions, including the Home Office Committee on persistent offenders and, in 1935, the unemployment committee, where she insisted that her view be recorded that women's and men's contributions and benefits should be equalised. (She later became Principal of Westfield College and a well-known broadcaster.)

Maude Royden, 1876–1956, was most famous as a preacher and campaigner for the ordination of women. Before the war she belonged to the NUWSS. She supported birth control along with family allowances, hoping that the latter would avoid the necessity for mothers to undertake paid work, and so avoid the need for nursery schools.

The leaders of the family allowances campaign underpinned their demand for family allowances by both feminist and socialist analyses of society. Many supported family allowances along with other linked proposals. The campaign aimed to stimulate debate and win sympathisers among those with influence in policy-making circles. It never attempted to become a mass movement.[25]

Of all the women involved in this campaign one, Eleanor Rathbone, was – and has remained – synonymous with family allowances. Rathbone brought an explicit gender analysis to all her public activities. The Victorian family ideal was, for Rathbone, at the heart of women's inequality. At first she thought that the state should ensure that men supported their families, but her experience of the way separation allowances worked in the First World War led her to the conclusion that the state should pay allowances direct to

---

25. John Macnicol, *The Movement for Family Allowances, 1918–45* (1980).

the mother. In calling for family allowances to be paid to the mother, she argued that it was vital for all women to have their own income; family allowances were not just a matter of preventing poverty in large families, of keeping up the birth rate, or of maintaining wage differentials while avoiding inflationary wage increases; certainly all these arguments were employed to win over a wide spectrum of political and industrial support, but they were secondary motives for Rathbone. Rathbone believed that women, as mothers, should be provided with direct state support. In the years before the First World War, she had come to the conclusion that the economic dependence of unwaged mothers lay at the heart of the unequal status of all women because all men as husbands benefited from the assumption that a man should earn a 'family wage', and all women were penalised. For Rathbone, women's second-class status resulted from the wage system in conjunction with the domestic organisation of life: provide mothers with a degree of economic independence and you can begin to change the gendered nature of society. In this sense, although working-class women would be the obvious beneficiaries of family allowances, the analysis was cross-class; gender, not class, was fundamental to her analysis. Rathbone saw all women as having common interests, even when this rather naively led her to campaign for Indian women, who neither appreciated her intervention nor agreed with it.[26]

Other supporters of family allowances, whether or not they represented women's organisations, all had their own agenda. Thus, for instance, Labour women tended to support family allowances because they believed that they would help to improve child health. The strongest appeal of family allowances certainly lay in the impact it was thought they could have on alleviating poverty. Although Rathbone never touched on birth control issues, NUSEC – in which she was highly influential – demanded birth control and family allowances in order to give women economic independence and control over reproduction. It was, therefore, part of an interlocking campaign which involved women's work during the General Strike and in the depressed areas, and demands for nursery schools and birth control.[27]

---

26. Susan Pedersen, 'Eleanor Rathbone (1872–1946) The Victorian family under the daughter's eye', in Susan Pedersen and Peter Mandler, eds, *After the Victorians: Private Conscience and Public Duty in Modern Britain* (1994), pp. 107–9.

27. The two key studies are John Macnicol, *The Movement for Family Allowances*, especially pp. 6, 25–8, 43, 48, 62; Susan Pedersen, *Family, Dependence, and the Origins of the Welfare State: Britain and France, 1914–1945* (Cambridge, 1993), especially pp. 13–145, 151, 168, 183–4, 318, 320–21. See also Susan Pedersen, 'Eleanor Rathbone', in Susan Pedersen and Peter Mandler, eds, *After the Victorians*, especially p. 117; Hilary Land, 'Eleanor Rathbone and the economy of the family', in Harold Smith, *British Feminism in the Twentieth Century* (Aldershot, 1990), especially pp. 104–5, 118.

Throughout the inter-war years the trade union movement was on the whole hostile to family allowances, fearing that they undermined the case for a man to earn a family wage, that is, sufficient income to keep a wife and family, and the effect of family allowances would therefore be to drive down wages. Within the Labour Party attitudes were mixed. While some in the Party were hostile, others saw family allowances as part of a strategy for introducing a minimum wage. Within the Liberal Party there was support, mainly from the women. The key to understanding the failure of the family allowance campaign lies within the Conservative Party. Leading Conservatives displayed no interest in family allowances. The costs of introducing family allowances ruled out any serious discussion within the Conservative Party or within government. According to John Macnicol, a government file was not opened on family allowances until 1938, when the policy was to express mild hostility towards them. From the mid-1930s Eleanor Rathbone managed to secure cross-party support for family allowances from MPs such as Harold Macmillan and others advocating a 'middle way'. By the outbreak of war she had, therefore, ensured that family allowances were under discussion within government and gaining growing support from MPs.[28]

In 1934 the women who were at the heart of the FES – Eleanor Rathbone, Marjorie Green and Eva Hubback – founded, and then ran, the CMC, which led the family poverty campaign in the 1930s with its publications, pamphlets, surveys, letters, articles, meetings, deputations to Whitehall and lobbying. As with the FES, the CMC focused on attracting the support of well-placed individuals. It also built bridges with other organisations, such as SCF and the NSA, with broadly similar interests, as well as with women's organisations, such as the WCG, Standing Joint Committee of Industrial Women's Organisations and NUSEC.[29] A huge number of societies supported the aims and work of the CMC, as well as prominent individuals, including those MPs of all parties who had voted against downward revisions to Unemployment Assistance Board (UAB) rates.

The CMC aimed to change government policies in order to help mothers and children in poor, and especially large poor, families, for it recognised that on mothers and children the 'sharpest edge of poverty falls'.[30] The CMC's emphasis changed over the years: at first it tried to get the government to recognise that malnutrition did actually exist; it then went on to advocate specific measures, calling for higher unemployment benefits; free or cheap milk for pregnant and nursing mothers and their children; free

---

28. The above is a synopsis of the argument in John Macnicol, *The Movement for Family Allowances*.
29. John Macnicol, *The Movement for Family Allowances*, pp. 26, 62–5.
30. CMC, *Special Areas Bill* (1937), p. 2.

school meals; family allowances, and rent rebates. The CMC focused on specific policies in the belief that this was more effective than a broad strategy, even though it recognised the artificiality of singling out individual programmes when the problems of poverty were far-reaching.

The depressed areas in the 1930s

Most historians of inter-war feminism are now agreed that it is wrong to label these years as the dark ages of British feminism. In the late 1920s, however, the women's movement split over the issue of protective legislation. Martin Pugh emphasised the internal weaknesses of the women's movement; Deirdre Beddoe argued that women's organisations increasingly fragmented into a series of special interest groups and in the 1930s their energies dwindled,[31] and Olive Banks pointed out that by the 1930s issues of war and peace were of escalating importance;[32] a weakened movement was then overtaken by events as unemployment and the worsening international situation marginalised all other issues. These analyses miss the important point that unemployment at home and a worsening international situation (see Chapter Five) did not eclipse a gendered analysis of society's ills but actually contributed to one. Historians have tended to ignore the research which was informed by a gendered analysis, perhaps because it had little impact on changing government policy or maybe because historians first became interested in poverty studies in the 1930s when researching the industrial male working class. Only occasionally did studies of unemployment consider women's position in the labour market, and then only as a side issue to male unemployment.

During the 1930s some studies adopted a thoroughgoing gendered analysis of the impact of poverty, while others recognised that poverty affected members of the same family differently, although a gendered analysis was only provided inter alia.[33] After Margaret Balfour's visits to the homes of the unemployed in Durham and Tyneside, she and Joan Drury drew attention to the gendered impact of poverty. They argued that although the mother was the centre of the household and the mainspring on which all

---

31. Martin Pugh, *Women and the Women's Movement in Britain, 1914–1959* (1992); Deirdre Beddoe, *Back to Home and Duty: Women Between The Wars, 1918–1939* (1989), p. 140.

32. Olive Banks, *The Politics of British Feminism, 1918–1970* (Aldershot, 1993), p. 17.

33. Margaret Balfour and Joan Drury, *Motherhood in the Special Areas* (1935); CMC, *Special Areas Bill* (1937); CMC, *Memorandum on milk for mothers and children* (1937); M. Green, *Evidence of Malnutrition* (1934); Industrial Christian Council, *The Fact of Malnutrition* (1938); HC Deb 8 July 1936 vol. 314 col. 1300 James Griffiths; Pilgrim Trust, *Men without Work* (1938).

depended, she received the least assistance. Her husband could be seen by a National Health Insurance GP, but the mother had to pay; the health visitor saw the baby and toddler but a mother had to look after her own health; school children were medically inspected and some received free milk and meals, but it could be difficult for a pregnant woman to attend ante-natal clinics on top of all her household work, such as washing, cooking, cleaning and mending; and for some women it involved a long walk or a bus fare, perhaps with a toddler in tow.[34] The Ministry of Health rejected their report on the grounds that Balfour and Drury were not qualified to undertake such research and the survey was too small. Although the Ministry of Health was dismissive of independent investigations, its own were no better.

Mothers were central to the debate over poverty and ill-health because of investigators' and lobbyists' focus on nutrition. Mothers were blamed by those on the government side for the poor nutrition of families; critics of government blamed poor nutrition on mothers' empty purses.[35]

During these years a major public debate over standards of health focused on the high maternal mortality rate (MMR). The arguments revolved around how far women were in part culpable by failing to attend ante-natal clinics and by not looking after themselves properly, and how far the high MMR reflected poverty and the lack of adequate government services.[36]

The health of mothers with frequent pregnancies and too little food was a matter of concern to women campaigners. In 1927 Gertrude Tuckwell and May Tennant had set up a Maternal Mortality Committee (MMC) to lobby governments to take action to reduce the rising MMR. Tuckwell lobbied the Ministry of Health over women's ill-health and disability and in the 1920s she sat on the Royal Commission on National Health Insurance. May Tennant who, as seen in Chapter Two, held one of the most senior positions of any woman in the country during the First World War, was well connected and pressed her views on ministers and civil servants when she met them socially.

All classes were hit by the high MMR. The MMC focused its demands on medical services, but also recognised the importance of other support for mothers, and along with women in the labour movement, pressed for home helps.

In the 1930s women campaigners saw the poor diets of mothers as contributing to their ill-health as well as to their death rate, an argument

---

34. Balfour and Drury, *Motherhood in the Special Areas*, pp. 9–10.
35. G.C.M. M'Gonigle and J. Kirky, *Poverty and Public Health* (1936); J. Boyd Orr, *Food, Health and Income* (1936).
36. Margaret Mitchell, 'The effects of unemployment on the social condition of women and children in the 1930s', *History Workshop Journal*, 19 (1985), pp. 105–27.

supported by the findings of a number of non-governmental reports. Despite the concern and expert knowledge which existed among women, when the Ministry of Health appointed committees to look into the problem it was rare for them to contain any women other than Janet Campbell, the Ministry's senior Medical Officer for maternal and child welfare. This absence of women's points of view was particularly significant as independent research tended to be ignored by the Ministry.[37]

Campaigners who were primarily concerned with child poverty recognised that mothers were especially hard-hit by poverty, and the harmful effects of poverty on mothers' health were widely recognised not just by the poverty lobby but also among some doctors, and even the occasional government minister. One CMC memorandum quoted the Minister of Health in the House of Commons: 'When you are looking for a place in the family where malnutrition will show itself and where the bad effects of unemployment and depression will show themselves, look at the mother . . . .'

The best-remembered of the surveys undertaken by women had least impact at the time. In 1939 The Women's Health Enquiry published *Working-Class Wives*, which gave a vivid description of the daily lives of working-class women, based on a sample of 1,250. The research was started in 1933 but because of various delays it took six years to be published. The enquiry comprised women from a range of women's organisations, from the Townswomen's Guild to the Women's Cooperative Guild, and included long-standing campaigners such as Gertrude Tuckwell and Barbara Ayrton Gould. The report aimed to expose the ill-health of women, especially married working-class women. Dame Janet Campbell (now retired on marriage from the Ministry of Health), although not sitting on the committee, penned the introduction, in which she reiterated the views of countless leading women in the inter-war years that the health and happiness of a working-class married woman, and her role in the family were of enormous importance to the health of the nation as a whole. 'On her depends very largely the success or otherwise of the family life of the greater part of our population.' The enquiry went on to assert that the growth and care of the family depended on the survival of the mother and a high MMR threatened the existence of the race. Chapters of the report covered the treatment of ill-health; attitudes to life and health; the day's work; housing, and diet. It concluded that poverty, poor health and a lack of trained knowledge all made the women's lives difficult and strenuous.[38]

37. Jane Lewis, *The Politics of Motherhood* (1980), pp. 118, 120, 125, 181.
38. Margery Spring Rice, *Working-Class Wives* (1981), pp. xiv–xv, xviii, 19, 21, 22, 26, 27, 188. First published 1939.

Government attitudes towards women's demands

To understand why politicians and civil servants failed to be moved by these campaigns it is essential to understand the dominant priorities of government. The policies advocated above did not involve radical or Keynesian economic policies to solve the problem of unemployment. Rather, women had developed policies to deal with the consequences of unemployment, not its causes. The policies to alleviate the worst effects of unemployment and poverty did involve increased government spending, and this flew in the face of government economic policies which were to balance the budget and to keep taxation and spending low in order to promote stability in trade and avoid inflation. None of the parties in Parliament, whether in the National Government or on the opposition benches, offered an alternative economic strategy. Further, in the 1930s poverty and unemployment were concentrated in those areas of the country which had been at the forefront of Britain's industrial and economic success in the nineteenth century. Job losses were greatest in coalmining in south Wales; in coalmining and shipbuilding in the northeast; in textiles and engineering in Lancashire; and in engineering and shipbuilding on Clydeside. The reasons for the job losses were international competition, markets lost during the First World War and never regained, the high cost of the pound in the 1920s, lack of investment and outdated machinery. A further aspect of government economic policy was, therefore, to encourage migration among young workers from the declining, depressed areas to those areas of the country, such as Greater London and the Midlands, where newer industries, primarily aimed at the domestic market, were developing. Concern was expressed within Whitehall that social policies should not negate the spur to young families to move for work. In 1934 a senior Ministry of Labour official warned that it was 'important to waste neither sympathy nor public funds on any activity which may anchor or attach young or middle-aged people more firmly to the depressed areas'.[39] As well as not wishing to do anything to make the depressed areas attractive to the unemployed, governments also tried to ensure that unemployment would never be more attractive than employment. Financial support for the unemployed, therefore, always had to be lower than the income of unskilled labourers.[40]

---

39. Quoted in Frederic Miller, 'The unemployment policy of the National Government, 1931–36', *Historical Journal*, 19, 2 (1976), p. 465.
40. Margaret Mitchell, 'The effects of unemployment on the social condition of women and children in the 1930s', p. 114.

Social policies in general and health policies in particular developed within the framework of economic policies. Health policies were further influenced by assumptions within Whitehall about working-class ill-health. Civil servants and ministers repeatedly voiced the assumption that mothers were themselves responsible for their poor health and even death in child-birth. A 1932 departmental report on maternal mortality claimed that an analysis of 5,000 maternal deaths showed that 45.9 per cent were avoidable. Of these avoidable deaths, 15 per cent were due to the absence or failure of ante-natal care, 19 per cent were due to an error of judgement on the part of those responsible for managing the patient (i.e. the midwife or doctor), 4 per cent were due to a lack of reasonable facilities for the birth, and 7 per cent were due to the 'negligence' of the mother or her friends in not follow-ing advice or in failing to detect obvious signs of serious illness. Their recom-mendations were, therefore, for more appropriate education for medical students and midwives, proper supervision of pregnant women and coordina-tion of existing maternity services. Three years later a Department of Health for Scotland report on maternal morbidity and mortality claimed that 57 per cent of antenatal deaths in its survey were the 'fault' of the women them-selves for not following advice, and in nearly half the postnatal deaths the women or their relatives were at 'fault'.[41]

The causes of death identified above and the recommendations which flowed from them sidestepped the crucial issue which was exercising those campaigning outside Whitehall to reduce the MMR, that of women's poverty, which meant lack of nourishment and frequent pregnancies, and women's subsequent ill-health. Hilton Young, the Minister of Health, was so ready to blame women for their ill-health that he tripped himself up and admitted that malnutrition existed (which his department spent much energy adamantly denying). In 1934 a deputation from the MMC raised the issue of malnutrition as a cause of maternal deaths. Hilton Young denied the claim but went on to say, 'Nevertheless, the question of maternal mortality must be watched. We all know how it is with the mother, you cannot prevent her when she gets anywhere near the poverty line from feeding her children and starving herself. . . .'[42] Dr Thomas Carnwath, Deputy Chief Medical Officer at the Ministry of Health in the early 1930s, blamed poor nutrition among working-class families on the mothers' bad cooking, and Sir Arthur Robinson, Permanent Secretary at the Ministry of

---

41.   PRO MH 55/265 Maternal Mortality; C. Douglas and P. McKinlay, *Report on maternal morbidity and mortality in Scotland*, Department of Health for Scotland, 1935.
42.   PRO MH 55/262 Maternal Mortality Mrs Tennant's Committee 1928–36.

Health, claimed that malnutrition was due as much to ignorance as to insufficient income.[43]

Government strategies to counter its critics

Ministers and civil servants developed various strategies for withstanding the logic and power of the poverty lobby's arguments and for bolstering their own narrow views. Departments ensured that they kept control over policy decisions by pre-empting criticism. So, at the beginning of 1928 when the Ministry of Health heard that the MMC was whipping up interest and the BMA formulating proposals on the subject, civil servants decided to undertake their own enquiries into maternal mortality and the training of midwives 'to anticipate useful suggestions'.[44] The Ministry of Health excluded those known to be critics of its policies, so in 1931 when Hilton Young set up a new committee on nutrition he ensured by its composition and by its terms of reference that it would not come up with any new policies. Civil servants also tried to undermine the credibility of documents which criticised government policy. Thus, in 1933 the BMA's nutrition committee report was dismissed as a 'stunt' and as a 'Labour Party tract'.[45] In 1936 the government was so disconcerted by the claims of the CMC that the Prime Minister, Stanley Baldwin, personally dismissed CMC figures as unreliable and lacking adequate research. He also claimed that CMC figures took no account of the support which the unemployed received from the Unemployment Assistance Board, and statutory and voluntary social services.[46]

While undermining the work of those outside government, the Ministry of Health hid behind misleading statements and figures. The Chief Medical Officer in his annual report wrote in upbeat terms about national mortality and morbidity trends, but as the problem of poverty-related ill-health was largely a regional one, national figures obscured as much as they revealed. The CMC criticised the 1934 report on these grounds and for a section headed 'unemployment and national health', which the CMC argued should have addressed the nub of the problem, namely, 'unemployment and the health of the unemployed'.[47]

---

43. Madeleine Mayhew, 'The 1930s nutrition controversy', *Journal of Contemporary History* 23 (1988), pp. 447, 450.
44. PRO MH 55/266 January 1928.
45. Madeleine Mayhew, 'The 1930s nutrition controversy', pp. 447, 451.
46. PRO MH 55/688 19 August 1936 Prime Minister to Secretary of CMC.
47. PRO MH 55/275.

Whitehall tried to ignore outsiders, unless they were thought to be useful. Between 1932 and 1937 when the WI was demanding that cheap milk be made widely available it was directed from Department to Department, and only seen in 1937 by Ministry of Health officials when they thought the WI could be of some use to them.[48] Hilda Chamberlain, the sister of the Prime Minister, Neville Chamberlain, was a leading member of the WI and for this reason it may well have suited the Department in 1937 to meet the WI. The Ministry of Health initially welcomed the MMC with its focus on maternity facilities, but when it raised the issue of nutrition and women's ill-health the Ministry was furious and called off friendly relations.[49] In 1937, when Eleanor Rathbone was part of a CMC deputation to the Ministry of Health about unemployment assistance levels being too low to maintain adequate nutrition, she complained that the CMC had been fobbed off for three years: it always met with the reply that the matter would be sympathetically considered.[50]

One of the most serious tactics of government was to try and silence critics by threatening their livelihood. This ploy could not be used against independent women, but it was used against working doctors. When Ministry of Health officials discovered from a newspaper report that an assistant Medical Officer with the London County Council had dared to speak at a CMC meeting, the Ministry made sure she received a warning against doing so again. Charles Webster has recounted how the Ministry of Health threatened to get both John Boyd Orr, an eminent medical researcher and Director of the Rowett Research Institute in Aberdeen, and G.C.M. M'Gonigle, Medical Officer of Health for Stockton-on-Tees, struck off the medical register if they continued to produce research which was embarrassing to the government. (Boyd Orr ignored the threats as he did not wish to practise again but M'Gonigle was forced to back down.)[51]

It is not surprising that reports which pointed to the effects of poverty on women had little impact on government policy, for this was true of most of the poverty research of these years. These reports were highly contentious and governments usually denied their validity. It was not that the reports were either too limited or insignificant, or that they made outrageous recommendations, but rather that they flew in the face of governments' economic and social policies. Carefully reasoned arguments backed by evidence were not enough to change government policies if they challenged

---

48. PRO MH 55/639.
49. PRO MH 55/679.
50. PRO MH 55/688 27 July 1937.
51. MH 55/275, Charles Webster, 'Healthy or hungry thirties?' *History Workshop Journal*, 13 (1982), pp. 112–21.

governmental assumptions. Government was not, however, impervious to challenge.

When governments were faced with violence, or the threat of violence, then they moderated their policies. In October 1932, when there were serious riots in a number of cities over means-tested benefits, the government made some concessions in the regulations for granting benefits. Again, in the winter of 1934–35, protests against government efforts to standardise relief rates forced it to back down and introduce the changes gradually. The Cabinet overruled the Unemployment Assistance Board for fear that dissatisfaction with its rates would develop into a general uprising, and unrest was especially unwelcome with the approaching Silver Jubilee celebrations of King George V and Queen Mary.[52]

Conclusions

Women's political activism around questions of health and welfare were successful to the extent that they placed issues such as birth control, family allowances and nursery schools on the political agenda. One cannot explain the failure of women's campaigns to make greater headway in terms of the narrow social class base from which they operated, for where one does see major mobilisations, as for instance during the General Strike or demonstrations in the 1930s against unemployment and the means test (i.e. working-class men's campaigns), little was achieved, except in the 1930s when demonstrations were accompanied by violence and government feared widespread disorder. Governments operated with a set of assumptions about first, economic policy, which influenced their social policies; second, the nature of governance, which excluded people and ideas which did not accord with ministers' and civil servants' pre-existing mind-set; and third, working-class behaviour, especially that of mothers.

Although the networks between women were impressive, there was no effective relationship between campaigners and governments. Women such as Eleanor Rathbone, Eglantyne Jebb, Marie Stopes, Margaret McMillan and their co-campaigners were not a part of the policy decision process, so they could not effectively challenge the vested interests and assumptions of policy makers. Instead, Whitehall actively excluded them and their supporters by using the range of ploys discussed above.

---

52. Frederic Miller 'The unemployment policy of the National Government, 1931–1936', *Historical Journal*, 19, 2 (1976), p. 461; Helen Jones, ed., *Duty and Citizenship* (1994), pp. 123, 125.

CHAPTER FIVE

The European Stage

Introduction

Throughout the inter-war years, as is often the case, events abroad and at home were closely linked in many minds. The losses and sufferings of the war did not end with the peace treaties, and various other issues, such as the nationality of women married to foreigners, and refugees from Nazi Germany, kept domestic and foreign affairs closely intertwined. The activities of the League of Nations Union, the peace campaigns, the sufferings of post-war continental Europe and the rise of fascism kept foreign affairs firmly on the domestic agenda. These issues and events, all with an important welfare dimension, were influenced directly or indirectly by the war.

Throughout the 1920s and 1930s a small band of British women in voluntary and religious organisations undertook welfare work on the Continent. As with welfare work in Britain, this focused mainly on the welfare of mothers and children. Where British women were successful it was in small-scale voluntary projects which were largely independent of, and at times in direct conflict with, governments. Although strong networks existed between British women, they did not reach into the heart of the policy process. An alternative network of women worked and campaigned over European welfare issues, which in some cases continued wartime welfare work, although now it was directed primarily at the middle class. The middle-class women involved in welfare formed part of a wider network of women who, although supporting the whole gamut of political parties, were connected through religion, pacifism, ex-suffrage activities or current involvement in women's organisations.

Evidence of women's interest in foreign affairs

That certain women were interested in foreign affairs is no more or less remarkable than the fact that some men were also interested in foreign affairs. Women's interest could not, however, be translated into taking decisions over foreign policy. There were no women in the foreign and diplomatic service and although women demonstrated an (at times passionate) interest in the League of Nations, and they attempted, through personal connections, to influence League policies for women and children, they had limited influence because they did not hold positions of power where key decisions were taken.[1] The popularity of the Women's International League for Peace and Freedom (WILPF), the involvement of women in the Peace Pilgrimage in June 1926 when thousands of women descended on Hyde Park from all parts of the country, and women and men's commitment to the Peace Pledge Union in the 1930s demonstrate a widespread concern with peace, disarmament and international relations.

Welfare was frequently central to women's international activities and interests although the WILPF quickly withdrew from supporting welfare work. Initially, in the early months of peace it campaigned with Fight the Famine Council to have the blockade against the old enemy lifted, and it was also involved in an appeal to send 1 million rubber teats to Germany. After internal debate it severed its links, however, on the grounds that it was not a welfare organisation and from then on it avoided all welfare-related activities; this helps to explain why, in the 1930s, its response to the plight of Jewish refugees was tardy.

Gender and Germans

The wartime indignities inflicted on British women married to Germans continued into the peace. Under the peace treaties any property of a British woman married to a German was seized as part of the British government's reparations from Germany. As a result of the requisition of women's property, and the injustices of the law during the war, the campaign for women to retain their nationality on marriage to a foreigner got underway with the formation of the Pass the Bill Committee (PBC) which collected evidence of

---

1. For women and the League see Carol Miller, 'Lobbying the League: Women's International Organisations and the League of Nations', Oxford D. Phil., 1992.

hardships suffered by the women, and put pressure on the government to change the law.

Although most of the PBC's records were accidently destroyed in the 1930s, there is evidence that public opinion, reinforced by government action, made British-born women with German husbands vulnerable to poverty and isolation. In 1921 one British-born woman living in Britain with her two children wrote that her husband refused to support her unless she went to live in Germany. She did not want to do this, but her securities (money left her by relatives) were seized under the peace treaties and she found it impossible to find paid work in Britain because of continuing hostility to anyone with a German name.[2]

The campaign's leader, Margery Corbett Ashby, 1882–1981, was a life-long Liberal and interested in women's welfare issues both at home and abroad. Before the war her suffrage campaigning involved membership of the International Woman Suffrage Alliance, renamed in 1926 the International Alliance of Women for Suffrage and Equal Citizenship. Through this she became aware of issues around the position of women in Palestine (to which she alerted Eleanor Rathbone MP), and women in India. She also opposed legalised prostitution. Corbett Ashby was no pacifist and strongly supported collective action through the League of Nations. Her opposition to fascism was rooted in her feminism. Within the National Union of Societies for Equal Citizenship (NUSEC) she supported Eleanor Rathbone over family allowances and she helped to persuade the Liberal Party to take up the issue. Along with Eva Hubback she helped to launch the Townswomen's Guild.

In the early post-war years, governments appeared reasonably open-minded about changing the law on women maintaining their British nationality if married to a foreigner, but gradually loosely argued points hardened into immoveable principles. In 1922 a select committee of the House of Commons and in 1923 a Joint Committee of both Houses examined the issue.[3]

While the campaigners' memories of the war played a part in their desire for a change in the law, for others the experiences of the war led them to oppose change. Home Office civil servants argued that a German-born wife of a British husband could shelter under her British status and thus 'work mischief' against British interests without any restrictions, whereas a

---

2. Fawcett Library Nationality of Married Women Pass the Bill Committee, uncatalogued. File: Hard cases.
3. PRO HO 45/12243 History of the movement in favour of separate nationality for wives. Unsigned, undated March 1925.

British-born wife of a German was subjected to restrictions and humilia-tions. On the other hand, civil servants argued that the danger to Britain from enemy-born British wives was easily exaggerated; there were powers to act against anyone known to be a danger. One Home Office civil servant argued that British-born women married to Germans could not always be trusted. He believed that the war had shown that the loyalty of these women to their husbands was as strong an influence over their feelings and conduct as loyalty to the British state.[4] Another civil servant thought it right and reasonable that a British woman who voluntarily threw in her lot with an alien by marrying him, ought to be prepared to assume his nationality as part of the transaction; losing her right to vote was a hardship she was bringing on herself by the voluntary act of marriage.[5]

These conclusions easily fed into the argument that the unity of the family was paramount. In 1930 J.R. Clynes, the Labour Home Secretary, told a deputation of women that if a child could choose either paternal or maternal nationality it would lead to international and domestic confusion and would be contrary to the true interests of the family; and if members of a family did not all have the same nationality one could be deported but not the others.[6] This point about the unity of the family continued to be used in the 1930s by the National Government, which gave it as the reason in 1938 for opposing a Private Member's Bill.

More important than arguments over the unity of the family, however, was the perceived need to maintain the unity of the empire. Throughout the 1920s and 1930s when the issue of women's nationality on marriage was raised at Imperial Conferences, it was either postponed or there was no agreement over change, and for this reason British governments refused to alter their position. In 1930 the Dominions Office pressed the case of imperial solidarity and Sir John Anderson at the Home Office explained to Edith Picton-Turbervill MP and Margery Corbett Ashby that it was vital for the law on British nationality to be uniform throughout the empire 'so as to maintain the common citizenship of British subjects who owe alle-giance to the king. There would be great danger of breaking up the Empire if in regard to any particular part of our nationality law we in the United Kingdom went back on the principle of uniform enactments through the commonwealth.' The Home Office, he claimed, was bound to examine the question from the point of view of the state, unlike women who tended to

---

4. PRO HO 45/12243 n.d c.1922.
5. PRO HO 45/15148 History of the movement in favour of separate nationality for wives. Unsigned, undated c.March 1925.
6. PRO HO 45/15145 Report of a meeting 13 January 1930.

concentrate too much on women's rights and to forget that they belonged to a nation and that the nation also possessed rights. In 1933 the government reiterated its objection to change on the grounds that it needed to keep the imperial character of the law.[7]

Women's organisations maintained that governments' arguments over the need to maintain the unity of the family and the empire were both fallacious. They argued that the governments' use of the word 'unity' confused harmony within the family with judicial unity. In essence women criticised this point because it postulated that the woman should be the subordinate partner in marriage; marriage, they argued, should be no reason for penalising a woman by refusing her the right to her own nationality.

The women campaigners also maintained that governments' arguments over the unity of the empire meant that governments accepted that the most retrograde member of the commonwealth should have the power to veto progress in all other parts of the empire. They also pointed out that there was no unity within the empire, as each country had moved at its own pace (Canada in 1931, Great Britain in 1933, New Zealand in 1934–35, and Australia in 1936) to ratify the 1930 Hague Convention which allowed women to keep their nationality on marriage to a foreigner if they did not gain his nationality. South Africa had failed to ratify it at all. Eire had no interest in maintaining imperial unity.[8]

Women's arguments in favour of allowing women to keep their own nationality on marriage to a foreigner were based on the principle of equality between men and women, but in the 1930s their campaign gained an added practical urgency with the rise of Nazism. In 1933 Flora Drummond, c. 1879–1949, an ex-suffragette who moved from supporting the Independent Labour Party before the war to becoming an ardent campaigner against trade unions, strikes, and state welfare, claimed that the position of women married to non-Nazis was already 'impossible'; by 1938 a number of British-born women married to German Jews had lost their German nationality and were refused passports.[9] The link between the principle of equality and the practical issue of German politics was kept alive throughout the 1930s by various publicists, and received a good deal of popular attention in the late 1930s with the publication of Madeleine Kent's *I Married a German*, which described everyday life for an Englishwoman in Nazi Germany. One further argument in favour of changing the law was put anonymously in

---

7. PRO HO 45/15145 27 January 1930; HO45/15366 16 June 1933 Brief for the Lord Chancellor.
8. Fawcett Library Nationality of Married Women Box 2 Memorandum on the Nationality of Married Women. Eva Hartree.
9. PRO HO 213/378 Harold Nicolson MP to Home Office 17 March 1938.

Labour Woman: as there were more women than men in the country, a woman marrying a foreigner was doing her sisters a favour by increasing their chances of finding a husband, and surely she deserved a reward, not a punishment for this act.[10]

In 1930 at the Hague Convention, the International Council of Women (ICW) and International Alliance of Women for Suffrage and Equal Citizenship arranged a pageant with girls representing different countries dressed in black or white according to their nationality rights; Great Britain's representative wore black with two tiny white spots which represented small concessions.[11] Women's groups campaigned vigorously against the Hague Convention because they felt it reaffirmed the unequal treatment of men and women.

The tactics of some of the women revived memories in the press of the suffrage campaign, although in truth this was a false parallel. Flora Drummond was described in the *Daily Express* as campaigning on behalf of the 'alienettes', and was quoted as saying 'it's like the old days again!' The *Evening News* reported women attempting to see Sir John Simon, the Foreign Secretary, at his house and him having to force his way through the crowd of women to his car. One woman threw herself on the bonnet and had to be removed. Later, women demonstrated outside the German embassy as Sir John and Lady Simon arrived for a reception.[12] The campaign was not a repeat performance of the suffrage campaign: that potentially affected all women, this a relatively small number. Numerous women's organisations, representing thousands of women, backed the campaign, but it never attracted a mass following. In this sense it had much more in common with many other post-suffrage campaigns: thousands of women behind them in theory, but only a few middle-class diehards actively campaigning. This campaign, as with suffrage, emphasised women's legal position, but in common with so many others between the wars it linked gender and family relations in the private sphere with state control.

Welfare work on the Continent

The image of middle-class women's charitable efforts in the inter-war years is one of locally based interests, an image fostered by *Mrs Miniver* and *The*

---

10. *Labour Woman*, October 1933.
11. NCW, *Annual Report* 1930–31 pp. 64–5.
12. PRO HO 45/15366.

Diary of A Provincial Lady; this is, however, only half the story. In the era of the two world wars, British women were interested in, and a small group actively involved with, welfare in continental Europe to an unprecedented extent. They attempted unsuccessfully to persuade British governments to intervene with welfare-based foreign policies.

Responses to the aftermath of Armageddon

The end of the war did not bring an end to instability and hardship for Germans. The 1919 winter of discontent saw demonstrations and uprisings; dislocation resulting from demobilisation and the breakdown of the transport system; shortages of every conceivable basic item, and near-starvation. Shortages were aggravated by the Allied blockade, which continued until July 1919 and the signing of the Treaty of Versailles. In Austria there was a similar tale of political instability, dislocation, shortages and suffering. In October 1918 the Habsburg monarchy was overthrown and the Austro-Hungarian empire disintegrated. This had two immediate effects; first, there was a stream of soldiers going home to the successor states and of Austrian civil servants coming back to Austria; second, the empire's integrated economy collapsed, which contributed significantly to the economic problems of the whole of Austria, and of Vienna in particular. The returning soldiers increased the pressure on housing and jobs, and many women who had taken up factory work during the war suddenly found themselves unemployed. Street riots and strikes flared up intermittently for years, largely as a protest against severe shortages, in particular of food and homes. Inflation and unemployment soared. The suffering of the population, especially in Vienna, was intense. The mortality rates among the civilian population were alarmingly high; in 1919 influenza alone carried off thousands.

A number of well-placed British observers drew attention to the political instability, and the suffering of Germans, especially of women and children.[13] Eglantyne Jebb and her sister, Dorothy Buxton, founded Save the Children Fund (SCF) as a direct result of the failure of their campaign to have the blockade against the defeated enemy raised.

At the end of the war Jebb suggested that she and her friends should publicise the appalling conditions on the Continent in the hope that public opinion would force the government to raise the blockade. To this end, the

---

13. See, for instance, PP 1919 vol. LIII. Army Reports by British officers on the economic conditions prevailing in Germany. Cmd 52; 54.

women tramped the country addressing public meetings, and helped to form the Fight the Famine Council, which held its first public meeting on 1 January 1919 at Central Hall, Westminster. The campaign was to no avail. In April 1919 Dorothy Buxton argued for the establishment of a sub-committee to raise funds for the relief of children's suffering: children were suffering most and no-one could hold them responsible for the war. On 15 May 1919, a few days before SCF's first public meeting, it received a shower of publicity when Jebb was prosecuted under the DORA and fined £5 for distributing a handbill with a picture of a starving Austrian baby, for which she had not obtained the Censor's permission.

From its inception SCF provoked controversy. It challenged government policy towards Germany at a time when anti-German feeling was still running high, and this is why Jebb was prosecuted. SCF then worked with the Society of Friends during the Russian famine, 1921–23, at a period when Anglo–Russian relations were still very frosty.[14] Governments across western Europe feared that if they provided relief for Russia during the famine they would be helping to prop up the Soviet regime. They had already had their fingers burnt when the Bolsheviks reneged on loans to the czarist regime.[15]

While the work of Quaker and SCF women was highly 'political' in overtly questioning the foreign policies of British governments, the middle-class women who went abroad were not constrained by their personal sympathies in political struggles. In January 1921, for instance, the Quaker Ruth Fry wrote of the help the Quakers were giving to students in Germany; the students were reactionary, but she felt this was an added reason for working with them as it could bring them under Quaker influence.[16] Similar attitudes were described in Chapter Four among those women who focused on the welfare needs of women and children in Britain, for they challenged government policy implicitly by their practices and explicitly by their campaigning.

It is hard to disentangle the motives of individuals who went abroad, partly because what they wrote at the time was for public consumption. Often letters the Quakers wrote home were read in meetings, so their content is somewhat predictable. The motives of SCF workers appear to be mixed. Edward Fuller of SCF listed compassion for suffering children; an act of national contrition for the suffering which the war had brought on

14. SCF archives. SCF DB/5.
15. Wm Barnes Steveni, *Europe's Great Calamity: The Russian Famine An Appeal for the Russian Peasant* (1922), pp. 2–4.
16. Society of Friends (SF) FEWVRC 4 January 1921.

innocent victims; self-interest (fear of disease spreading), and a desire to create friendship out of enmity.[17]

In the 1920s welfare was perceived as a goodwill gesture, and this justified for the women the very limited impact they had on conditions. They were not under any illusion about what they could achieve, in contrast to women working in the welfare field in Britain, many of whom assumed that if only the lives of working-class mothers could be improved, society would be transformed. One way of trying to understand what motivated these women, is not to look at the reasons they gave, but at the issues which they prioritised, and these were children, the middle class, and women.

The work for children was primarily relief work. Jebb recognised from the outset the limitations of such an approach, arguing that relief alone could not save children; there was also a need to stimulate a new outlook so that money needed for children's food and education was not spent on luxuries and amusements.[18] At first SCF collected money for relief work among children which was administered through existing societies. For instance, the Quakers distributed milk and clothes for children in Vienna. In 1922 milk, cocoa, fats, cereals and soap were distributed monthly to 1,200 'needy' (mainly middle-class) children.[19]

Soon SCF was running its own schemes. It inaugurated 'adoption' schemes, whereby British sponsors would agree to make a regular contribution for a specific child, or a British school would send money for a particular children's institution in Germany. In 1924 SCF was running kitchens in Cologne for 1,250 children, helping to feed 4,000 children in Berlin and making small, regular donations to 70 children's institutions across Germany.[20]

In the 1920s many continental schemes specifically targeted distressed gentlefolk, for whom relief workers frequently expressed their admiration and concern. Despite taking up the cause of poor children in Britain, SCF often expressed its empathy with the continental middle class, who were seen to be especially hard-hit by wartime and economic misfortune. In 1922 SCF women compared favourably the poor middle-class women of Vienna with poor working-class British ones over the way they dressed their children. Instead of adopting a judgemental attitude towards the British mothers, however, they tried to explain the reason for the Viennese children being so well dressed, concluding that appearances were overwhelmingly

17. Edward Fuller, *The Rights of the Child* (1951), pp. 35–8.
18. SCF SC/SF/18 Jebb to Susanne Ferriere n.d. but early 1920s.
19. SCF EJ's papers. Austria 11/11 Mary Houghton, Friends' Relief Mission, Vienna. Letter received 30 May 1922.
20. SCF 2/20 Miss Sigdwick's notes; SCF SC/MH/8 Jebb to Margaret Hill 2 March 1924.

important, and poor middle-class families probably knew other, not so poor, middle-class families to give them nice clothes.[21]

One recurring theme of Quaker relief workers was their concern for the middle class in the cities in which they worked. On 13 September 1919 Hilda Clark, a Quaker doctor working in Vienna, wrote of her anxiety over the plight of the Austrian middle class to her lifelong companion, Edith Pye, 1876–1965, also a Quaker, who was a nurse and midwife and had run a maternity hospital for refugees in France during the First World War. Special schemes targeting the middle class were set up in both Austria and Germany; intellectuals and students were especially popular groups for Quaker aid. Depots for professionals were a feature of their work. In 1920 a *Mittelstand* (middle class) training scheme was inaugurated. By the end of 1922 a programme to help the intellectual classes, in accordance with an American Friend's suggestion, was under way. Soon after, criticisms were aimed at a milk scheme, on the grounds that the money could be better spent on intellectuals. Early in 1920 relief was given to individual middle-class families, and in the spring there was a scheme to feed teachers. The Friends Appeal for Central European students and professionals became the Universities Committee of the Imperial War Fund. Berlin students were given a special grant, and in 1920 an appeal was made for university books.[22]

Those women who went abroad were almost always well-to-do, and the prominent organisers in Britain were predominantly female and middle-class. SCF relied on voluntary, middle-class and upper-class support; it was backed by a wealth of well-known names, the blessing of all the churches, and yet it still managed to appeal to all classes of British society.

Middle-class women were at the forefront of British relief work in Germany and Austria immediately after the First World War and in the related campaign to force the coalition government of Lloyd George to raise the blockade against the defeated enemy. Smaller women's organisations, such as Lady Muriel Paget's Mission to eastern Europe, eventually joined forces with SCF. Numerous women not only organised relief from Britain but also continued to work in the field; Evelina Haverfield, for instance, worked with women in Serbia. Women extended the rough and unpleasant work usually associated with their activities on the Continent during the war. From the outset many of SCF's key organisers were women, although men

21. SCF 5/4; 7/4; 17/3.
22. SF FEWVRC 24 February 1920; German sub-committee 19 February 1920, 22 April 1920. Box 425/27; FEWVRC 1 April 1920; FEWVRC 4 January 1921. Elizabeth Howard, *Across Barriers* (1941), p.13; SF Box 425/27.

were not excluded. In the mid-1920s Lady Cynthia Mosley chaired a special German committee.[23]

As well as women offering their services to work for SCF, there were a number of well-placed women from across the political spectrum, including Lady Astor (Conservative), Margaret Bondfield (Labour), and Violet Markham (Liberal), who publicly supported SCF's work. Evelyn Sharp, 1869–1955, a suffragette, journalist, writer and pacifist, provided eyewitness accounts of conditions in Germany and Austria after the war and in Russia during the 1922–3 famine.[24] Sharp had been a member of the Anti-Sweating League and a suffragette before the war. In 1911 she switched to being a suffragist and during the war continued to campaign vigorously for the vote. After the war she joined the Labour Party and while continuing to pursue her career as a journalist, she took a special interest in poverty and unemployment, and birth control.

Prominent feminists, some of them old hands from the suffrage campaign supported SCF. Emmeline Pethick-Lawrence, 1867–1954, had undertaken philanthropic work and been a leading suffragette. During the war she was a pacifist and member of the WILPF. In the 1920s she campaigned against restrictions on women's employment and supported calls for birth control. She was a leading member of the Women's Freedom League (WFL), Six Point Group and Open Door Council. Charlotte Despard, an ex-suffragette was also a member. Lilian Lenton, before the war a member of the Women's Social and Political Union, went to Russia in 1922 with Boyle and two other women. On her return she toured the country talking about the Russian famine. Between 1924 and 1933 she was travelling organiser for the WFL. Nina Boyle, a suffragist, novelist, and SCF Council member for 22 years, visited Russia from 1921 to 1922 on behalf of SCF; Ray Strachey and Katharine Bruce-Glasier were also active in SCF. The Marchioness of Aberdeen, another leading member of SCF, was president of the National Council of Women, a member of the International Council of Women (ICW), and patron of the National Society for the Prevention of Cruelty to Children.

At times SCF's appeals for assistance were targeted specifically at women. Jebb believed that the responsibility for the next generation lay with women, both in their own families and in the wider world. She argued that women determined what aspects of the culture were preserved and handed on to the next generation; and women influenced children's expectations of

---

23. SCF 20/2; CB 13/6; SCF 13/1; SCF *Annual Report* 1924.
24. SCF M1/3, 17/4; Evelyn Sharp, *Unfinished Adventure: Selected Reminiscences from an Englishwoman's Life* (1933), pp. 233–49.

standards of living and their sense of responsibility for others. In 1925 Eglantyne Jebb sent an open letter to British women's organisations on behalf of Greek refugees from Turkey. She argued that it was vital for women to recognise their international responsibilities as women towards the weak and suffering of the human race. She wrote in high-flown language of the way British women might save civilisation if they made a distinctive contribution to public policy in international affairs and used their recently won influence and opportunities to win over people of the world to principles of mutual service, righteousness and goodwill. She appealed for British women's organisations to save the Greek women and children from poverty in order that they might have the opportunity of an 'honourable' and self-supporting life. She had already referred to the fact that women of a 'semi-oriental character' had limited possibilities to fend for themselves and this led to a lowering of moral standards and to prostitution among the refugees.[25]

This assumption that poverty led to prostitution among continental women was unusual among relief workers. The hysterical racist campaign after the First World War over the alleged peril faced by German women when the victors sent Black troops as part of the army of occupation, or the alleged prostitution among Cologne women for the British army of occupation, was never taken up by relief workers. They never used these allegations as a means of whipping up sympathy and money for their work or expressed as one of their motives the need to combat 'immorality', perhaps because their main concern was with the middle class, whom they judged unlikely to resort to prostitution. (The Greek women were peasants.) They feared that if they mentioned immorality among the defeated enemy it would reinforce hostility rather than attract support. By focusing on the needs of children they were less likely to face hostility; children could hardly be blamed for starting the war, and they represented the future.

The network of women in Britain supporting welfare work on the Continent extended to those in the field. Many of the women who went abroad under the auspices of the Society of Friends provided each other with strong support. They knew each other personally, shared homes both in Britain and abroad, and their stream of letters reveal a strong sense of community and comradeship. Although the Society of Friends sent both women and men abroad to undertake relief work, the network of women

---

25. Eglantyne Jebb, *Save the Child: A Posthumous Essay*, ed. D.F. Buxton (1929), pp. 49–50. SCF Eglantyne Jebb papers Greece 17/9 From Eglantyne Jebb 7 January 1925.

was especially tightly knit. The women showed no interest in challenging gender relations, and indeed worked in harmony with the men.

As well as offering to help save the children of Europe, SCF women also recognised the crucial role played by the Austrian and German mothers in saving their own children, and expressed great respect for their efforts. One woman working for the Quakers in Vienna commented that she wished a 'Save the Mothers Fund' could be started because mothers bore the brunt of suffering. In a radical suggestion she argued that mothers should be paid a salary for the amount of work they undertook for the family.[26] Quaker women were thrown into close contact with German and Austrian mothers as projects focusing on children inevitably brought them together. Often, too, they used local women to organise and help distribute the aid. There is no evidence in SCF records that the British women thought that they would teach other European women how to be good mothers in the way that working-class mothers in Britain were being so taught by those who offered them charity. Respect for the other Europeans to whom they provided assistance and with whom they worked was a strong feature of SCF. One example of this is the way in which they tried to 'screen' those women who went abroad by, for instance, looking for women who could speak German if they were going to Germany or Austria.

SCF's international credentials existed from the outset. Eglantyne Jebb and Dorothy Buxton had established SCF as a British organisation to help starving children in Austria and Germany. The organisation quickly spread to other countries which established organisations in their own right, not simply as British outposts, and with Geneva as the international headquarters.[27] In 1921 a separate home fund was established in recognition of the fact that Britain faced similar problems to its European neighbours, although the suffering on the Continent was recognised as worse and therefore received priority.

Middle-class women worked on the Continent with the defeated enemy in a welfare role. Although inevitably brought into conflict with their own government, they avoided political engagement on the Continent. There were, however, soon to be small stirrings over political developments in Italy and, later, in Germany. As with welfare work on the Continent, campaigning against fascism remained the active concern of middle-class women; it never turned into a mass mobilisation of support.

---

26. SCF 11/11, 7/2.
27. SCF *Annual Report* 1920.

In the shadow of fascism

The history of foreign policy in the 1930s has been largely confined to accounts of (male) politicians as 'appeasers' or 'anti-appeasers'. Historians examining the influence of pressure groups and individual campaigners have focused on pacifist activities, but they barely mention women's role, or the history of WILPF.

There are exceptions to this male and/or pacifist approach. Johanna Alberti has drawn attention to the activities of British feminists who were not necessarily pacifists. She has argued that opposition to fascism brought together women of various political persuasions; many women undertook relief work with refugees. She draws a number of parallels between the new feminism and fascism, particularly their common emphasis on mother-hood. Alberti notes that feminists recognised fascism's attack on women's independence and right to paid work, and they linked their campaign with demands for equal pay and the right of married women to retain their nationality on marriage to a foreigner. She points out that many of the women's anti-fascist activities were not necessarily feminist, and for many women socialism seemed a more effective means of challenging fascism than feminism.[28] Carol Miller has also undertaken interesting work on women's strong support for, and involvement in, the League of Nations' disarmament and peace activities, as well as its work to improve women's welfare and status, and to bring about legal equality between women and men.[29]

Women's response to fascism falls into two main categories. First, there were those women who campaigned to expose the nature of fascism through, for instance, their publications; such writings normally drew attention to the inherent attack on women within fascist ideology and practice. Second, there was relief work on the Continent and work with refugees in Britain. In both cases the emphasis was primarily on helping women and children through women's traditional work of offering shelter and care. This approach fitted with welfare/maternalist feminism although the women did not necessarily express explicitly feminist motives. Their reasons for challenging fascism complemented the nature of the women's activities.

---

28. Johanna Alberti, 'British feminists and anti-fascism in the 1930s', in Sybil Oldfield, ed., *This Working-day World: Women's Lives and Culture(s) in Britain, 1914–1945* (1994), pp. 111–22.
29. Carol Miller, '"Geneva the key to equality": interwar feminists and the League of Nations', *Women's History Review* 3, 2 (1994), pp. 219–45.

Women's reaction to fascism went through a number of stages. First, from the early 1920s there were the anti-Italian fascist activities of a small British group, headed by Sylvia Pankhurst. Stirrings of a wider concern began after a socialist uprising against the Austrian dictator, Dollfuss, in February 1934 was brutally suppressed, but the response remained largely confined to the same groups (SCF and the Quakers), and indeed individuals (Hilda Clark and Edith Pye), who had undertaken relief work after the war. Their response remained in the tradition of pacifism and humanitarianism, rather than feminism or socialism. At the same time, feminist and other commentators were beginning to expose the nature of the Nazi regime in Germany. It was not until the outbreak of the Spanish civil war in 1936 that a far wider challenge to fascism was mounted, which overshadowed the previous welfare work spearheaded by women. Spain was an aberration in the majority of British women's response to continental fascism. The new activists were more likely to be socialists, not necessarily pacifists or linked with pacifist organisations, as well as women in the labour movement who were able to mobilise support, albeit mainly home-based.

From 1938 the plight of refugees from Nazi Germany came to dominate British responses to fascism, but as there was no clearly identified socialist opposition in Germany with whom British socialists could identify, concern was more muted than in the case of the Spanish victims of fascism. Mobilising support for Spanish anti-fascists was easier in that it did not pose a challenge to British lifestyles; the support offered was, on the whole, to people a safe distance from British shores who did not threaten British jobs. The needs of Jewish refugees from Nazi Germany could not be so easily accommodated and for this reason we see a gap between the humanitarian and anti-Nazi sentiments publicly expressed and the actual welcome which refugees experienced. Sympathy for the victims of fascism was always greatest when those victims did not present a threat (perceived or real) to standards of living of the British population.

Italian fascism

In 1922 when Mussolini seized power there was no great outcry in Britain. In 1924 when fascists murdered Giacomo Matteotti, a leading opposition parliamentarian, there was barely a flicker of interest in Britain, with the notable exception of the best-known British activist against Italian fascism, Sylvia Pankhurst, now remembered for her suffragette campaigning rather than for her anti-fascist stance. In response to Matteotti's murder, Pankhurst formed the Women's International Matteotti Committee, which publicised the nature of the Italian fascist state. It also put pressure on governments to intervene on behalf of Matteotti's widow, whom Pankhurst described as living under 'extraordinary and inhuman treatment', with her home under police observation and few daring to visit her. Pankhurst wrote letters to the press highlighting the position of women under fascism, in particular the way in which their legal and social status was being undermined.

Contemporary British women writers were quick to draw attention to the gendered nature of fascist ideology and practice. Women who wrote warnings about fascism were informed by their own feminism, although those publicising the nature of Italian fascism remained a small and elite group. In 1932 the feminist playwright, novelist, actress, travel writer, translator, suffragist and peace campaigner, Cicely Hamilton, 1872–1952, published *Modern Italy As Seen By An Englishwoman*. In her biography of Hamilton, Lis Whitelaw draws attention to Hamilton's intimate knowledge of the Continent; she spoke French, German and Italian and travelled widely, usually alone. Between 1931 and 1950 she published nine books on modern Europe. One of her main objections to fascism, according to Whitelaw, was that it was anti-feminist.[30] Hamilton drew attention to a number of aspects of Italian fascism which denigrated women: fascism was hostile to birth control; it emphasised a woman's duty to the state, and claimed that her self-fulfilment lay in childbearing and childrearing; women were discouraged from public affairs; they did not have the vote; they were encouraged to join women's fascist groups which took their orders from the male units; and *fascio femminile* were confined to the relief of distress such as providing clothes for the poor, child welfare, care of the sick, and care of the dependents of dead soldiers or fascists. Such activities also acted as fascist propaganda by showing the good works of fascists. It was also, according to Hamilton, a means of chipping away at the influence of the Catholic Church, which had in the past undertaken similar work. After 1929, preference in employment was given to the married over the single, and to parents over childless couples. The tax system favoured marriage, and family allowances favoured those with children.[31] All these aspects of Italian fascism were abhorrent to Hamilton, whose feminism was based strongly on the belief that women should be able to choose whether to be dependent on men or not. In Britain she campaigned for women's economic independence, for birth control and, through the Open Door Council, against protective legislation. Those criticising the regime in Italy did not, however, offer practical

---

30. Lis Whitelaw, *The Life and Times of Cicely Hamilton* (1990), pp. 225–8.
31. Cicely Hamilton, *Modern Italy As Seen By An Englishwoman* (1932), pp. 76–89.

suggestions for opposing it. In contrast, events in Austria offered some limited scope for action.

Austria, 1934

The February 1934 revolution in Austria, when an uprising against a right-wing government was brutally suppressed, prompted the first awakenings of women in the British labour movement to the nature of fascism. From October 1934 *Labour Woman* carried accounts of the activities of Austrian socialist women, who were portrayed as both activists against, and victims of, fascism. Mention was made of women assisting men in the underground movement, distributing banned socialist literature and helping the victims of the February 1934 revolution. Calls were made for the British women to protest against the imprisonment of two socialist women MPs, Gabriele Proft and Helen Postranetzki, both of whom allegedly suffered nervous breakdowns in prison.[32] There is no way, however, of knowing what proportion of women actually read the articles on Austrian women. There is no evidence of a concerted campaign in Britain to assist the Austrian women. *Labour Woman* made no mention of relief work undertaken by British women under the auspices of SCF and the Quakers.

Concrete assistance to Austrians remained in the hands of those women who had worked in Austria after the war. After the events of February 1934 Hilda Clark, representing the Quakers, and Mosa Anderson, for SCF, undertook a preliminary survey. In 1934 Edith Pye and Hilda Clark both returned to Vienna. Alice Nike, an American who had also worked in Vienna after the First World War, returned to help distribute aid supplied by foreigners for the victims of the February 1934 revolution. British trade unions raised money, which was used in Vienna and Graz.[33] Criticisms were voiced of the Quaker relief in Vienna on the grounds that it was slow, inadequate and not reaching the families in need. The relief agencies, however, had to walk a precarious tightrope; after a trip to Graz in 1934 Anderson commented on the problem of not appearing too close to the socialists while at the same time needing their confidence.[34] Aid to the victims of Italian and Austrian fascism by foreigners was severely constrained, and remained low-key. The rise of Spanish fascism transformed the nature and extent of British responses.

---

32. *Labour Woman*, October 1934; October 1935; February 1936.
33. SF Yearly meeting 1935–36.
34. SF FSC 14 March 1934.

Spain, 1936–39

Between July 1936 and March 1939 Spain was engulfed in a civil war between Republicans, defending the democratically elected government, and the Falangists, led by General Franco and backed by the army. Before 1936 the majority of Spanish women's lives had been hard and subject to repression. After the establishment of the Republic in 1931 some progress had been made, with universal suffrage for those aged over 23, education measures, some secularisation and the possibility of divorce as well as a shorter working week for agricultural workers and maternity compensation. Women, however, remained a low priority on all parties' political agendas. Even so, in the early months of the civil war women played a full part, sitting on committees, serving in militias in the front line and undertaking the traditional work of women in wartime, nursing, cooking and looking after the men. This traditional role was soon to be their only one. As the war dragged on and defeat overtook them, the lives of women became ever harder due to shortages, queues and the daily struggle for existence in a civil war. Both the years of the Republic and the civil war had a distinctive gendered impact.

Unlike women's responses to fascism in other countries, a specific gender analysis appears absent from British women's critiques of developments in Spain. British women, nevertheless, were at the forefront of the campaign to collect aid for Spain and to help Spanish women and children, that is, to help Spanish women in their traditional role as mothers. While the British government resolutely held back from aiding the forces of democracy, a massive wave of support swept the length and breadth of the country. All political parties, but predominantly the Labour Party, all classes, but predominantly the working class, Christian organisations, but predominantly the Quakers, along with pacifists, voluntary organisations, and women's organisations all responded to appeals for aid.

Women MPs of all parties took up the issue. The Spanish government invited Edith Summerskill and Ellen Wilkinson to see conditions for themselves. Summerskill, a medical doctor, Labour MP, 1938–61 (Parliamentary Secretary to the Minister of Food, 1945–50, and Minister of National Insurance and Industrial Injuries, 1950–51), went alone, because Wilkinson was ill, and subsequently toured the USA describing the conditions she had found. Wilkinson was a strident critic of Nazism and of Conservative foreign policy.

In April 1937 an all-women delegation – comprising the Duchess of Atholl, Conservative MP, 1923–38, and Parliamentary Secretary at the Board of Education, 1924–9; Rathbone, Wilkinson and Rachel Crowdy – went on a fact-finding mission to Spain. On her return Atholl broadcast an appeal for the children of Madrid and then published a bestseller, *Searchlight on Spain*. In April 1938 the Conservative whip was withdrawn from her and soon she lost the support of her constituency. She sought the Chiltern Hundreds and unsuccessfully fought a by-election in December 1938 as an Independent candidate. Even at the end of 1938 a Conservative who defied the Party and actively campaigned against fascism was not supported by the women and men of her party.

The Spanish civil war presented a clear-cut issue where British people could easily identify 'right' from 'wrong', and where there was obvious scope for them to respond. It brought the working class into a discourse on international affairs and foreign policy and for this reason it was perhaps more of a break from the past for them than for the middle class or upper class. Spain, however, did not signal a popular consensus; although there was agreement over the need to provide aid to Spain, the motives of those involved varied greatly. On the left, supporting the Republicans was an extension of anti-fascist activity at home and an expression of class solidarity; for others it was a humanitarian concern over the sufferings of those caught up in the war.

The majority of British people who helped the Spanish Republicans were women at home; a small minority of British people actually went to fight, yet the image we have of British people's involvement is of men going off to fight. Spain provided opportunities for a wide range of people to make a contribution; there was scope for politicians to campaign, and to put pressure on the government, for women to collect money and make clothes to send; for volunteers to go out to Spain in a medical, nursing or administrative role, and for charitable organisations with a tradition of relief on the Continent, such as the Quakers and SCF, to organise relief. Opportunities existed to work with the relief organisations whatever one's class, gender, circumstances or motives.

There were three main relief organisations. The General Relief Fund for Displaced Women and Children of Spain sought to avoid political involvement and gained much of its support from the churches. The National Joint Committee for Spanish Relief was started after a group of MPs visited Spain. It was launched at the Houses of Parliament in January 1937, with the Duchess of Atholl in the chair and Rathbone as vice-chair. Ellen Wilkinson and Leah Manning, not at this time an MP, but Labour MP, 1931 and 1945–50, joined along with a number of other women and men within and outside Parliament. Both the Quakers and SCF were represented on these bodies. Medical Aid for Spain was the most overtly political group, organised by the labour movement. Isobel Brown, a member of the Communist Party launched it, and Leah Manning acted as honorary secretary until she was replaced by a paid official, George Jeger.

The Quakers and SCF quickly became involved in relief work. Although supposedly neutral, in practice the Quakers' aid went to Republicans: the Nationalists controlled the more fertile areas and were constantly on the attack. Much of the Quaker work was with refugees – large numbers of refugees from the south in the early part of the war, later evacuees from Madrid, and at the end of the war vast numbers of refugees in northern Spain and southern France. Both women and men were involved in all these organisations, including old hands from the 1920s, such as Edith Pye and Francesca Wilson. Women-only organisations outside the labour movement, such as the NCW and WILPF, played only a marginal part in providing aid. In the autumn of 1937 when Eleanor Rathbone tried to get women's organisations to sign a telegram to Franco she was unable to send it for lack of signatures.[35]

In contrast, women in the labour movement were at the forefront in working for the Republicans. Almost every women's section of the Labour Party, local Labour Party and Women's Co-operative Guild was involved in collecting money and making clothes. Milk tokens were on sale at Co-operative Stores for 6d.[36] The emphasis on milk is instructive; while the motivation of those helping Spain was a mixture of humanitarianism and political sympathy, not feminism, the bulk of aid was collected by women and sent to women and children together; indeed appeals often emphasised the interlocking needs of women and children.[37]

In April 1937 Leah Manning and Edith Pye went to Bilbao to help arrange to bring nearly 4,000 Basque children out of the war zone and over to Britain. In the summer a rally to support the children was held at the Albert Hall, but the reception which the children received in Britain was a very mixed one and foreshadowed the response to those children who arrived in rural areas following the evacuation of the cities once Britain was at war, and to Gibraltarians who arrived in Britain after the evacuation of Gibralter (see Chapter Eight).

The bulk of women's activities for Spain took place in Britain, but a significant number of women also went to Spain in medical, nursing, administrative, teaching or relief worker capacities. Those who went out to Spain were usually initially motivated by humanitarianism; political awareness followed once they were in Spain. Alexander asserts that the dominant

35. NCW vol. xvii no. 1 Jan 1939; WILPF Annual Report 1937 2/7, 12 Jan; 13 April 1937, September/October 1937 1/13 Executive Committee.
36. *Labour Woman*, December 1937, July 1938.
37. Committee Against Malnutrition; Francesca Wilson, *In the Margins of Chaos* (1944); *Labour Woman*, July 1938.

political impulse in support for Spain was anti-fascism.[38] This impulse, how-ever, remained firmly focused on Spain.

Mobilisation for the Spanish Republicans was an extension of anti-fascism at home and a defence of working-class interests which could not so easily be incorporated into aid for the victims of German fascism: there was no clear class solidarity, no working-class German opposition with which the British could identify, and helping refugees was not seen as comple-menting the class struggle, but rather the opposite, for it was seen as a threat to British jobs and standards of living. Boycotting German goods was supported by trade unions, an act which worked to their own advantage, and Jewish businessmen who moved to the depressed areas were acceptable because of the jobs they created. While the labour movement demonstrated its wholesale support for Spanish anti-fascists, reactions to German fascism were far more muted and complex because of latent anti-German feel-ing and anti-semitism; the fear that refugees would take jobs from British workers, and the absence of a clear alternative within Germany to which critics of fascism could attach themselves. So, while Jim Fyrth claims that the Spanish civil war awakened a new understanding of fascism[39] – and certainly it did lead many to abandon their earlier pacifism – it did not translate into widespread support for the victims of German fascism.

Nazi Germany, 1933–38

Those women who provided a critique of fascism focused on the racist and gendered nature of the Nazi regime. Hitler came to power on a platform of recovering Germany's standing in the international arena and of reviving the economy, part of which involved reducing unemployment. Winifred Holtby, 1898–1935, a feminist and novelist whose play attacking fascism *Take Back Your Freedom* was published posthumously in 1939, noted at the time that one ploy for reducing the unemployment figures was to remove certain groups, such as women, from the labour market. British women could immediately identify with the struggle against such a strategy; pro-moting women's paid work and fighting against prejudice was part of their campaigning in Britain. While both women and men were involved in helping, or hindering, refugees from Nazi Germany, the focus of aid was children, traditionally a concern of women; it also reflected the priority of

---

38. Jim Fyrth and Sally Alexander, *Women's Voices From the Spanish Civil War* (1991), p. 15.
39. Jim Fyrth, *The Signal was Spain: The Aid Spain Movement in Britain, 1936–39* (1986), p. 309.

German families who tried to save their children, and of the organisations, such as SCF, which was one of the first to intervene.

On 31 May 1933, soon after Hitler had come to power, Eleanor Rathbone chaired a NUSEC meeting of women's organisations at the Houses of Parliament where a unanimous resolution was passed, expressing dismay at the dismissal of women from the civil service, for 'any injury done to the women of one nation must be deeply felt by the women of all nations'.[40] This was sent to the German ambassador. The Open Door Council warned that 1933 was a black year for women, with sweeping attacks on their political and economic rights, and glorification of their return to the home, there to be the 'recreation of the tired warrior'.[41] In 1933 Cicely Hamilton wrote that National Socialism was essentially anti-feminist, as one of its principles was that women's place was in the home. As a result of its campaign against women wage earners, she believed there would be an increase in 'kept women' and prostitutes, an inevitable accompaniment of the dependence of one sex on the other.[42]

In 1934 Winifred Holtby warned of the evils of National Socialism. She argued inter alia that Hitler's promise of reviving German vitality and prosperity and solving the problem of unemployment involved removing non-Aryans, Jews, left-wingers and women from the labour market. While National Socialism employed financial inducements to encourage women's domestic interests, she warned that confining women to motherhood defeated its own ends by making women less capable of successful motherhood. Holtby did not, however, single out fascist regimes for criticism. She believed that the political subjection of women under the Nazis was accepted because of the ingrained social theories of women's subservience which preceded the Nazis; and she identified not only Germany and Italy, but also France and Ireland as countries where fecundity was revered as a patriotic duty. 'The mother who fills the cradle enables her sovereign to rule the world.'[43]

While contemporary British feminist writers were in no doubt that German women were the victims of the Nazi state, historians are not so sure.[44] The key determinant of a woman's experience was not her gender or her class, but her 'race'. For Jewish women the situation was distinct from that of the majority Gentile population. Non-Jewish women and men could

---

40. *The Times*, 2 June 1933.
41. Open Door Council 8th *Annual Report* 1933–34.
42. *The Times*, 2 June 1993; Open Door Council 8th Annual Report 1933–34; Cicely Hamilton, *Modern Germanies As Seen By An Englishwoman* (1933), pp. 265–7.
43. Winifred Holtby, *Women* (1934), pp. 153–69.
44. Claudia Koonz, *Mothers in the Fatherland: Women, Family and Nazi Politics* (1987).

be both victims and perpetrators. An Aryan woman might be denied an abortion because she was of a 'superior' race, and at the same time she might be implementing Nazi anti-semitic policy on a daily basis by her boycott of Jewish shops because they were run by an 'inferior' race. While some women were pushed out of professional posts, others, such as social workers, nurses and midwives, were identifying targets for sterilisation and euthanasia.

British women's initial response to National Socialism was spearheaded by women on the left, but embraced women of all political persuasions. In 1934 the Women's World Committee against War and Fascism was formed, with broad social demands linked with anti-fascism. It was backed by Charlotte Despard; Sylvia Pankhurst; Ellen Wilkinson; Vera Brittain, 1893–1970, a journalist and writer, member of the Six Point Group, and a pacifist who also campaigned for an end to the marriage bar and equal pay; Storm Jameson, a writer; Evelyn Sharp, and Sybil Thorndike, 1882–1976, an actress. In late 1934 Selina Cooper and Monica Whately went to Germany with an interpreter to try to help women in gaols and camps; they achieved nothing in Germany but on their return they were armed with more information with which they could address meetings and warn a widening circle of women of the evils of fascism.[45] Sheila Grant Duff, a left-wing journalist, publicised the threat posed by Nazi Germany and met Churchill to brief him.[46] Similarly, the Duchess of Atholl drew attention to the sections of *Mein Kampf* which advocated an aggressive foreign policy and had been omitted from English translations. She briefed Churchill on parts of *Mein Kampf* and supplied him with extracts of Hitler's speeches not circulated in the British press. She, too, made known the aggressive nature of Nazism. As Churchill played such a pivotal role in bringing to an end the policy of appeasement and mobilising the country for war from May 1940 onwards, Atholl's role in arming Churchill with information proved more useful than knocking on ministers' doors.

Eleanor Rathbone was one of the most active parliamentarians to attack fascism and to support its victims. She railed against British people taking holidays in Germany and attacked British participation in the 1936 Olympic Games in Berlin. She supported a boycott of German goods. In Parliament she frequently asked awkward and searching questions about passports, visas, finance and conditions for refugees and she sent a stream of letters to the press. She exposed MPs, including Labour ones, whom she believed

---

45. Jill Liddington, *The Life and Times of a Respectable Rebel: Selina Cooper, 1864–1946* (1984), pp. 410–15.
46. Sheila Grant Duff, *The Parting Ways: A Personal Account of the Thirties* (1982), pp. 169–95.

displayed sympathy towards General Franco, leader of the Spanish fascists, and kept a dossier on the attitude of peers. In the months leading up to the outbreak of war she harrassed the Foreign Office over the plight of refugees from Czechoslovakia. Rathbone made a point of seeing conditions for herself. She visited Spain during the civil war; in 1937 she and Atholl travelled to Yugoslavia, Czechoslovakia and Rumania; and in 1938 she went to Czechoslovakia. Women recognised the limited impact they and welfare organisations could have on the plight of victims of fascism and on the international situation, and for this reason women such as Rathbone constantly urged the government to take a more interventionist and supportive role, in particular by expediting the flight of refugees and by offering more financial support to them. Rathbone believed that much of what she was doing was educating the British public to the anti-semitism and other evils of fascism.[47]

The sum total of what British women in their welfare and political work achieved in terms of supporting the victims of fascism was inevitably limited, and far less than could have been achieved if women's priorities had been those of governments. Nevertheless, women helped to raise the British public's awareness of the evils of fascism and thus contributed to breaking down the revulsion against embroilment in another war which had followed within a few years of the end of the First World War, and the strong pacifist sentiment which had swept the country in the early and mid-1930s. They helped to generalise the specific anti-fascist sentiment displayed during the Spanish civil war, and thus to firm up the country's support for the government when war broke out. Neither the volte-face which this change involved nor women activists' part in changing opinions and policies should be underestimated.

The Jewish experience

While many in Britain were distracted by the Spanish civil war, the situation in Germany had deteriorated significantly. In 1934 Lady Helen Bonham-Carter, 1887–1969, prominent member of the Liberal Party, member of the League of Nations executive and anti-appeaser, spoke out against Nazi Germany, drawing attention to the cruelties and humiliations suffered by Jewish children, and the duty of non-Jews to rally to their aid. She called

---

47. Eleanor Rathbone papers, University of Liverpool xiv.2.6 (1–16) xiv.2.10 (1–70) xiv.2.11 (34–50) xiv.2.12 xiv.2.15.

for as many Jewish children as possible to be removed from their surroundings in order that they would not grow up 'warped' and 'bruised' and 'embittered by injustice'.[48]

The bald facts of Hitler's campaign against the Jews cannot do justice to the horrors of the regime; all they can do is to highlight the situation from which an increasing number of refugees tried to escape. In the 1930s the Nazi regime launched random attacks on the Jews rather than implementing a systematic policy of genocide. Jews lived in an atmosphere of menace and exclusion, never knowing where the next attack on their lives would come from, or what form it would take. From the 1920s Nazi thugs had attacked Jews, but in the 1930s these attacks became institutionalised, with the full backing of the state. From April 1933 Jewish shops and businesses were boycotted; Jews were excluded from the civil service and from certain professions. In 1935 the Nuremberg Laws removed their remaining rights as German citizens, excluded them from public places, and imposed restrictions on marriages between Jews and Gentiles. In November 1938, on what became known as *Kristallnacht*, Jewish synagogues, homes and businesses were torched and ransacked, and numerous Jews were murdered.

Refugees from Germany

In the course of the 1930s Germany came increasingly to dominate European foreign affairs. In the 1920s the quality newspapers had reported Nazi activities, and after 1933 the popular press provided coverage, albeit uneven, raising the awareness of a growing section of the British public. No lead was given by the government in enlightening the population about the nature of Nazism, mainly because it did not want to worsen Anglo–German relations. Until 1938 few Christian leaders publicly condemned the regime. An increasing number of British tourists visited Germany, seeing what they wanted to see and coming away with a wide variety of impressions: sympathisers were impressed, others remained indifferent to the menace posed to certain sections of the population, while critics had their fears reinforced. Germany often appeared to be remarkably 'normal' to tourists, and indeed the regime went to some pains to give the impression of normality and stability to visitors. Not for nothing did Eleanor Rathbone rail against travel firms operating trips to Germany. Even those who were not taken in could feel restrained from speaking out. One woman who worked in

---

48. Lady Helen Bonham-Carter, *Child Victims of the New Germany* (1934), pp.1, 4, 5–8.

Germany as a language teacher in the early 1930s kept her feelings on the regime to herself when she returned to England, because she did not want to be branded a war-monger or accused of having swallowed anti-Nazi propaganda.[49]

Interest in the political situation in Germany and help for refugees came mainly from sections of the middle class, in contrast to the Spanish civil war when so many of the working class responded. Those refugees who came to Britain were less of a financial threat to the middle class, and indeed often a positive advantage to them. Whereas trade unions and professional organisations showed hostility to the entry of refugees, women were encouraged to come as domestic servants. The shortage of domestic servants was a perennial complaint among the middle class and the importing of women willing to work as domestic servants fitted in with the concerns of women's organisations and the policy of inter-war governments who tried to encourage more working-class girls to take up domestic work. Children, who also posed no immediate threat to jobs, were accepted in Britain. The Home Office was highly sensitive to pressure groups' demands to limit the number of refugees. For this reason it adopted a cautious approach towards the mass entry of refugees, relying heavily on the advice of voluntary organisations for the actual administration of the system. Where different interests were in conflict the Home Office acted as mediator, for instance when it bowed to pressure from women's organisations to allow refugees to enter the country as domestic workers to meet the apparently insatiable demand of middle-class households for domestic servants, and ignored the hostility of the TUC and the Union of Domestic Workers to refugees working in domestic service.

The Quakers undertook some work in Germany; they ran a rest home to which British helpers would go for varying periods, say a couple of months. Most of the work was, however, carried on in Britain, through a variety of organisations helping refugees. Both the SCF and Society of Friends worked with refugees, and Jewish women worked through the Union of Jewish Women. The Refugee Children's movement is the best-known voluntary effort of the time. Refugee committees were established in all major cities.

Bloomsbury House, run largely by volunteers, coordinated the refugees who came to Britain and all refugee organisations worked through it. Until 1938 a steady trickle arrived, 60 per cent of them women. After *Kristallnacht* the trickle turned into a flood as women and children scrambled to leave Germany and Austria, assisted in large part in Britain by the Refugee Children's Movement. *Kristallnacht*, according to Margareta Burkhill, one of

---

49. IWM Hughes PP/MCR/129.

the key organisers of the Cambridge Refugee Committee, sent an electric current through Britain. Since 1933 the Cambridge Committee had been assisting refugees. It began in the house of a Quaker, Hilda Sturge. Sturge was in charge of the adults and a committee consisting of Burkhill, Mrs Hartree and Mrs Sybil Hutton took over the care of the children. The committee was responsible for finding guarantors for the children, as all refugees had either to find work or be formally supported; they were not to be a burden on taxpayers. Burkhill herself came from an Austrian/Russian background and was brought up in an international environment. Early on she was aware of the problem in Germany. Others began helping refugees more by accident: one woman advertised for a lodger and found herself with a refugee; thus alerted to the plight of Jews she visited the refugee's family in Germany and later took in another refugee couple.[50]

The political outlook of women made little difference to how willing they were to offer help; pacifist Quaker women offered help far more quickly than pacifists in the WILPF, who were slow to respond. Women from all political parties spoke out against fascism. The bulk of those who took in refugees were middle-class, who had space, time and money to help in this way.

All those individuals and groups working for refugees operated within certain limitations: trade unions' and professions' hostility; anti-semitism, anti-Germanism; government policies; and the desire of the Jewish leadership in Britain to limit the numbers of Jews entering the country in order to maintain their assimilationist policy and to prevent a backlash of anti-semitism from those resenting the arrival of refugees.

Throughout the inter-war years there is evidence of anti-semitism, not only from fascist organisations, such as the British Union of Fascists, led by Oswald Mosley, but also from more mainstream opinion. There was discrimination in employment, on occasions job advertisements excluded Jews from applying; there was discrimination in housing; and Jews were banned from certain clubs and insurance policies. Problems for Jewish refugees were more obvious in public, but even in the privacy of their new homes they were not necessarily welcomed or happy.

The experience of refugee domestic servants was not a happy one. They left home in harrowing circumstances. Most of them were from middle-class backgrounds and would never have dreamt of working as domestic servants under normal circumstances. They moved out of domestic work as soon as possible. There is evidence of friction between British Jews and

---

50. IWM Miscellaneous 818 Mrs M Burkhill The Refugee Children's Movement 1938–48. Sound Recordings 004588/08 reel 1. IWM Mary Blaschko.

refugee Jews; usually those who did not speak English wanted to stick together and this was often interpreted as aloofness, which was consistent with the long-standing animosity between central European Jews, now refugees and east European Jews, now well established in Britain. According to Kushner, the worst experiences of Jewish refugees were with Jewish and lower middle-class families. He has argued that although many refugees who came over to work as domestic servants were from a middle-class background, and thus of the same or higher class background than those for whom they worked, their class origins had to be denied because domestic service required inequality.[51]

Conclusions

European affairs were not a distinct entity from domestic politics; at a number of points they meshed together. The issue of the nationality of British-born women married to foreigners mixed domestic legislation, the empire and events in Germany. Hostility to German refugees in the 1930s was partly due to the high level of unemployment in Britain. The high percentage of refugees who came as domestic servants reflected Britain's labour market needs. The reaction of Jews to other Jewish refugees was constrained by their strategy of integrating within British society. Working-class support for the Republicans in the Spanish civil war was an extension of working-class activism in the British labour movement.

While British involvement in the Spanish civil war is the best-known of Britain's active relations with the Continent, it was not part of a consistent response to international fascism. Except in the case of Spain, whose civil war was seen as an extension of the socialist struggle in Britain, the working class displayed a limited commitment to the victims of fascism. In other fascist countries civil war did not break out, so the needs of opponents and victims of fascism, and how the British working class might help meet these needs, were not so obvious.

In contrast, throughout the inter-war years, middle-class women were caught up in European affairs in a variety of ways. There was a clear class division between women in their perceptions of the rest of Europe and in their activities with other Europeans. There was, too, a common feeling between British middle-class women and continental middle-class women,

---

51. Tony Kushner, 'Asylum or servitude? Refugee domestics in Britain, 1933–1945', *British Society for the Study of Labour History* 5 (1988), pp. 19–27.

which contrasts with women's welfare campaigning in Britain, where a much closer interest was displayed by middle-class women in working-class women. The success of women was, however, limited to small-scale welfare and refugee projects. Many of the women discussed in this chapter presented arguments which foreshadowed the 1940s, when governments took a more serious interest in international welfare organisations. Although women were excluded from the Foreign Office and almost every senior civil service and political post, and a culture of hostility to women as policy makers permeated Westminster and Whitehall – as discussed in the following chapter – women did find ways to affect relationships with other Europeans, by making a practical contribution to welfare and refugee work, and by publicly voicing their critiques of fascism.

CHAPTER SIX

Westminster and Whitehall
between the Wars

Introduction

It was in Westminster and Whitehall that central government's welfare policies were framed. (Westminster is shorthand for the Houses of Parliament with elected MPs in the House of Commons and unelected members in the House of Lords. Whitehall refers to the geographical area where departments of state with civil servants and government ministers were located.) Here it will be argued that the legislative changes, mainly in family law, usually identified as marking a temporary increase in women's political power in the 1920s, owed little to women's direct role in policy making. Women MPs supported, with varying degrees of enthusiasm, the welfare campaigns of women outside Parliament for family allowances, birth control and nursery schools (discussed in Chapter Four). Women MPs, however, suffered from the twin constraints of their limited numbers, which reflected the difficulties women faced (and still face) in entering Parliament, and the barriers erected by their male colleagues against women's advancement once in Parliament. If there had been more women MPs, especially in senior positions, they might have been able to move women's issues from the realm of pressure group politics to party and thence government policy. Instead, men continued to monopolise government posts and take policy decisions. Westminster politics divided along male-dominated party lines, and women's political advancement depended on their assimilation into the existing structures, which required abandoning exclusively feminist projects. It cannot be assumed, moreover, that all women in Westminster or Whitehall were interested in furthering any of the variously nuanced feminist policies of the period.

Women civil servants banded together to increase their collective influence, not on policies but on their career opportunities. They had limited success, although the separation of the legislature and the executive in Britain meant that success or failure had implications for middle-class women's employment opportunities, but not other areas of women's welfare. In both Westminster and Whitehall there were women taking decisions which were not necessarily to the advantage of other women, and this underlines the importance of analysing women's contribution not only by their presence but also by their attitudes and policies.

During this period women joined organisations in huge numbers. Many of these were, in a broad sense, 'political'. In part, this high degree of organisation reflected the political culture across Europe, manifested in its most menacing form in the fascist regimes. It also reflected the way in which women chose to carve public spaces for themselves outside the workplace and the home, although the organisations were often closely linked with the home and family matters.

Many individual women, and women's organisations, saw their interests impinging on a wide range of political issues, and their class and gender interests going hand in hand. This is not to suggest either that there were no conflicts over the two or that the relative importance of each did not fluctuate between groups, individuals and over time. Throughout the period gender remained significant for many women. In the Labour Party of the 1930s, however, women's issues were subsumed under a class analysis, which was itself highly gendered, reinforcing a male-dominated culture which Labour women in the 1920s had, to some extent, managed to temper.

Women promoted what they perceived to be their interests through a range of organisations, including the political parties, the Women's Institute, Townswomen's Guild, Girl Guides, National Union of Societies for Equal Citizenship (NUSEC), Women's Freedom League (WFL), the Six Point Group and Open Door Council (ODC). Many of these, with the exception of the political parties, provided a woman-friendly space where women could pursue their interests and concerns, frequently within the local community, but also at a national level. The organisations mixed political and social functions.

There was often overlapping membership between the women's organisations, which frequently worked in concert to promote policy changes. All were represented in the National Council of Women (NCW), an umbrella body. NUSEC and the Six Point Group called for more women police; all women's groups demanded equal franchise, equal guardianship of children, the right of peeresses to sit in the House of Lords, the right of married women to work, and the right for women to maintain their British nationality if they married a foreigner. Most organisations in the 1920s campaigned on a number of issues. In the 1930s they became more focused on single issues, although these were often very wide-ranging in their implications. The London and National Society for Women's Services always concentrated on opening up professional employment and the higher grades of the civil service for women; the League of Church Militant campaigned for the ordination of women, and the Association for Moral and Social Hygiene demanded that the age of consent be raised to 16 and that the soliciting laws be applied to women and men equally. The National Union of Women's Suffrage Societies (NUWSS), the main constitutional pre-war suffrage organisation, renamed itself NUSEC after the war and was led by Eleanor Rathbone, with Eva Hubback as secretary. In the 1920s it was at the forefront of promoting legislation of particular interest to women. It had close ties with MPs other than Rathbone, such as Nancy Astor.

In 1921 Nancy Astor formed the Consultative Committee of Women's Organisations to coordinate women's political activities and lobby MPs over a range of issues of concern to women's groups. It did not attract the full support of organised women. The Labour Party put pressure on its women members not to join women-only organisations, and for this reason the Standing Joint Committee of Industrial Women's Organisations never joined Astor's committee. The representatives of other women's groups worked together for a number of years in Astor's committee until 1928 when NUSEC withdrew following disagreements over protective labour legislation; Astor then refused to stand again for election as president and the committee was wound up. What is remarkable is not that it split up but that it lasted so long. With women holding strong and differing views on strategy and policies it was a well-intentioned experiment, but one doomed to failure. In the first few years of a tiny number of women working in an overwhelmingly hostile Parliament it made sense to experiment, but in the longer term it proved more effective for women to come together on the specific issues which genuinely united them.

At one time historians divided inter-war feminists into two distinct camps: 'new' or 'welfare' feminists on the one hand and 'old' or 'equality' feminists on the other hand. Welfare feminists argued that, because of women's reproductive role, women and men's needs were different, and social policies, such as protective labour legislation and family allowances, should be framed to meet these different needs. Equality feminists maintained that, in order for women to gain equality, policies should not differentiate between women and men; they therefore advocated equal pay and labour legislation. Nowadays, historians are far more likely to argue that while feminists had different priorities, so-called 'welfare' and 'equality' feminists often demanded the same policies. Harold Smith asserts that feminists did, nevertheless, conceptualise gender issues differently: welfare feminists claimed that equality feminists were trying to ape men and adopt their values and priorities while equality feminists countered that welfare feminists, by making women's natural reproductive functions their starting point, reinforced traditional roles and women's inequality.[1]

Despite overlapping issues and personnel, disagreements were real enough and came to a head in 1926 over the issue of protective legislation when a number of members left NUSEC to form the Six Point Group and campaign against protective legislation for women in the workplace. It was symptomatic of, and contributed to, reduced cooperation among women's groups. In the 1930s political activities were conducted less through long-established women's organisations, but this does not denote a lack of interest in politics among women. NUSEC declined but out of it grew the Townswomen's Guild, which proved enormously popular. Women were active in all the political parties and although women in the labour movement tended not to combine with other women's groups, they often had similar priorities.

The two strands of feminist thought have been identified with different women's organisations and the division between these has been interpreted as a sign, and cause, of their decline. The range of organisations in which women were involved, however, was a sign of flourishing thought among women and a means of them trying to order competing priorities. The fall in membership of bodies such as NUSEC and the WFL over the course of the inter-war years is not a reflection of an overall decline in women's associational life, or of women's lack of interest in politics. Even if women had been more one-dimensional in their thinking, their concerns would not have transformed into government policies because of the political culture of the period, illustrated below. Cheryl Law rightly maintains that during the 1920s difficulties placed in the way of women made it harder for them to achieve their reforms but, on balance, she provides an upbeat analysis of the role of women's organisations in policy making. Law has explained how NUSEC would draft bills, try to get backbenchers to adopt them as private member's bills (PMBs) and then lobby MPs to support them. She argues that women's groups gained attention, and put issues on the parliamentary and public agendas. She claims that this was a means whereby women accessed and utilised the political machinery.[2]

Here it will be argued that women's role in policy making did not really move beyond that of pressure groups; women remained the supplicants,

---

1. Harold Smith, 'British feminism in the 1920s', in Harold Smith, ed., *British Feminism in the Twentieth Century* (1990), pp. 47–9.
2. Cheryl Law, *Suffrage and Power: The Women's Movement 1918–1928* (1997), pp. 100–1.

albeit well-organised, articulate, and dynamic ones. This marginalisation of women's organisations in the policy-making process was the result of attitudes among those already entrenched in policy-making roles. Administrative grade civil servants had a strong antipathy to anyone outside Whitehall (and often outside their own Department) playing a part in policy making. This prejudice inevitably worked to the disadvantage of women. There is evidence of senior Home Office civil servants, for example, regarding women's groups and individual women who put pressure on government to improve women's position vis-à-vis men as unreasonable, unrepresentative and extremist. In 1925 the Home Office turned down a request from the WFL for a deputation of women's organisations to be received in order for them to argue against excluding women from courts of law when cases of sexual violence were being heard. One civil servant dismissed the WFL's views because

> The women who join the League or similar associations – which certainly do not represent accurately the views of the majority of the female population – are apt firmly to believe that justice is not done as between the sexes, that men guilty of assault on women and children are acquitted because at present the administration of justice is almost entirely in the hands of men and that this evil can only be remedied by women attending the Courts, whenever a case affecting the interests of a woman is concerned. However unreasonable such a belief may be, it would be useless to attempt to persuade a deputation such as is proposed. . . .[3]

The cordial reception which women often received from civil servants hid an underlying distrust and animosity. In 1925, another senior Home Office civil servant, John Anderson, was livid with the Foreign Office for letting Eleanor Rathbone's name go forward for appointment as an assessor on the League of Nation's Women's and Children's Advisory Committee, and he wrote to the Foreign Office:

> We know Miss Rathbone well. She is the President of a Body – the National Union of Societies of Equal Citizenship – which is always engaged in urging and promoting extreme legislation in matters affecting women and children and we at the Home Office, though on perfectly friendly terms with the Society, constantly find ourselves at issue with them. The prospect of having to sit in conference with this lady in the presence of representatives of other States who are always ready to make capital out of our domestic differences is, to put it mildly, disconcerting.[4]

---

3. PRO HO 45/22907/450239.
4. PRO HO 45/12310/475441. Anderson to Sir Eyre Crowe 1 April 1925.

If senior civil servants were willing to write down the comments expressed in the above quotations, it is not unreasonable to surmise that stronger and even more hostile views were not committed to paper. In the 1920s at least, the culture of one of the channels which women used for promoting social policies was fundamentally antagonistic. The other channel, that of the political parties, was no more sympathetic.

The political parties

Women contributed to the flourishing associational life of Britain and there were organisations to cater for a wide range of interests. For women wanting to pursue explicitly political ends the main channel for them was not now the women's-only groups but the mixed, party-political ones. This was a difficult project for women as the parties offered limited scope for the full expression of women's interests. In all the political parties 'glass ceilings' and 'glass doors' prevented women occupying more than a confined space.

At first glance the Liberal Party offered the most sympathetic welcome to women, but those women who advanced in the Liberal Party were the least committed feminists.[5] Once Parliament had partially enfranchised women, the Liberal Party constantly underlined the relevance of liberalism for 'women' as a group; they asserted that Liberal Party policies had a positive impact on all aspects of women's lives. Campaigning explicitly for women's interests, as perceived by Liberal women, was integral to their attempts to halt the decline of the Liberal Party. As well as supporting overall Liberal Party strategy, Liberal women advocated policies explicitly affecting women, such as pensions for widows with dependent children.[6]

Other non-party women's organisations which followed the Liberal Party philosophy, such as the Open Door Council, opposed protective legislation for women because it hindered women's job opportunities. A 'fair field and no favour' was also carried over into arguments against protective legislation for working-class women's jobs, but there is little evidence of support from working-class women for such a policy. Although these organisations campaigned for equal treatment for women and men under national insurance and national health insurance, which would have benefited all women, they threw most of their energies behind campaigns against the dismissal of

---

5. Martin Pugh, *Women and the Women's Movement, 1914–1959* (1992), p. 157.
6. *Women's Liberal Magazine,* January–February 1924.

teachers on marriage, the exclusion of women from certain medical schools, and against pensions for single women from the age of 53 because it would adversely affect women's chances of obtaining responsible posts.

The culture of the Conservative Party, with its emphasis on social activities, the absence of macho trade unionists, and little overt conflict between the women and men, gives the impression that women were encouraged by male officials to participate actively in the Party. The social activities in which women played a central role were important to the party machine because they promoted a sense of belonging, they boosted morale and they helped fund-raising. Behind the scenes, however, men displayed hostility to women activists. Some men complained that women ruined the atmosphere and effectiveness of constituency work, and that women's contribution was trivial and irrelevant to the need to fight socialism head-on. Male agents feared that women undermined their authority.[7]

The Conservative Party portrayed women's interests as best served by the Party because it stood for home life and domesticity for women. The Party emphasised that women had responsibilities beyond themselves, such as looking after their families and mothering the children of the empire. The family, and women's role as mothers in it, was central to both Conservative and Labour women, but under the umbrella of the 'family' Conservative and Labour Party women often pursued different policies. There were, too, differences among Labour Party women over what was in the family's, and women's, best interests.

According to Graves, women's issues were not part of mainstream Labour Party policy in the 1920s and this led to conflict in the Party. From 1923 to 1930 issues such as birth control, which women saw as raising standards of living for the whole working class, were regarded by men as women's 'special interests'. Women's groups within the Labour Party, as well as the Women's Cooperative Guild (WCG), had to fight within the labour movement for the subject of birth control to be taken seriously. It was not a narrow sectional issue as the mainstream Party argued, but integral to the wellbeing of working-class women, men and children. In the 1920s neither the women leaders, nor the male-dominated Party, were willing to put the topic of birth control on the conference agenda, let alone act on the matter when in government: they feared that in view of the substantial Irish Catholic support for the Labour Party, the subject would wreak

---

7. David Jarvis, 'The Conservative Party and the politics of gender, 1900–39', in Martin Francis and Ina Zweiniger-Bargielowska, eds, *The Conservative Party and British Society, 1880–1980* (Cardiff, 1996), pp. 174–88.

havoc on Party unity and damage the Party's electoral chances. Graves also points to the fact that men in the Party may well have seen birth control as a threat to their authority in the home. (They were already busy maintaining their authority over women within the Party.)[8] Birth control information was a subject which bitterly divided both Labour women and women's sections from the Labour Party as a whole. In the 1930s the issue was overshadowed by unemployment and fascism which became the two central concerns of both women and men, and women's voices became less often heard and less oppositional.

Although the majority of women in the Labour Party favoured the employment of married women, this was not a unanimous view. Women who were not wage earners were more concerned about maintaining high rates of wages for men, on whom they were dependent, and less inclined to insist on equal pay. Yet, as Marion Phillips, the women's organiser, argued, it was impossible to hope for the economic independence of women unless the principle of equal pay for equal work was established.[9] Not all Labour women were convinced: when a resolution against the London County Council (LCC) dismissing married women teachers was put to the 1923 National Conference of Labour Women, it was carried by a large, but not unanimous, majority.[10] Despite differences over birth control and married women in paid work, Labour Party women campaigned unanimously around a range of issues which affected women's welfare in the labour market and in the home.[11]

Women in all three parties were interested in a wide range of subjects, but the family, women's health, and the labour market headed the list. Perhaps these priorities reflected powerful attitudes in society which most adversely affected working-class women's health, and middle-class women's employment opportunities. The most potentially radical thinking among women, reflected in the campaigns related to women's poverty – family allowances, birth control, and nursery schools – was never wholeheartedly pursued by the political parties. The male-dominated parties failed to take up key concerns of women and turn them into party policy. Women's struggles to enter Parliament thus took place in the context of all three parties sidelining women and women's issues.

---

8. Pamela Graves, *Labour Women* (1994), pp. 81, 84–94.
9. *Labour Woman*, November 1918.
10. *Labour Woman*, June 1923.
11. Pat Thane, 'Women in the British Labour Party and the construction of state welfare, 1906–1939', in Seth Koven and Sonya Michel, eds, *Mothers of a New World: Maternalist Politics and the Origins of Welfare States* (1993), pp. 348–9.

Westminster

All the women MPs, with the exception of Eleanor Rathbone, who was an Independent member for the Combined Universities, had to balance the demands of their parties, which often worked against women's interests, with the advantages which a woman MP might gain for women in pressing women's issues, and in the mere fact of being a woman and an MP herself. For a woman to be successful enough in a party to be selected to fight a seat she had to assimilate into the party. Those women who were adopted in their husbands' seats enjoyed greater freedom, however, not having had to work their way up the party machine; instead they were elevated to the top of the hierarchies by virtue of being married to an MP. Nancy Astor took over her husband's seat when he inherited a peerage on the death of his father; Margaret Wintringham, Liberal MP, 1921–4, took over her husband's seat when he died; and Mabel Hilton Philipson, Conservative MP, 1923–9, took over her husband's seat when he had to resign over his agent's wrongdoing. Thus, a most anti-feminist route to the top of a party worked to the advantage of some women. In 1919 Nancy Astor became the first woman to take her seat at Westminster when she won the Plymouth Sutton by-election. Astor's riding to Parliament on the back of her husband was not an auspicious start for the feminist cause and her bumptious style alienated many who would have been natural sympathisers.

In Chapter Three the importance of an occupation's male culture, its hierarchy and its heterogeneity for impeding the advancement of women was underlined. These constraints also held true for women MPs. The parliamentary system obstructed women's success as MPs. The growth in the number of women MPs was painfully slow; until the end of the Second World War there were never more than 15 in the House at any one time. Constituency parties were loath to adopt a woman in anything other than an unwinnable seat. Women often found it financially difficult to pursue a parliamentary career, and they had either to juggle the competing demands of a family and Parliament, or do without a family.

Once an MP arrived at Westminster she had to contend with spoken and unspoken male hostility towards women's issues and women MPs. Nancy Astor commented in her maiden speech, 'I know it is very difficult for some hon. Members to receive the first lady MP into the House. [HON. MEMBERS: "Not at all".] It was almost as difficult for some of them as it was for the first lady MP herself to come in.'[12] Numerous women referred to the

---

12. HC Deb. vol. 125 24 February 1920 col. 1623–24.

atmosphere of the House. Thelma Cazalet, Conservative MP, 1931–45, and PPS, at the Board of Education, 1937–40, wrote that there was something 'slightly freakish' about a woman MP and she frequently saw male MPs pointing her out to their friends as though 'I were a sort of giant panda'.[13] Jennie Lee, a Labour MP, found other MPs almost 'stiflingly affable' with the exception of a number of Scottish miners' MPs whose 'faces curdled up like a bowl of sour cream whenever we accidently collided'.[14] Leah Manning, Labour MP, 1931, 1945–50, 'walked into an atmosphere which was stung by a cold lash. Bitter hostility there was where there should have been comradeship.' She detailed the lewd comments the Labour MP, Ben Tillett, shouted to her, Marion Phillips and Susan Lawrence, in both the Chamber and Annie's Bar, to the delight of other male MPs.[15] (The one exception to this picture of male hostility comes from Mary Agnes Hamilton, Labour MP, 1929–31, who claimed that she found a warm and friendly fraternity and an equality in the House of Commons that she had not met elsewhere except in journalism.)[16]

Women MPs carried an unusually heavy workload because women saw a woman MP as their representative, whether or not they were constituents. Mary Hamilton bemoaned the fact that, as there were so few women MPs, they counted as national speakers for the Labour Party and suffered from the idea that every good platform should have one woman on it. The Labour Party whips put pressure on the women MPs to trail up and down the country at weekends on speaking engagements.[17]

Not only did women MPs have a heavy burden of work but also their working conditions were worse than the men's. It was only after the Second World War that a lady members' room was set aside. In the 1930s the women worked in what Leah Manning described as a dank, dark dungeon with a washbasin with a jug of water and pail underneath it, and with no women's toilet.[18] None of the women MPs entered the smoking room, where rumour had it as much business was transacted as on the floor of the House.[19]

Some of the women MPs, such as Nancy Astor, took up issues on which particular women's organisations outside Parliament were campaigning, and which have already been discussed in previous chapters. In the early 1920s Nancy Astor and Margaret Wintringham both spoke against cuts to

13. Thelma Cazalet-Keir, *From the Wings* (1967), p. 126.
14. Jennie Lee, *The Great Journey: A Volume of Autobiography, 1904–45* (1963), p. 99.
15. Leah Manning, *A Life for Education: An Autobiography* (1970), pp. 87–90.
16. Mary Agnes Hamilton, *Up-Hill All The Way: A Third Cheer for Democracy* (1953), p. 46.
17. Mary Agnes Hamilton, *Up-Hill All the Way*, pp. 46, 52.
18. Leah Manning, *A Life for Education*, p. 91.
19. Thelma Cazalet-Keir, *From the Wings*, p. 126.

the number of women police, a subject dear to the heart of a number of women's organisations for whom women police linked the two concerns of morality and employment opportunities for women. Astor spoke up for equal opportunities and equal pay for women civil servants, for more women on public bodies and in the prison service; for greater protection for young people from indecent assault; for the suppression of prostitution and brothel-keeping; for the control of venereal disease (VD), and as mentioned in Chapter Four, for nursery schools.[20]

On occasion the women MPs joined forces to defend women's interests, as for instance in the 1930 nationality debate when the women called for a British woman married to a foreigner to be allowed to maintain her British nationality; in 1932 they defended married women's unemployment benefit, in 1936 they voted for equal pay for women, and in 1938 they demanded pensions for single women at 55. Astor, Rathbone and Summerskill repeatedly pressed for women's statutory representation on public bodies.

In general, women took an especial interest in welfare campaigns, both in Britain and abroad. Along with women campaigners outside Parliament, women MPs linked foreign affairs and welfare issues. Astor spoke in Parliament about the evils of female circumcision in Kenya, and defended the welfare of dockers and sailors during navy debates. Rathbone spoke up for Indian women's franchise. Atholl set up a Committee for the Protection of Coloured Women in the Colonies with members coopted from outside Parliament as well as MPs. Rathbone and Edith Picton-Turbervill, Labour MP, 1929–31, were especially active members.

Many of the women MPs spoke, wrote and campaigned against the evils of fascism, as discussed in Chapter Five. Labour MPs took an especial interest in the Spanish civil war. Mavis Tate, Conservative MP, 1931–45, was an early advocate of rearmament. Tate fought against women's unfair treatment under national health insurance and pension schemes; she called for equal pay, an end to the marriage bar, and women's entry to the Foreign and Diplomatic service. In 1935 she presented a petition to Parliament on behalf of thousands of women who demanded that women be allowed to keep their own nationality on marriage to a foreigner. She also supported the birth control movement and abortion law reform. However, none of this received the high profile of her involvement during the war with the demand for equal compensation for war-inflicted injuries on civilians. Other notable critics of fascism included Thelma Cazalet MP, Edith Summerskill MP and Megan Lloyd George, Liberal MP, 1929–51, 1957–66. Astor, on the other hand, supported appeasement, and Agnes Hardie, Labour MP,

---

20. Christopher Sykes, *Nancy: The Life of Lady Astor*, 2nd edn., (1979), pp. 263, 328.

1937–45, was a pacifist. Rathbone, as already discussed in Chapter Five, was one of the most prominent campaigners for refugees from fascism.

The small number of women MPs, the even smaller number who reached government, and the combative nature of Westminster party politics meant that, although the women avoided personal attacks on each other and formed a cross-party network of mutual support and friendship, this never developed into an effective network for advancing either their own position at Westminster or those policies which most interested them and which they identified as being of special concern to particular groups of women. With never more than 15 women in Parliament, and often only a handful, even if the women had formed a solid block, they could never defeat government policy or change its outcome.[21]

There was no political mileage in women MPs forming a block because towing the party line was a sine qua non for personal advancement and office. Labour women MPs were more loyal to the party line than other women. When Nancy Astor invited all the women MPs to lunch after the 1929 general election and suggested that in effect they form a women's block the Labour women were enormously hostile to the suggestion. It was naive, anyway, of Astor to think that when Labour had just formed a government with Margaret Bondfield in the Cabinet and Susan Lawrence a junior minister, the nine Labour women MPs would want to split their loyalties.

So few women reached high office that those who did do so were isolated from other women. It is not surprising that women MPs could not reverse policies or change the tone of the House. Any influence they exerted came from working through the parties and assimilating into them. In 1924 James Ramsay Macdonald appointed Margaret Bondfield Parliamentary Secretary to the Ministry of Labour in the first, minority, Labour government. In 1929 he appointed her the first woman – as Minister of Labour – to the Cabinet and, with Cabinet rank, she also became the first woman Privy Councillor. Bondfield wrote in her autobiography that when in 1929 she accepted office, she knew that it touched more than herself as it was part of a great revolution in the position of women, which she had helped to forward. She remembered feeling initially depressed at the complexity and difficulty of the task, but as she went through the congratulations which flooded in from all over the world, many from women's organisations and some from opponents, she felt a jumble of pride and humility. At no point in her autobiography, however, does Bondfield refer to her experiences as a woman MP or woman member of government. It would have been

---

21. Brian Harrison, 'Women in a men's house: the women MPs, 1919–45', *Historical Journal* 29 (1986), pp. 634–5.

interesting to read her account of how she felt colleagues treated her; Leah Manning wrote that the men were often malicious about female colleagues and, when Bondfield was Minister of Labour, Manning heard more than one man maintain that Bondfield had only been appointed because no-one else would take the job and because she was sure to make a mess of it.[22] This anecdote underlines the fact that male MPs tried to undermine rather than support Labour colleagues, if they were women. The idea that all the men turned down a Cabinet post is, of course, risible.

In 1924 Stanley Baldwin, the Conservative Prime Minister, appointed the Duchess of Atholl Parliamentary Secretary at the Board of Education, under Lord Eustace Percy. Atholl later wrote 'I need not say how honoured I felt, for there had only been one woman Minister before me. . . .'[23] Atholl's biographer claims Percy resented the appointment of a woman and ensured Atholl's appointment was unsuccessful. According to Atholl's biographer, Percy denied Atholl any power or encouragement, which made Atholl nervous and unable to perform effectively in the House. Atholl was not reappointed in 1931 when the Conservatives returned to power in the national government, but by then she was already on a path which veered increasingly away from party policy on foreign affairs.[24]

As much divided as united women MPs. The Duchess of Atholl and Florence Horsbrugh, Conservative, 1931–45 and 1950–9, who both enjoyed government office, criticised women MPs (Astor, Rathbone and Summerskill) who pressed for women on statutory bodies.[25] Horsbrugh was a loyal party supporter and regarded by senior party men as a safe pair of hands. In 1936 she had been the first woman to move the address in reply to the King's speech. Between 1933 and 1935 she represented Britain at the League of Nations. (Between 1939 and 1945 she was Parliamentary Secretary at the Ministry of Health. In 1945, when Labour walked out of the coalition government following VE Day, Churchill appointed her Minister of Food. In 1949 she was the first woman to present a party political broadcast on behalf of the Conservatives. When the Conservatives returned to power in 1951 Churchill appointed her Minister of Education, a post she held for three years. In 1959 she became a life peeress.) In 1925 Ellen Wilkinson spoke and voted against the Widows' Orphans and Old Age Contributory Pensions Bill; Astor spoke and voted for it; Mabel Hilton

22. Margaret Bondfield, *A Life's Work* (1950), pp. 276–8; Leah Manning, *A Life for Education*, p. 90.
23. Katharine, Duchess of Atholl, *Working Partnership* (1958), p. 143.
24. S.J. Hetherington, *Katharine Atholl 1874–1960 Against the Tide* (Aberdeen, 1989), p. 110.
25. Brian Harrison, 'Women in a men's house', p. 652.

Philipson thought it better than nothing and voted for it; the Duchess of Atholl neither spoke nor voted. Wilkinson attacked the Bill for embodying the contributory principle, which women inside and outside the labour movement opposed. She argued that a non-contributory scheme would not be dispensing charity but a definite payment for services that a widow had rendered to the state and it should enable a widow to bring up her children (to the age of 16 and not 14 as in the Bill) properly. Wilkinson also argued that, instead of a pension being given to a young widow, it should be given to a woman with an incapacitated husband. She criticised the provision for taking a pension away from a widow convicted of a crime which might have no bearing on her ability to bring up children. Wilkinson also thought it unfair that single women had to contribute to a scheme from which they could not possibly benefit. Astor, on the other hand, argued that it was part of a wide range of social policies which the government would introduce to attack poverty.[26]

Not all women MPs believed in speaking up for those issues which especially affected women. Mary Agnes Hamilton claimed that the best women MPs in her time never represented the woman's point of view.[27] (This is not true as she included in this group Eleanor Rathbone, who did speak up and defend women's interests.) Women MPs were divided, as other women, over what constituted 'women's' interest, and they shifted their views over the years.

Both contempories and historians have assumed that feminism was initially influential after the war, but then declined. The Duchess of Atholl claimed that, once women gained partial enfranchisement, their influence could be seen in various pieces of legislation.[28] Picton-Turbervill wrote that some legislation was repeatedly rejected before women obtained the vote, but that once women were enfranchised parliamentary values changed. She listed a whole string of Acts which she believed demonstrated the changed values and influence of women.[29] Harrison argues that feminism declined over the period and that from the mid-1920s the political climate was unsympathetic to feminism. This presupposes that the climate was sympathetic before then, but the motives behind granting a limited number of women the parliamentary franchise and the male MPs' treatment of the first women MPs does not suggest a period of sympathy with feminism

26. HC Deb. vol. 183 29 April 1925 col. 163; vol. 184 18 May 1925 cols. 181–87 Ellen Wilkinson; vol. 184 19 May 1925 cols. 302–303 Astor.
27. Mary Agnes Hamilton, *Up-Hill All the Way*, p. 46.
28. Duchess of Atholl, *Women and Politics*, p. 98.
29. Edith Picton-Turbervill, *Life Is Good: An Autobiography* (1939), p. 221.

among men MPs. In 1920, when an unsuccessful Bill for the equalisation of the franchise was debated, Gideon Murray, Conservative MP, 1918–22, spoke against it on the grounds that women's suffrage was still on trial; 'girls' of 21 were far more emotional than 'men' of the same age; and if women were given the vote at 21 there would be more female than male voters, which was not *equal* opportunities for women but *greater* opportunities for women.[30] With such ideas circulating in Parliament it is hard to see it as a time of political strength for women. This was also a period when women were sacked wholesale from civil service posts, when they were unable to compete on equal terms with men, and when Parliament voted to exclude government service from the 1919 Sex Disqualification (Removal) Act.

Harold Smith has shown that when women gained full enfranchisement in 1928 it was not inevitable, and it only gained the overwhelming support of MPs because they feared that, if the legislation should pass, and they were seen to have voted against it, they would lay themselves open to women reacting against them by voting for other candidates.[31]

An analysis of the legislation passed in the 1920s which has been used to demonstrate the influence of women's enfranchisement does not support the claim. Some of this legislation was the result of PMBs which are notoriously unpredictable in their pass rates. They could equally well have failed. Much of the family law of the 1920s was a development of earlier legislation which does not of itself suggest that women's enfranchisement was crucial to the legislation. The 1920 Employment of Women, Young Persons and Children Act, the 1922 Criminal Law Amendment Act, the 1923 Bastardy Act, the 1925 Summary Jurisdiction Act and Guardianship of Infants Act, and the 1926 Legitimacy Act were all introduced under Home Secretaries with no particular interest in women's equality or protection. Women MPs were obvious more for their absence than presence in the crucial second reading debates, and women MPs did not necessarily agree on legislation relating to women, as has been seen with the Widows, Orphans and Old Age Contributory Pensions Act.

The 1920 Employment of Women, Young Persons and Children Act was not the result of pressure from women's organisations, but of the need to give effect to a draft convention of the 1919 Washington International Labour Conference. This concerned the age of admission of children to industrial employment, the employment of women on night work and, most controversially, the employment of women over two shifts, which involved

---

30. HC Deb. vol. 125 27 February 1920 cols. 2077–78.
31. Harold L. Smith, *The British Women's Suffrage Campaign, 1866–1928* (1998), pp. 70–81.

one shift starting very early and the other finishing very late. The Home Office received mixed messages from women about the desirability of women working on a two-shift system. It went along with the views which fitted with the draft convention, and the evidence supplied by its own women Factory Inspectors. The Home Office chose to ignore the views of women in the labour movement who strongly opposed the continuation of the two-shift system.[32]

The 1922 Criminal Law Amendment Act contained one clause around which controversy swirled; the clause removed a defendant's plea that he had 'reasonable cause to believe' a girl with whom he had sex was 16 or over. A massive head of steam had built up from women's organisations, ranging from women's religious groups to NCW, NUSEC, the Medical Women's Federation, the Association of Head Mistresses, the Federation of University Women, the WI, the Six Point Group, the WFL, the Women's National Liberal Federation, as well as the AMSH, in favour of the Bill and this clause in particular. The government wanted the legislation to be acceptable to women's organisations, perhaps so that the issue would be laid to rest, and the women's groups were willing to negotiate and compromise. Opponents of the clause – who were well represented in Parliament and did not therefore have to rely on their views being taken up by others – were unwilling to compromise, and could possibly have wrecked the Bill. As a result, the plea was allowed to stand for men aged 23 and under. (The men who opposed the abolition of the clause argued that it might cause hardship to young and inexperienced men!)[33]

On the second reading of the Matrimonial Causes (England and Wales) Bill 1923, drafted by NUSEC, no women MPs spoke or voted. The Act represented a piecemeal extension of earlier legislation and brought divorce law into line with the law over judicial separations. Until 1923 a wife could only divorce her husband for incestuous adultery, bigamy with adultery, or adultery coupled with desertion or cruelty. The 1923 Act made adultery alone sufficient cause for a woman to divorce her husband. This legislation was – as the promoters of the Bill asserted – a step towards justice and equity, and it certainly enjoyed the support of women's organisations, but this alone could not have ensured its success.[34]

The 1923 Bastardy Act was one of a series over a number of years relating to payments by putative fathers, and again cannot be explained by the presence of women MPs or the strength of women's organisations.

32. PRO HO 45/11021/403897.
33. PRO HO 45/11084/430126.
34. HC Deb. vol. 160 2 March 1923 col. 2355–2357.

Despite friendly correspondence between the Home Office and NUSEC in the early 1920s, discussions in 1920 over new legislation had revealed the Home Office to be suspicious of women and sympathatic to men in the context of the welfare of illegitimate children. In 1920 a memorandum by the Home Secretary (drafted by civil servants) to the all-male Cabinet Committee on Home Affairs, argued that a Bill to make a putative father pay up to 40s 0d a week to maintain an illegitimate child would encourage women to bear illegitimate children and to 'find a father for every bastard – if the true father, so much the better – but in any case fix paternity upon someone and then make him pay a weekly allowance . . .', who would be the richest person the woman knew, and in the case of domestic servants this would be the employer.[35]

The 1925 Summary Jurisdiction (Separation and Maintenance) Act amended an Act of 1895. Eva Hubback, on behalf of NUSEC, had been pressing the case for reform for a number of years. There was an assumption within the Home Office that legislation to give women equality with men was actually favouring women over men. In 1924 one civil servant noted that, although existing legislation did not always give women protection against bad husbands, 'it may be doubted whether society will as a whole gain by continuous legislation in favour of one sex against another. . . .'[36] No women MP spoke in the debate on the second reading. The Act abolished the requirement that a married woman should have left her husband before she applied for an Order on the grounds of persistent cruelty or wilful neglect by the husband; of cruelty to the children; or if the husband had forced her into prostitution. If a wife committed adultery because the husband failed to support her, in accordance with an Order, he could no longer get the Order discharged as in the past. An Order could also be obtained if either spouse was a drug addict, whereas in the past only habitual drunkenness was covered by the Act. The clause to allow either a wife or husband to obtain an Order against the other on grounds of persistent cruelty to the children was added at the request of NUSEC, which does indicate it was exerting some influence, but this was not such a big concession as courts already often regarded cruelty to children as tantamount to cruelty to the wife.[37]

The 1925 Guardianship of Infants Act complemented the Summary Jurisdiction Act and confirmed to the mother the same rights as the father possessed if a dispute ended in the courts. It was backed by large numbers

---

35. PRO HO 45/11190.
36. PRO HO 45/11936.
37. HC Deb. vol. 180 col. 1978–1979 25 February 1925.

of women's organisations, but as Ellen Wilkinson, the only woman to speak on the second reading, pointed out, they were critical of the Bill because 'where people are living apparently quite happily, whatever goes on behind the lace curtains, the fact still remains that the woman is not regarded as an equal . . . unless there is some dispute, the whole assumption of the law is that the man, as always, remains completely the head of the household'.[38] It was in fact a compromise following a series of failed Bills – supported by women's organisations, Nancy Astor and Margaret Wintringham – which would have given mothers and fathers equal guardianship rights within marriage, not just after a marriage had broken down. During the early 1920s NUSEC appeared to have the ear of government over the issue, for a great deal of correspondence and discussion took place between NUSEC and civil servants. This should not detract from the fact that the legislative process automatically operated to women's disadvantage. There were no women on the Cabinet Committee looking at the matter (no women civil servants or politicians were senior enough). Members of the House of Lords opposed equal guardianship and lobbied the Home Office against it. As women were excluded from the second chamber they were systematically disadvantaged and men privileged. The presence of two women backbenchers could not compete with the combined Lords and Commons' prejudices in full flight.[39]

Astor claimed in the debate on the Widows, Orphans and Old Age Contributory Pensions Bill that if women had had the vote sooner widows' pensions would have been introduced sooner.[40] Yet, this legislation was a continuation of a principle embodied in separation allowances introduced during the war before women were even partially enfranchised. Pedersen has argued that separation allowances were based on the needs of those fulfilling the functions of male citizens. They assumed a wife's dependence without regard to her economic status. The notion that a husband had a right to a state benefit for his wife was extended to pensions for war widows and children and then in 1925 to civilian widows. In 1925 this assumption was also incorporated into the insurance system.[41] Widows' pensions were attractive to the government as a cheap alternative to family endowment. Thus, government was motivated by a desire to limit its support for mothers. While the 1925 Act held attractions for government, according to Pedersen, it originated neither with government nor with Parliament, but with

---

38. HC Deb. vol. 181 col. 541 Ellen Wilkinson 4 March 1925.
39. PRO HO 45/11566/404730.
40. HC Deb. vol. 184 19 May 1925 col. 303.
41. Susan Pedersen, 'Gender, welfare, and citizenship in Britain during the Great War', *American Historical Review* 95 (1990), 1005–6.

Sir Alfred Watson, the government actuary. It was Watson's idea to have contributory financing and the extension of benefits to women without children on the basis of a man's right to maintenance. Pedersen has argued that financing pensions through insurance-linked pensions to the working man meant that eligibility depended on a man's insurance status, not on a woman's needs; thus, the system excluded women whom men had not maintained, such as deserted or separated wives, wives of invalids and unmarried mothers. The civil servants who drew up the plans were thinking about men's rights; women's rights as citizens did not cross their minds.[42]

No women spoke on the second reading of the 1927 Legitimacy Act. The Act meant that children born out of wedlock could be legitimised when the parents subsequently married, so long as neither was married to someone else when the child was born. The 1929 Age of Marriage Act, which raised the age of marriage for girls from 12 to 16 and for boys from 14 to 16, was introduced in the House of Lords, from which all women were banned. It was already a criminal offence for a man to have sexual relations with a girl aged under 16, and already an unacceptable defence to claim that the girl looked at least 16.

Although women MPs' contribution to the oft-cited family law legislation in the 1920s was limited, they did make a positive contribution to the House by speaking in a range of debates, in particular over welfare issues, such as housing, health and benefits. On occasion they spoke up for particular groups of women, such as the unemployed. Throughout the 1930s there were women MPs who promoted the interests of wives and mothers, with the support of male colleagues. In 1930 the Labour government approved in principle local authorities providing contraceptive information to mothers for whom further pregnancies would be a hazard to their health. In 1931 Edith Picton-Turbervill steered a Private Member's Bill through Parliament which prevented the death sentence being passed on pregnant women. (It was already the practice for such sentences to be commuted.) In 1936 the Midwives Act turned midwifery into a salaried service under local authorities. The system was not, however, free to women, who were expected to pay if they could afford to do so, and as the service was run by local authorities it inevitably varied in quality and in the extent to which it was integrated with other services for mothers. In 1937 A.P. Herbert's divorce reform extended the grounds for divorce to include desertion for three years, cruelty, insanity, rape, bestiality, and sodomy. A marriage could be declared null and void if a spouse suffered from VD, epilepsy, or if the

---

42. Susan Pedersen, *Family, Dependence and the Origins of the Welfare State, Britain and France, 1914–1945* (Cambridge, 1993), pp. 169–75.

1. Nancy Astor visiting the Margaret McMillan nursery school in Plymouth.
Source: The Western Morning News Co Ltd.

2. Eglantyne Jebb, the founder of Save the Children Fund.
Source: Save the Children.

3. Eleanor Rathbone, Independent candidate for E. Toxteth, Liverpool. Source: The Hulton Getty Picture Library.

4. Clementine Churchill.
Source: The Hulton Getty Picture Library.

5. Margaret Bondfield, the first woman Cabinet Minister, and J. J. Lawson, M.P., 1929. Source: The Hulton Getty Picture Library.

6. Women's Voluntary Service store, London.
Source: Mary Evans Picture Library/Bruce Castle Museum.

7. Marie Stopes, pioneer of birth control.
Source: Mary Evans Picture Library/Fawcett Library.

8. Stanley Baldwin, the Prime Minister, with Margaret McMillan at her nursery school. Source: Lewisham Library.

marriage was not consummated. After failed Bills in 1931 and 1933, wives and children were finally supported by the 1938 Inheritance (Family Provision) Act, which prevented a husband from disinheriting his wife and children.

As well as holding different views on family law, women MPs were ambiguous in their attitudes towards women in paid work. In 1936 Ellen Wilkinson introduced a motion on equal pay in the civil service which passed the House, with the support of Astor, Cazalet, Megan Lloyd George, Horsbrugh and Wilkinson, but not with the support of Atholl or Rathbone. The government was determined to maintain inequality in its own service and the motion was put again a few days later as a vote of confidence. On this occasion the vote was inevitably lost; Wilkinson and Megan Lloyd George were the only two women to stand their ground.[43]

Given the hostility of their colleagues, women MPs' contributions would not necessarily have helped the policy they were advocating. Often it is the speaker rather than what they say, and certainly not how much they say, which influences the listener. For this reason, Harrison's calculations of the number of words spoken by women MPs on different subjects is limited in its usefulness.[44] His study is limited, too, because we do not know how women's welfare interests compared with those of men in the House.

The very presence of women in the House was a slap in the face for those MPs who had opposed women's enfranchisement and who remained hostile to women MPs. The women who sat in the House of Commons present a remarkable group portrait of determination. Jean Mann's (Labour MP, 1945–59) sweeping criticism of other women MPs' standard of competence and lack of leadership skills does not seem justified.[45] 'Success' can be judged in three ways: first, how successful the women were as MPs and second, how far, as pioneers, they encouraged others to follow in their footsteps. Third, it is not just the women who should be judged but also the parliamentary system: did it facilitate and enable the women to perform to a high standard?

A good MP needs to be a good constituency MP and here there is no evidence that the women performed less well than their male colleagues and indeed some of them, such as Astor and Rathbone, were regarded very highly in this respect. MPs need to contribute to the work of Parliament and Harrison's anaysis of women's contribution to speaking and voting shows that they acquitted themselves well. Their debating skills were mixed.

---

43. HC Deb. vol. 310 1 April 1936 cols. 2017–23, 2068; 6 April 1936 cols. 2472–2562.
44. For details of women MPs see Brian Harrison 'Women in a men's house', pp. 623–54.
45. Jean Mann, *Woman in Parliament* (1962), p. 39.

Atholl was not very good and tended to ramble. Rathbone was excellent: Picton-Turbervill commented that Rathbone drove her points home like a sledge-hammer.[46]

As pioneers, the women MPs should have encouraged other women to follow in their footsteps. There is no evidence of this happening specifically, but they set an example of competence. It was difficult for the women to encourage other women when the political parties and the parliamentary system erected barriers to their success. This links to the third yardstick, for when judging the parliamentary system there is copious evidence of the system making life awkward for the women. It was difficult for them to be selected for winnable seats and therefore the number of women MPs was paltry, which in itself created problems for women working in a totally male-orientated environment. The atmosphere of the House of Commons was uninviting; and the physical facilities were worse for women than men.

Whitehall

While women MPs struggled to establish themselves, and some tried to advance the cause of other groups of women, women in the civil service were also defending their careers. Tensions existed over what was to the benefit of women civil servants and over what was considered to be in the interests of government. While women civil servants were active in defending their perceived interests, these perceptions varied. In general, the more senior women supported equal pay, scrapping the marriage bar and opening the Foreign and Diplomatic Service to women.

At the end of the war the government sacked women wholesale from the civil service, and gave ex-servicemen employment priority. The traditional view, which presented women cheerfully abandoning work they had undertaken in the war, has now been rejected by those who argue that demobilisation was actually forced on women. Women civil servants argued for their own retention on the grounds of women's sacrifice in the war, their economic needs and the debt of honour owed to them by society.[47] What women civil servants found particularly galling was that all men benefited from positive discrimination and all women lost out. The specific situation

---

46. Edith Picton-Turbervill, *Life is Good*, p. 233.
47. Meta Zimmack, '"Get out and get under": the impact of demobilisation on the civil service, 1918–1932', in Gregory Anderson, ed., *The White Blouse Revolution* (Manchester, 1988), pp. 88–120.

of some men was generalised to all men (just as the argument for a family wage was generalised so that, as Eleanor Rathbone pointed out, all men were winners and all women were losers).

From 1919 to 1924 open competition for the administrative grade was suspended and women were banned from the men's selection process. In 1925, when women were allowed to compete with the men, 80 men and 27 women sat the examination, 19 men and 3 women were successful, a figure for the women which Hilda Martindale, civil servant and historian of women in the civil service, thought 'encouraging'. Soon, however, the number of women declined. Martindale pointed to what she felt deterred women from applying: they usually finished university at the age of 21 and considered the chance of winning a civil service place too remote to wait a year until they were aged 22 to compete; often they had no funds for the coaching which was widely assumed to be essential; and women were often discouraged from taking the examination or did not have their attention drawn to it. Gradually, publicity and a loan fund for examination coaching attracted more women, but even so the numbers were miniscule. In 1936, 17 women competed and 6 were successful, and in 1937, 29 women competed and 8 were successful.[48]

Women civil servants had a mixed experience of discrimination. Alix Kilroy, who was one of the first women to enter the administrative grade after successfully sitting the examinations in 1925, commented that women experienced discrimination at the point of entry and at points of promotion. Her sister sat the entrance examinations with Kilroy, did not gain marks as high as Kilroy, but was top of the reserve list. Over the course of the following year she waited for a vacancy to be announced but none was made. When the departments saw that a woman was at the top of the list they decided not to declare a vacancy and Kilroy's sister never gained entry to the civil service. Kilroy learned later that her own appointment was greeted with horror by the men at the Board of Trade. In 1932 when Kilroy applied for promotion to the grade of Principal she was at first told that she did not have wide enough experience, which she knew to be nonsense. She suspected promotion would have been a foregone conclusion if she had been a man. Kilroy recalled having to nag to get fair treatment over promotion. Once she had reached a particular grade, however, she did not feel discriminated against in her daily work. When Kilroy joined the Board of Trade she remembered being slightly nervous and very much

---

48. Hilda Martindale, *Women Servants of the State, 1870–1938: A History of Women in the Civil Service* (1938), pp. 104–6. In 1926, 12 women sat the examination and 1 was successful. Between 1927 and 1935, 88 women sat and only 8 were successful.

aware that she was the first woman in the administrative grade at the Board of Trade and she was determined not to fail. At first she was put in an office with a secretary, who presumably was meant to act as a chaperone. Kilroy wrote that her male colleagues showed generosity of spirit to her and to Evelyn Sharp, another successful woman in the 1925 intake, and Kilroy was never made aware of any objections or difficulties they may have felt about working with her.[49]

Hilda Martindale was well placed to comment on women in the civil service. Before the war she had been a Factory Inspector, rising to a Senior Factory Inspector. After the war she became a Superintending Inspector in the newly amalgamated women's and men's branches, and then in 1925 the first woman Deputy Chief Inspector. In 1933 she became Director of Women Establishments at the Treasury, where she unsuccessfully pressed her views for equal pay and against the marriage bar for women civil servants. In 1934 she sat on an interdepartmental committee investigating the possibility of allowing women into the Foreign and Diplomatic Service, where she and Muriel Ritson, the other woman member, put the case for women. She championed women civil servants on the Whitley Council Committee on Women's Questions and on the Council for Women Civil Servants. Although she believed in protective legislation for working-class women, in 1932 and 1934 at the International Labour Conferences, she put Britain's case for an exemption for professional women from the ban on night work.

Martindale had personal experience of the institutionalised gender bias, which operated even when individual male colleagues were supportive. The senior men at the Home Office held Martindale in high regard, yet in 1932 she herself had to set out the case for her salary to be raised above that of a male Superintending Inspector whose work she supervised.[50]

It has often been suggested that in order for women to succeed in a man's world they have to take on the mores of men; they in effect become coopted into the male system. Janet Campbell, following experience at London hospitals, was appointed assistant Medical Officer in the London School Medical Service. In 1907 she was appointed the Board of Education's first full-time woman Medical Officer. With the creation of the Ministry of Health in 1919, she became its Medical Officer in charge of maternal and child welfare. Here she fitted into the Ministry's culture and withstood the demands of various women's groups for more action first and foremost to improve the health of mothers and reduce the maternal mortality rate,

---

49. Alix Meynell, *Public Servant, Private Woman: An Autobiography* (1988), pp. 82–3, 85, 87, 128–9.
50. PRO HO 45/14995.

and to improve the health of babies born into poor families. Campbell, like Sir George Newman, the Chief Medical Officer of Health, believed that infant welfare clinics should be centres for educating mothers in good practices, not outlets for financial support, as women's groups demanded. She stood out against birth control advice to poor women, drawing conclusions from her own research which flew in the face of the evidence she presented. Her study of 1924 showed that a woman was at high risk of dying after her fourth child, and yet Campbell concluded that there was only a risk after the eighth child. In 1932 she did, however, concede that nutrition was more important to mothers' health than was often realised. Her work was, on occasion, used to promote causes of which she would not necessarily have approved. In 1924 she produced a report which showed that miners' wives had poorer health than that of other occupational groups. The next year the Family Endowment Society demanded family allowances for miners' families, citing Campbell's evidence.[51] Campbell's experience and loyalty to the Ministry's ethos was not enough to save her career in 1934 when she married and was forced to resign.

While Campbell is an example of a woman civil servant not taking up issues of concern to large swathes of the female population, women civil servants did display a concern with their collective advancement. The few senior women in the civil service tried to stand apart and organise themselves in order to advance the opportunities of women civil servants; they did not simply strive individually for promotion. Struggles took place formally and informally. In 1920 women in the higher grades formed the Council of Women Civil Servants to promote a common policy on women's work in the civil service. The first chair was Dame Adelaide Anderson, the Principal Lady Inspector of Factories, who was followed by Frances Durham CBE, Assistant Secretary at the Ministry of Labour, then Hilda Martindale OBE, Deputy Chief Inspector of Factories, and then Miss E. Sanday OBE, Superintendent of Women Staff, Accountant General's Department of the General Post Office. Adelaide Anderson always saw her work as pioneering; she, along with other women Factory Inspectors, had entered an overwhelmingly male, and often hostile, profession in which the few women, even when scattered across the country, made it their business to keep in contact, and they developed a strong ethos of pioneering work, both in terms of their own careers and in terms of the influence they could exert over women's industrial working conditions.

The Council of Women Civil Servants was open to women in the administrative, executive and professional grades. The Council aimed to be a

---

51. Jane Lewis, *The Politics of Motherhood* (1980), pp. 104, 171, 174, 208, 212.

means of communication between women; to act as an organisation through which their views could be ascertained and expressed and joint action taken; and to work for equal opportunities, status and pay between women and men. It demanded that all restrictions on grounds of gender should be removed, and that the principles governing the employment of women and men should be the same. With the senior women spread thinly across the country, however, they were often isolated from each other.[52] The scarcity of women in the administrative grade was a problem in itself. Many years later Dame Evelyn Sharp recalled that when she first entered the civil service in the 1920s it was 'horrible' being treated as an 'object of curiosity'. The reactions of her male colleagues were not, however, uniform. Older ones, she believed, just resigned themselves to the presence of a woman in the office, while younger ones, seeing women as a potential threat to their own prospects, feared them far more. Luckily, as a trainee she was allocated to a man who took women's equality seriously and believed in giving juniors responsibility.[53]

The assumption that the *gradual* entry of a new group of workers somehow eases problems is a false one: it does not ease the problems of the new group. Administrative grade work involved constant contact with colleagues rather than beavering away alone, so the attitude of colleagues towards new entrants was important. A civil servant's day was highly interactive, as can be seen from Evelyn Sharp and Alix Kilroy's description. At the start of the day the in-tray would be stacked with papers: some were requests from junior staff for instructions, with draft replies to letters with minutes suggesting action for approval; and there were letters from other departments. A deputation would be met and a note made afterwards of what took place; then there might be a discussion with a colleague from another department or a conference called by a senior officer to settle a point of policy. On some days answers had to be hurriedly prepared for Parliamentary Questions, on other days briefs urgently drafted for the minister or a senior official. Throughout the day junior staff were in and out for instructions, and there were telephone queries with which to deal.[54]

Further evidence of the problems which accompany piecemeal breakthroughs is provided by Barbara Wootton, an academic rather than a civil servant, who recalled that as the only woman member of a departmental

52. Fawcett Library. Council of Women Civil Servants (higher Grades) Statement prepared for the Royal Commission on the Civil Service (1929–30) October 1930.
53. BBC Sound Archives 15 March 1977 Broadcast November 1977. AC LP 37553 f01.
54. Alix Kilroy and Evelyn Sharp, 'The civil service', in Margaret Cole, ed., *The Road to Success: Twenty Essays on the Choice of A Career for Women* (1936), pp. 50–1.

committee to look into the national debt and taxation she was hounded by the press and pestered with questions about her private life.[55]

Women civil servants presented robust criticisms of the civil service system to the 1929–31 Tomlinson Royal Commission on the Civil Service. They criticised the paucity of women in senior posts; they catalogued the departments which employed no women in the higher grades; they pointed to the failure of the civil service to respond to the recommendations of the last Royal Commission's recommendations in 1915 on the employment of women in the civil service; they criticised the exclusion of women from the Foreign and Diplomatic Service; they condemned the selection and promotion boards which had been devised for men and had not been modified sufficiently for the recruitment and advancement of women; and they demanded equal pay, and the abolition of the marriage bar.

Women civil servants were divided over the marriage bar. Women in senior posts wanted the bar lifted, those in junior positions were keen to retain it. Those who were not going to marry saw it as a protection: they feared that their meagre promotion prospects would be even worse if more women stayed on after marriage as there would be more women competing for promotion. Most of the women in junior grades were not interested in staying on after marriage in a job that was not very interesting or well paid.[56]

The women calling for changes identified two reasons for women's poor prospects, one related to attitudes, the other to organisational structures. First, and most importantly, they asserted that 'traditionalism' meant that official opinion was often mistrustful of women's value and their ability to perform the highest class of work; second, they claimed that the actual conditions of service worked to the disadvantage of women. They argued for a better use of women because they had the education and qualifications; public opinion demanded it; there was value in cooperation, and inequalities fostered injustice and inefficiency in public life. In the 1930s attitudes gradually began to change: segregation ended, and in 1935 women were granted equal pension rights with men. Other changes bore no immediate fruit, such as the support male civil servants' organisations gave to women's perennial call for equal pay. Even when individual departments of state wanted to offer equal pay they could face a Treasury rebuff on the grounds of expense.[57] Women struggled not only in the civil service as a whole but also within their departments, where attitudes divided along

55. Barbara Wootton, *In A World I Never Made* (1967), pp. 64–5.
56. Dorothy Evans, *Women and the Civil Service* (1934), p. 61.
57. PRO HO 45/17957.

gender and generational lines. Each department operated its own ethos and attitude to women. The most senior women were often found in specialist areas, such as inspection of factories, schools and Poor Law Infirmaries. The experience of women at the Board of Education was discussed in Chapter Three.

Although women Factory Inspectors operated together to promote their careers, the older and younger generations held differing views on the way their careers could best be advanced. By the end of the First World War disagreements existed between the women Inspectors over the appropriate role for them within the inspectorate. The senior men at the Home Office and the junior women Inspectors were united in advocating the amalgamation of the women's and men's branches, and thus the ultimate equality of the women and men Inspectors. The junior women Inspectors wanted to swim in the mainstream, not be caught in a side current. Adelaide Anderson, who had entered the Home Office in 1894, fought against the change; those who supported her believed that the old system was satisfactory and was essential for the protection of women's interests. The women had provided a specialist service within the inspectorate and now feared that the investigation of the needs of women workers, which they had pioneered, would be swamped by the many general duties of inspection. Anderson argued that 'any change of organisation can . . . be weighed and judged only by the result in increased effectiveness and finess of inspection, not by greater official convenience, nor by a theory of equality of men and women'. It was also thought that she opposed the scheme because her own personal standing would have been impaired if she had been forced to confine herself to a comparatively small section of the country as a Superintending Inspector. It was not a clear-cut case, therefore, of Anderson and her supporters putting the interests of working-class women first and the younger Inspectors prioritising their career prospects.

A Departmental Committee on the reorganisation of the inspectorate came out firmly in favour of amalgamation, arguing that the alternative would confirm the women in positions of less responsibility and status, and continue to bar them from the highest positions. It assumed that its recommendations were swimming with the tide of widening opportunities and higher status for women. The amalgamation of the women's and men's branches reflected the recognition, reinforced by the war, that women could act in as competent a fashion as the men Inspectors, and the temporary changes which had taken place in industry during the war made it impossible to separate women's and men's inspection duties. Changes came gradually and erratically. In 1933 Isabel Taylor became Deputy Chief Inspector of Factories, a post she held for 14 years, during which time men leap-frogged over her three times to take up the post of Chief Inspector.

In 1919 when the Ministry of Health was created it incorporated the Local Government Board (LGB) and the National Health Insurance Commission. The only women in the LGB were Assistant Inspectors of Poor Law Infirmaries and Inspectors of committees for boarding out Poor Law children. Women doctors were only employed in the maternity and child welfare section of the Ministry. Until 1936 they were kept on separate work from their male colleagues. A few nurses were appointed Inspectors to assist women Medical Officers. In 1925 the two sets of women Inspectors merged, but with no promotion. The NHI employed the largest number of women Inspectors. They worked separately from the men and were restricted to trades largely employing women. In 1928, after an enormously detailed investigation, the women and men NHI commissioners were amalgamated.

Women could not even compete for a place on the lowest rung of the administrative grade of the Foreign Office. Women's organisations outside the civil service campaigned against the exclusion of women from the Foreign Office and diplomatic and consular services. Although this was an opening which would affect relatively few women it was of symbolic importance to women's groups, and their exclusion was perhaps more galling in the 1930s when women demonstrated a strong interest in foreign affairs. In the early 1930s when tariffs were introduced Alix Kilroy worked on negotiations with Sweden, undertaking work which in other countries came under their Foreign Office. Thus, a woman civil servant was already undertaking diplomatic negotiations with no detriment to the country.

There was, however, deep hostility among key Foreign Office officials as well as from the bulk of heads of overseas missions. One diplomat referred to the idea of women diplomats as 'tiresome' and 'ridiculous', and the general tone of the Foreign Office towards women was high-handed and arrogant, as, for instance, when the National Union of Women Teachers was told that its letters were receiving attention while a civil servant minuted that they were not. Diplomats' reasons for opposing the appointment of women varied. The Prague embassy regretted women's suffrage, women MPs and women JPs, while other embassies pointed to the difficulty of women working in certain countries because of the local culture. Sir Robert (later Lord) Vansittart, Permanent Under-Secretary at the Foreign Office, for instance, opposed the appointment of women diplomats, which he said was not the fault of women but of foreigners. Certain senior women civil servants also opposed women's entry to the Foreign Office. The press, in the main, was also unsympathetic to women's demands. The experiences of women working abroad during the war or as missionaries, doctors, nurses, relief workers or even in an unofficial capacity, as Gertrude Bell had done, cut no ice. So, despite the wide range of arguments in favour of opening up the last male bastion of government to women, their campaigns stood little chance of success. Entry to the Foreign Office was never going to affect large numbers of women, but as a point of principle it attracted strong support from women's organisations. In the 1930s an inter-departmental committee was set up to look into the question, but the only members of the committee to support opening up the service unconditionally to women were the two women, Hilda Martindale and Muriel Ritson. Despite women's interest in foreign affairs they continued to be excluded from policy making.

Not only was women's entry to, and promotion within, the administrative grade of the civil service extremely slow, but they were also less likely to be incorporated into the policy process on an ad hoc basis. This was true even on issues, such as the protection of children, which virtually everyone agreed was women's particular province. Thus, the departmental committee on sexual offences appointed in 1925 had three women and five men members.

In contrast to the difficulties experienced by career civil servants and politicians, Violet Markham – neither a career civil servant nor a politician – influenced national and local politics throughout the period. Unlike so many other women whom the government shook off after the war, Markham's war work opened doors to permanent influence. Throughout the 1920s and 1930s she chaired the Central Committee on Women's Training and Employment (CCWTE); from 1934 she was the statutory woman member of the Unemployment Assistance Board (UAB) and from 1937 its deputy chair. During the Second World War the government used her on various committees.

Markham claimed that she wanted to see working-class women's field of employment expanded and their wages improved, but as a member of the CCWTE she presided over schemes confined to domestic work. Her ideas for widening opportunities for middle-class women received more concrete expression. She pressed for more women in senior civil service posts, and sat on the committee which recommended the amalgamation of the women's and men's sections of the Factory Inspectorate, on the optimistic assumption that this would open up more senior posts for women. She also made recommendations to the Lord Chancellor's Office about the appointment of the first women JPs. While pressing for the expansion of middle-class womens' employment opportunities, she never wavered in her belief that women's chief joy in life was procreation.

Markham's pre-war anti-suffrage stance gave way during the First World War to support for women's enfranchisement, but she remained diffident about women in politics. During the 1918 general election, when standing unenthusiastically, and unsuccessfully, as an Asquithian Liberal candidate in her dead brother's Mansfield constituency, she announced that, if elected, she would resubmit herself for election after two years because if the electors made the 'novel, and very sporting venture' of electing a woman, they should have the chance of getting out of the bargain if they did not like it.

She exploited her many connections to gain influence for herself and her views. During the 1930s she attended weekend house parties with those influential in political circles. In the mid-1930s, when she wanted her views on unemployment taken seriously, she revived her acquaintance with Neville Chamberlain, now Chancellor of the Exchequer, and tried to influence Cynthia Colville, lady-in-waiting to the Queen. In almost every instance Markham had forged her own connections, and she expressed irritation with women who held posts through their husbands: 'I get dreadfully bored with the type of woman who "presides" just because she is her husband's wife.' Indeed, Markham never let her marriage impinge on her public life: her public work snowballed after her marriage in 1915 at the age of 43, and she symbolically kept her maiden name for her public work. While Markham's pre-war anti-suffrage campaigning never hindered her subsequent public work, some women's pre-war suffrage activities barred them for life from certain employment; former suffragettes, for instance, could never gain employment in the police.

Markham's role in policy making did not signal expanded political opportunities for women. She could as well have been appointed to the posts she held without women's enfranchisement, and although she exploited her connections to her own advantage, she did not use them to help other women's careers. Her influence, therefore, offers a cautionary tale to those who believe that the mere presence of a woman will advance other women's interests.[58]

Conclusions

The foregoing discussion does not support the contention that women MPs dented the masculine world of Parliament. The presence of women did not, as Rowbotham asserts, shift the discourse of politics or pioneer social reforming conservatism.[59] (The latter goes back at least as far as Disraeli.) The small number of women MPs and senior civil servants is a measure of the difficulty women faced in accessing well-paid and high-status work. Both Parliament and the civil service offered only very limited opportunities for women to play a direct part in policy making. The number of women MPs

---

58. See Helen Jones, ed., *Duty and Citizenship: The Correspondence and Political Papers of Violet Markham, 1896–1953* (1994).

59. Sheila Rowbotham, *A Century of Women* (1997), pp. 122–3.

and senior civil servants was too small to overcome an ingrained culture, manifested in policies and procedures, which was at best indifferent and at worst hostile to women's individual and collective ambitions. In its adaptation to women's demands for a share in central government's powers, the British system was painfully slow; in this it was not alone.

CHAPTER SEVEN

British Women's Experiences Compared

Introduction

This chapter aims to reinforce the arguments of the preceding four chapters by looking at the political experiences of women in the USA, Australia, France, Germany and Italy. These countries have been selected for both their similarities with and differences from Britain. They provide a mix of European and non-European, fascist and non-fascist countries, as well as representing three countries where women were enfranchised and two where they were not. While women in politics, in health and educational employment, and in welfare campaigns enjoyed varying fortunes, the factors determining their success were similar to those in Britain.

Women in the countries discussed below campaigned over broadly similar issues, relating to their role both in the family and in the labour market. The extent to which women's issues were taken up by governments reflected less women's inherent organisational and campaigning strengths and weaknesses, than the extent to which governments chose to appropriate women's issues for their own ends. When women's organisations and governments promoted similar policies, they did so for dissimilar reasons. Women's political participation did not usually equate with policy-making powers. It was more important for women to be both well placed and part of an effective network of women pursuing goals which were in close accord with those of government. Women were frequently disempowered both in the social policy-making process and in health and education occupations through isolation, division, and a male-dominated hierarchical culture. It was rare for an individual woman to make a difference.

USA

As in Britain, so in the USA, in the years immediately after the First World War the political culture appeared to favour women's professional advancement. In 1919 women were granted the vote; and in 1920 Congress established a Women's Bureau in the Department of Labor. By 1925, 20 states admitted women to jury service and two had equal pay legislation. From then on, however, women's professional advancement ground to a halt and even went into reverse. Barbara Harris argues that this was due to the fact that it was almost unanimously held that men's employment should be prioritised over women's because men had families to keep. This aspect of domestic ideology played a large part in the ability of states and cities to sack women, sometimes en masse.[1] Between 1932 and 1937 Congress prohibited more than one member of a family from working in the federal civil service (a measure aimed at excluding women).[2] During the depression, professional and business women suffered more than other groups of women workers for, according to Wandersee, they failed to receive the support from New Deal policies which non-professional groups of women received.[3]

In 1920 the Women's Bureau in the Department of Labor was set up, and professional women were brought into government specifically to promote working women's interests. As there were never more than 80 employees in the Women's Bureau it did not herald a breakthrough, either in terms of the numbers of women employed in government or in terms of women's power, for, along with those employed in the Children's Bureau, the women never found an effective means of determining government policy. Government in Washington operated as a hierarchy of male legislatures, Cabinets and Courts. In the 1920s, a range of women's professions were linked together in the common bond of children's welfare. In the 1930s these groupings became fragmented, largely as a result of the political culture of the New Deal, when the range of government intervention widened and spread into related fields. Women were unable to control this expansion of state intervention. Thus, the professional autonomy of women vis-à-vis other agencies, and male professionals, weakened.[4]

---

1. Barbara Harris, *Beyond the Sphere: Women and the Professions in American History* (Westport, CT, 1978), p. 141.
2. Rosalind Rosenberg, *Divided Lives: American Women in the Twentieth Century* (Harmondsworth, 1993), pp. 74–5, 103.
3. Winifred Wandersee, *Women's Work and Family Values, 1920–1940* (Cambridge, Mass, 1981), p. 95.
4. Robyn Muncy, *Creating a Female Domain in American Reform, 1890–1935* (Oxford, 1991).

Glazer and Slater have focused on the varied experiences of women according to the profession they attempted to enter. They argued that men institutionalised patronage practices for younger men, favouring people similar – in terms of race, gender and social background – to those already in the profession. Women did not develop this patronage system and a lack of professional unity meant that each generation, group, or individual had to fight for position and influence anew. Women, therefore, continued to be isolated. The vulnerability of women in the professions meant that women tended to play down their gender.[5] This argument accords with Ehrenreich and Trolander. The former maintains that in the 1920s social workers saw a need to professionalise more and more in order to legitimise themselves; the key to this professionalism lay in emphasising the scientific nature of social work with a theoretical underpinning and discrete body of knowledge; psychoanalytic theory served the purpose.[6] Trolander, too, asserts that social work emphasised psychology as it turned away from its social reforming roots of the progressive era.[7]

When American women campaigned for changes which did not clearly fit in with federal government policy their success was limited. The history of the American birth control movement paralleled that in Britain. As in Britain, so in America, one woman, Margaret Sanger, became synonymous with the campaign. Influenced by her mother's early death, which she blamed on too many children and too few dollars, from 1915 Sanger campaigned through her speeches and the opening of a birth control clinic run by women in a poor part of New York. The clinic was short-lived. In 1921 Sanger founded the American Birth Control League, which aimed to make the subject of birth control respectable. However, she faced hostility from the medical profession, from radicals (especially men) who thought birth control a low priority set against the working-class struggle, and from many feminists who feared that by making the consequences of sex safer for women, men would assume that they had a carte blanche for sex. Sanger's main support, therefore, came from eugenicists. In 1923 she opened the Clinical Research Bureau in New York, the first birth control clinic in the USA staffed by doctors. Most of the women who visited it were poor. During the 1920s infant welfare clinics opened across America under the 1921 Shephard-Towner Act but, as in Britain, the clinics would only give advice

---

5. Penina Migdal Glazer and Miriam Slater, *Unequal Colleagues: The Entrance of Women in the Professions, 1890–1940* (New Brunswick, New Jersey, 1987), pp. 231–9.
6. John Ehrenreich, *The Altruistic Imagination: A History of Social Work and Social Politics in the USA* (1985), pp. 57, 60.
7. Judith Trolander, *Professionalism and Social Change: From the Settlement House Movement to Neighbourhood Centers, 1886 to the Present* (New York, 1987), p. 23.

to women on how to care for themselves and their children, they would have nothing to do with birth control. Gradually, birth control clinics opened around the country, and in 1937 the American Medical Association officially endorsed artificial contraception. As in Britain, although the birth control campaign was aimed primarily at working-class women, middle-class women were the first to reap the benefits.[8]

The 1920s began hopefully for American feminists when, in 1921, Congress passed the Sheppard-Towner Act, following pressure from poor women, women's organisations and Children's Bureau officials. It provided federal funding to match state funding for information and education on nutrition and hygiene in pre-natal and child health clinics, and for health visitors. No material help or medical care could be given, but even so it prompted outrage from medical associations and right-wingers who condemned the Act as the product of communism and as the first step on the road to a dreaded state health service. As a result of ferocious opposition when the Act came up for renewal in 1926, it was only accepted for two years, and in 1929 it was repealed. Fear of the power of the women's vote had prompted many Congressmen, who would not otherwise have supported the legislation, to vote for it in 1921, but when no women's electoral lobby emerged, Congress dispensed with sops to women.[9] American women never formed a single lobby group. Class, race and ideology divided more than gender united them. The most public disagreement within women's groups occurred over protective legislation, but when women rallied behind the Democrats in the 1930s this diverted attention from this divisive issue.

During the early years, 1932–36, of Franklin D. Roosevelt's presidency, 1932–45, white, though not native American or Black, women enjoyed unprecedented influence over policy. Susan Ware has shown how a network of 28 women, headed by the First Lady, Eleanor Roosevelt, participated in the federal social policy process. They influenced the management of the economy; the provision of work relief; the making and implementation of the Social Security Act, and protecting the rights of consumers, labour and Black people. Three women held key posts: Molly Dewson, head of the Women's Division of the Democratic Party, 1932–37, and a member of the Social Security Board, 1937–38; Frances Perkins, Secretary of Labor, 1933–45, who was responsible for much of the social welfare legislation; and Ellen Sullivan Woodward, who set up relief programmes for women under the Federal Emergency Relief Administration and was later head of

8. Rosalind Rosenberg, *Divided Lives*, pp. 77–90.
9. Molly Ladd-Taylor, 'My work came out of agony and grief': mothers and the making of the Sheppard-Towner Act, in Seth Koven and Sonya Michel, eds, *Mothers of a New World: Maternalist Politics and the Origins of Welfare States* (1993), pp. 321–42.

Women's and Professional Projects for the Works Progress Administration. For six years she sat on the Social Security Board.

Ware argues that the women were able to determine policy because their reforming zeal fitted in with, rather than challenged, the ethos of the federal government's New Deal strategy, and the accompanying expansion of government services provided new openings into which they could step. The women, moreover, operated a close network, based on friendship and co-operation which went back to the pre-war days of the suffrage campaign and the Progressive movement, which worked to promote social reforms. These women clearly enjoyed an influence denied women in most other countries, who found themselves out of step with government policies.[10] Ware maintains that, as social welfare came under increasing fire from Congress in the late 1930s, the women's power receded along with the social welfare programme. There was little turnover in posts, so few opportunities arose for new women to enter government service. The 1939 Hatch Act curtailed political activity by government workers and this hit the Democratic women's campaign hard, for it relied on women in government to publicise the New Deal's successes. As the years wore on it was harder to gain access to the President, and Eleanor Roosevelt gradually became less involved in women's issues.

The importance of women being well placed in the political process is clear from the work of Frances Perkins, who as Secretary of Labor, managed to chip away at an ungenerous refugee policy, despite operating within a whole host of constraints, which included the existing immigration laws and regulations, State Department bureaucracy, and Roosevelt's unwillingness to fly in the face of public opinion, which was hostile to a flood of immigrants. Perkins was willing, and in a position, to argue on behalf of Jewish and other humanitarian organisations for a more liberal immigration policy. From 1933 she pressed for more Jewish refugees to be allowed to enter America, arguing that they could be absorbed almost everywhere, except on the east coast; they should be allowed in to relieve their suffering, and their presence would help the economy by boosting domestic demand. Behind the scenes, she engaged in a legal battle to prevent Consuls from barring refugees on the grounds that they would be a charge on the state, and she demanded that Consuls be less strict. She called on Roosevelt to permit refugees to enter the country, whether or not they would 'strengthen' the USA. After *Kristallnacht* in 1938 she pushed successfully for Jews on visitors' visas to be allowed to stay, and she pressed for Jewish children not

---

10. Susan Ware, *Beyond Suffrage: Women in the New Deal* (Cambridge, Mass, 1989), pp. 1–21, 127–30.

on the quota system to be allowed into the USA. Even at the eleventh hour, with the war clouds gathering over Europe, Perkins was attacked within her own department and by Congress. The House Judiciary Committee tried to impeach her for unpopular deportation and immigration decisions she had made.[11] Despite having few allies in the administration, she did wheel and deal privately and publicly for an unpopular cause with some limited success and, in the Jewish refugee field, she exercised more influence than other individual women or women's groups in countries of potential haven.

A number of other women made a stand against fascism by supporting the American Committee to Aid Spanish Democracy. Dorothy Parker chaired the women's section. A few women went over to Spain, including the journalist Martha Gellhorn, and others served in a medical and a nursing capacity.

At a time when women's organisations and employment prospects nosedived, other women's political influence rose. For over a decade women's political enfranchisement had not given them political muscle, but in the 1930s political circumstances and women waiting in the wings meant that a small group of women did gain access to the federal social policy-making process. No such circumstances existed in Australia, however, where women continued to be excluded from the federal policy process.

Australia

In 1901 Australian women had gained the federal franchise, but it was not until 1943 that a woman sat in the Australian federal parliament in Canberra. Over the course of the inter-war years only nine women in total were elected to state parliaments; in addition, nine women briefly served as appointed members of the New South Wales legislative council. Women, therefore, had to campaign with little or no female support in state and federal parliaments. The early success of Australian women in gaining the vote, maternity allowances, free mother and baby clinics, women's hospitals, old-age and invalid pensions, and boarding-out allowances for deserted mothers was a false dawn.

There is evidence that in Australia, as in Britain, certain issues of concern to women crossed class, interest group and party lines. Women in the

---

11. Richard Breitman and Alan M. Kraut, *American Refugee Policy and European Jewry, 1933–45* (Bloomington, Indiana, 1987), pp. 3, 19–20, 22, 26, 59, 62, 66–7.

Liberal and Labor parties, in the National Council of Women and the Housewives Association in South Australia all took a keen interest in the guardianship of children, equal divorce laws, representation of women on government boards, care of Aboriginal women, maternity care for poor women and maternity allowances.[12]

Women's success in influencing policy was patchy. Following a campaign among women, in 1912 a maternity allowance was granted to all white women on the birth of a baby. Not only were Aboriginal women banned from claiming the payment, they also had any mixed-race children which they bore removed from them. These children were then brought up either by white families or in institutions run by whites. The welfare campaigns, spearheaded by white working-class Australian women, were shot through with racist notions of white women as the 'mothers of the race'. As motherhood and claims to citizenship were closely interwined, Aboriginal women were thus excluded from any benefits accruing to mothers and from full citizenship. In Britain there were no obvious losers in campaigns to raise the standards of living of working-class women, but in Australia, these campaigns reinforced the marginalisation of the poorest group of women.

Australian women unsuccessfully called for a range of policies which aimed to benefit white women, whether in the home or the labour market, including the endowment of motherhood, child endowment and equal pay. Marilyn Lake has argued that women demanded support for mothers in their role as citizen mothers; they often equated women's role as mothers with the military service of men: both made sacrifices and risked injury and death for the future of Australia. In 1927 New South Wales introduced limited child endowment, but it was not extended to other states until the Second World War. Although a Royal Commission was set up to consider child and maternal endowment (indicating that the issue received more serious attention from policy makers than in Britain), the Commission unanimously rejected endowment of motherhood, and a majority rejected child endowment, on the grounds that the unity of the family would be undermined if mothers enjoyed any economic independence.[13] The Commission's recommendations reflected, according to Lake, widespread opposition to economic independence for women, which she believes highlights the contradictions of maternal citizenship in a patriarchal society: men's citizenship required the dependency and services of women.

---

12. Helen Jones, *In Her Own Name: Women in South Australian History* (Kent Town, SA, 1986), p. 235.
13. Marilyn Lake, 'A revolution in the family: the challenge and contradictions of maternal citizenship in Australia', in Seth Koven and Sonya Michel, eds, *Mothers of a New World*, pp. 382–8.

In the early years of the century Australian women's groups had established infant welfare centres and mothers' schools, which it was assumed would be run by women. Although the women succeeded in obtaining state funding for the clinics, they failed to keep treatment of women within the hands of women. As in Britain, the medical profession displayed hostility to any loss of control and insisted that women should be referred for treatment to local doctors or hospitals. In the 1920s, as in Britain, information and access to birth control remained largely in the hands of those with money. In the 1930s family planning clinics, known as Racial Hygiene Clinics, opened in the capital cities of each state, Sydney, Melbourne, Adelaide, Perth, Darwin, and Brisbane, strongly backed by eugenicists. As in Britain, Australian women failed to exert much impact on governmental social policies in the years of the depression, and their influence remained at the local level, where they distributed food and clothing, and Labor women set up work depots.[14]

In the 1930s, when the depression hit Australia, pressure was put on women to abandon paid work. Whereas in the 1920s feminists had emphasised 'citizen mothers', now they emphasised 'citizen workers', whether women or men, and made claims for women's equal rights with men to paid work. Constraints were imposed on women teachers. The law governing the employment of married women varied from state to state, but in New South Wales in the early 1930s women had to resign on marriage. Public opinion, and the Teachers' Federation, were divided in their opinions and the latter refused to oppose the new policy. Nurses and their representatives were also weak, and failed to exert collective pressure for improved wages and conditions. The main improvement in women's job opportunities came from more women moving into the lower-status and worst-paid professions. Social work was also turning into a paid career and from 1929 women active in welfare organisations, who had close links with women's groups, helped to establish social work training courses.[15]

While organised women in Australia displayed a range of political attitudes, they shared a common interest in the ways women in other countries organised themselves, and in the policies they pursued. The Country Women's Association (CWA), for instance, which was overwhelmingly concerned with the daily lives of women in rural areas, took an interest in women's

14. Patricia Grimshaw, Marilyn Lake, Ann McGrath and Marian Quartly, *Creating a Nation, 1788–1990* (Ringwood, Victoria, 1994), pp. 222, 227–8, 245–6, 243.
15. Judy Mackinolty, 'To stay or to go: sacking married women teachers', in Judy Mackinolty and Heather Radi, eds, *In Pursuit of Justice* (Sydney, 1979), p. 140; Glenda Law '"I have never liked trade unionism": The development of the Royal Australian Nursing Federation, Queensland Branch 1904–45', in E. Windschuttle, *Women, Class and History* (Auckland, 1980); Elaine Martin, 'Amy Wheaton and the education of social workers in South Australia 1935–46', *Historical Studies* 20 (1983), pp. 574–89.

lives abroad. Women in the CWA wholeheartedly accepted the domestic ideology. Involvement in the CWA offered a social setting which complemented that of the family and it thereby enhanced women's domestic role. It also gave women a sense of independence. Women in the CWA met together to support each other and develop a range of skills useful to women in the country and in isolated areas. The CWA was not primarily a campaigning organisation but it did influence the provision of local facilities.

White women were not formally excluded from the political process, they enjoyed civil rights and displayed an interest in politics way beyond their own immediate concerns, but isolation and domestic responsibilities excluded them from Federal politics. In contrast, French women lacked political rights, they were formally excluded from national politics and they were often isolated in their welfare work, and yet individual women were occasionally 'granted' positions within local and national government.

France

French women continued to be barred from certain educational and training establishments; although in this way their opportunities were more limited than those of British women, at least French women, unlike their British counterparts, were viewed as suited to commerce. In both countries openings in the civil service widened but still remained largely at the lower levels, and in France women continued to be excluded from a number of government departments. As in Britain, women entered nursing, teaching and social work, all careers viewed as suitable for women.

The experience of French teachers demonstrates the important interaction of the political climate with the hierarchy, discipline, extent of isolation and male domination of an occupation. Once trained, both women and men teachers could be sent to any school in France. Inevitably, this meant that teachers were often isolated. Posts in cities were harder to obtain as they were more popular than rural postings. Many teachers found themselves in remote areas where their every move was carefully monitored by a censorious local population. Hidebound by isolation and moral gazing, women teachers displayed neither the camaraderie nor the feminism of many British women teachers.[16]

During the 1920s and 1930s social work gradually shifted from being an outlet for philanthropic volunteers to a job with training, salary and a

---

16. James McMillan, *Housewife or Harlot: The Place of Women in French Society, 1870–1940* (New York, 1981), p. 122 and *passim.*

uniform. French social work grew out of what was really health visiting. It involved visiting (usually poor) families in their homes and doling out medical aid and advice. Middle-class women went on newly established training courses, so that until the Second World War the workers were both middle-class and relatively young. Once trained, the social workers were thrown in at the deep end, as they ventured into the poorest and roughest areas, with minimal back-up support. Men had little interest in social work, so the field was left largely free for women who, along with women coopted onto local municipal committees, negotiated the implementation of policy and inevitably enjoyed some scope for decision making. Even so, the women were restricted by their lack of formal political power. Their policy powers, moreover, while enhancing the status and influence of the individual women involved, did not signal a growth in political power and authority of other women.[17]

In countries where policies for which British women campaigned were implemented it was not because women there were more effective campaigners than British women, but rather that the policies were appropriated by the state for its own ends. The history of family allowances in France and Italy are cases in point. Susan Pedersen has shown how influential French employers set up welfare funds, *caisses de compensation* (*caisses*), from which family allowances were paid as a central part of their business strategy of keeping wages down; preventing absence from work, for instance, due to strikes, and recruiting workers. In some cases employers attempted to intervene directly in the families of their employees; for example, by paying the family allowance to the unwaged wife and so pitting her interests for the allowance against her husband's interests. Employers also developed home-based social services for mothers and infants which gave them a foot in the door of their employees' homes. Between 1929 and 1939 French governments gradually expanded the employers' system into a national one. In 1932 all employers in business and commerce had to affiliate to a *caisse*, and by the end of the decade, a national system of family allowances had been created, with the backing first and foremost of pronatalists (who wanted to spread the economic burden of children and restrict women's employment), along with social Catholics, civil servants, businessmen and feminists. The influence of pronatalists was crucial and far more important than in Britain where concern over the falling birth rate never reached French proportions.[18] French feminists supported family allowances, but

17. Sîan Reynolds, *France Between The Wars: Gender and Politics* (1996), pp. 132–55.
18. Susan Pedersen, *Family, Dependence, and the Origins of the Welfare State: Britain and France, 1914–1945* (Cambridge, 1993), pp. 285–8, 224–9, 273, 357–8.

they did not influence the government to take up the policy. The one women's group which did enjoy some success only did so by aligning itself with arguments which flew in the face of most feminists' views. Pedersen has argued that the introduction in 1938 of a state benefit for unwaged mothers followed a campaign led by the Union Féminine Civique et Sociale (UFCS), the Catholic women's organisation, which supported pronatalism and condemned married women's paid work. The Popular Front government introduced the benefit for unwaged wives not out of any concern for the women but out of a panic attack brought on by fears of population decline and the effects of male unemployment during the depression.[19]

Sîan Reynolds has shown how women did, nevertheless, influence social policy making and implementation in France at the local, and to a lesser extent at the national, level. At a time when French women were still unable to vote, they were coopted as municipal councillors to welfare and education committees. Women were appointed at all levels of French government, although relatively few were appointed to senior posts, for which they needed to be well connected, party members or wives of party members.

In June 1936 three women briefly served in Leon Blum's Popular Front government. Susanne Lacore joined the Ministry of Public Health, with responsibility for child protection, under Henri Sellier, who was willing to work with women even though he opposed their enfranchisement. Lacore, a socialist, had no experience of public office in Paris and her role was largely a public relations one. She enjoyed a great deal of publicity but little power. The beginnings of a coordinated approach to child protection emerged but little concrete policy was put in place. Irène Joliot-Curie was closer to the communists than Lacore. She had a national reputation as a scientist, having recently jointly won, with her husband, the Nobel prize for chemistry, but she lacked experience of political office. Although she was also in the press spotlight she only lasted a couple of months as Minister for Scientific Research. The third appointment, Cécile Brunschvicg, a radical, was used to public life and tried hard to be more than a public relations ornament for the government; this provoked hostility towards her from civil servants. She held the twin brief of welfare within the Ministry of Education and general responsibility for overseeing women's rights. Blum forced Brunschvicg to give up suffrage campaigning while in office. He was unwilling to contemplate a suffrage Bill because of the hostility of colleagues. Both Brunschvicg and Lacore appointed women advisors, including lawyers, but

---

19. Susan Pedersen, 'Catholicism, feminism and the politics of the family during the Third Republic', in Seth Koven and Sonya Michel, eds, *Mothers of a New World*, pp. 246–76.

their brief tenure of office did not have a domino effect for, when Blum resigned in June 1937, no women were reappointed. French feminists then, and since, have argued over the appointment of women to posts when they were still disenfranchised. Blum offered Louise Weiss a post if she would give up her suffrage campaigning. She refused: 'J'ai lutté non pour être nommée mais pour être élue.'[20] All three women were used as a political gesture; unlike women who were coopted at the local level for their expertise, the three government appointees were not meant to do any policy making, only stand as a symbol of Blum's theoretical commitment to women's rights. They did, nevertheless, enjoy some limited policy-making powers.[21]

Italy

In Italy, as in France, family allowances were introduced in order to keep wages down and the trade unions weak. In 1928 the government introduced family allowances, for children up to the age of 18, for wives, and even sometimes for parents, of all state employees. The aim was to offer a perk – there were numerous others – to those who were among the fascist regime's most loyal supporters.[22] In 1934, in order to ease the unemployment rate, the working week was cut to 40 hours with no increase in hourly pay. A fund was set up with contributions from employers and workers still working over 40 hours a week to pay an allowance to those workers on reduced time who had families to support. In 1936 as more workers were put on short time, and the original scheme appeared blatantly impractical and unfair, family allowances were introduced for all industrial workers; the state now shared the cost with employees and employers. Finally, in 1937 family allowances were extended to dependants of all employees in agriculture as well as industry and commerce. Victoria de Grazia argues that this system helped to keep the fascist trade unions weak while favouring male heads of households over their working wives and other family members who lived at home.

In the 1920s and 1930s, family allowances, briefly on the agenda at the turn of the century, were no longer one of Italian feminists' demands. The feminist movement was on a downward spiral in Italy. In the early 1920s the fascist regime suppressed any organisations with communist or socialist links. Bourgeois women's groups, forced to abandon suffrage demands in

---

20. Laure Adler, *Les Femmes Politiques* (Paris, 1993).
21. This section relies heavily on Sîan Reynolds *France between the Wars: Gender and Politics*, Chapters 6 and 7.
22. Victoria de Grazia, *How Fascism Ruled Women, Italy 1922–1945* (Berkeley, 1992), pp. 86–7.

1925, staggered on with a low profile until 1938 when the regime outlawed those which remained. In contrast, from the 1920s the Catholic women's movement grew among the urban working class and middle class. It offered a clear-cut alternative to women's *fasci*, and, although it campaigned against 'immorality' in its various guises, it never attempted to find a niche in mainstream politics, and was, therefore, tolerated by the regime. The fascist women's movement, which developed very slowly, boasting roughly 3 million members or one quarter of the female adult population by the Second World War, was no more able to play a part in government policy making than any of the other women's organisations. Organised on strictly hierarchical lines, the women leaders never enjoyed the same powers as male fascist leaders. The women leaders in Rome, who were middle-class or upper-class and titled, had connections with leading male officials, but the latter took all decisions which affected women. de Grazia has pointed to the contradictions of mass fascist politics, which on the one hand required women to participate, but on the other hand prevented women's full integration by its ambivalence towards women's role in public life. Custom and family life reinforced the exclusion of women from politics. Pockets of protest and resistance stood no chance of success.[23] Perry Willson has also drawn attention to the contradictions of Italian fascism for women, for while new opportunities opened up for middle-class urban women, who had fewer children and found openings in social welfare employment, the *massaie rurali*, the fascist organisation for peasant women, reinforced their traditional position in society. Far from bringing women together, Italian fascism drew women apart.[24] It did not enhance either their political power or their careers in the welfare field.

In countries where the state introduced family allowances for its own ends we see women's organisations unable to obtain their goals. In both France and Italy the state rendered the birth control movement impotent. In Italy disseminating birth control information and abortion were both crimes; official sanctions were backed by the Pope's 1930 encyclical (papal letter for public circulation), *casti connubi*. What effect this had on birth control practices is hard to gauge; it probably had less effect in the north and in the cities than in the south and in rural areas.[25]

Few Italian women entered the professions and those who did do so were concentrated in teaching. Fascist culture easily incorporated domestic ideology to the detriment of women's professional advancement. The regime

---

23. Victoria de Grazia, *How Facism Ruled Women*, pp. 237–46, 265, 275.
24. Perry Willson, 'Cooking the patriotic omelette: women and the Italian fascist ruralisation campaign', *European History Quarterly* (1997), pp. 531, 542.
25. Victoria de Grazia, *How Fascism Ruled Women*, pp. 55–7.

condemned women's paid work and it would have liked women confined to the home, breeding and rearing young fascists. In 1929, as part of the strategy of rewarding marriage and fecundity, priority in employment was given to married men and women, rather than the single, and to parents over childless couples. Women's entry into professions such as law and medicine became harder, although this caused barely a blip in the statistics because there were already so few women in these professions. The system for getting on the professional ladder was especially hard for women. Doctors, lawyers and writers often relied on government patronage for their advancement and as women lacked useful connections they were doubly disadvantaged.

The number of women in caring occupations, where motherly qualities were seen to be at a premium, increased. This trend did nothing, however, to improve women's position within the hierarchy of particular occupations. The fascist regime banned women from headships and gave men teachers boys to teach. Women were also more likely to be isolated. Once sent to a rural school they had difficulty in finding a husband because of the limited number of available men, and since an effort was made to give married couples schools near each other, as in France, it was hard for single teachers to transfer to more populated areas. At the same time as women were having their promotion to headships stymied, the education system became more rigidly hierarchical. As in Britain, political culture and domestic ideology offered a negative context in which women worked; the hierarchy and isolation of careers increased the disadvantages against which women had to struggle.

The fascist welfare state encouraged family welfare services which included three party-run schools for social work. Men made the policy for all these services but they were staffed by women, either unpaid and untrained volunteers, or increasingly, trained, uniformed and paid social workers. The key institution, ONMI, the National Institution for Maternity and Infancy, used a mixture of untrained women. Tensions existed between the trained party workers and the old-style volunteer philanthropists who resented the growth of an impersonal state welfare bureaucracy. The volunteers, who were middle- and upper-class, sought to impose bourgeois family behaviour on the women in the families they visited, which only helped to highlight the divisions in Italian society which fascism had aggravated. The party social workers saw their task as 'modernising' women's role in family and society, not something envisaged by the men who feared women's challenge to fixed notions of the family.[26] Although few argued that women should be treated equally in the professions, or that they could find complete

---

26.   Victoria de Grazia, *How Fascism Ruled Women*, pp. 59, 61, 82, 98–9, 261–2.

fulfilment in a career, women's professional groups did attempt to defend their members' interests. The National Fascist Association of Women Doctors and Surgeons, for instance, spoke out against discrimination against women in public competitions; and the Italian Federation of Women Jurists was affiliated to the International Federation of Women Magistrates and Lawyers.[27] The experience of French and Italian women was not dissimilar; greater contrasts existed between Italian and German women, despite the superficially similar political culture.

Germany

German women took part in the November 1918 revolution, which led to their enfranchisement and ability to stand in elections. In early 1919, 49 women were elected to the National Assembly in Weimar, where they contributed to discussions on social policy. After 1919 all the political parties made an effort to attract women voters, but the male-dominated party machines kept women at arm's length from active engagement in politics, and none of the parties put women in favourable places on election lists for the Reichstag, Land or local elections. Women constituted a paltry number of Reichstag members, ranging from 37 in 1920 to 27 in 1924 and 41 in 1930. Most female party members undertook 'non-political' and traditional welfare work. While failing to gain power through the parties, women flexed their muscles in women's organisations, and campaigned for women's political rights, abortion, contraception and equal pay. Throughout the 1920s there was a division between middle-class/liberal women and working-class/socialist women, and women's groups were ineffective vehicles for driving towards power beyond the localities. From the standpoint of the 1930s, however, women in the 1920s were making progress, if erratically.

In contrast to mainstream parties, the National Socialists unapologetically refused to select women for election lists. In 1933 all women's organisations were dissolved. National Socialists encouraged women to join the Nationalsozialiste Frauenschaft (NSF – the Nazi Women's Section) and the Deutsches Frauenwerk (DFW), but with only limited success. Women who joined the NSF were either committed Nazis, or more likely, women wanting to protect their careers. Most women who joined did no more than pay a subscription.[28]

---

27. Cicely Hamilton, *Modern Italy as Seen by an Englishwoman* (1932), p. 87; Victoria de Grazia, *How Fascism Ruled Women*, pp. 195–200.
28. Jill Stephenson, *The Nazi Organisation of Women* (1981), pp. 14–19.

Women were not banned from the Nazi Party but they were kept away from posts where they could have made policies. The various Nazi organisations, all characterised by a labyrinth of hierarchies, spawned a huge number of minor offices and women filled thousands of these posts in the women's Nazi organisations. None of the posts offered a route to decision making at the heart of the Nazi state.[29]

German women made some political advances in the 1920s but under the Nazis previous successes were reversed. Some historians both downplay women's political progress during the Weimar Republic, in contrast to Usborne, who emphasises the activities and influence of women at all levels, from local politics to the Reichstag. Usborne points to the continuities in official attitudes towards the family in imperial, Weimar and Nazi Germany but, she argues, young women ignored these attitudes, at least in the Weimar years. Usborne points to the positive aspects of Weimar's emphasis on the importance of women's role as mothers, and she argues that the 'protection of motherhood' reflected governments' new responsiblity for the 'weaker citizens'. At the same time she acknowledges that Weimar policy reinforced the ideology of motherhood. In the 1920s women campaigned for the decriminalisation of abortion and in 1926 the Reichstag reduced the punishment for abortion, so that Germany now had the most liberal abortion laws in western Europe. Women spearheaded the expansion of clinics for sexual and marital advice, and contraceptive information became more widely available. Maternity allowances introduced during the First World War continued, and a network of ante-natal, infant, youth, family care, birth control and marriage guidance clinics opened around the country. Benefits for women were usually accompanied by propaganda about the prime role of women as reproducers. In the early years of the Weimar Republic industry tended to pay employees according to marital status and number of children. Weimar governments gradually introduced family allowances for civil servants in the unrealised hope that they would have larger families, and help to reverse the trend towards smaller families.[30]

Under the Nazis abortion was again more seriously punished, the sexual advice clinics closed and contraceptives made more difficult to obtain. The Nazis introduced financial incentives for Aryan sections of the population to marry and have children, and divorce was made easier. While women in the past had campaigned for child benefit, for women's work in the home

---

29. Ute Frevert, *Women in German History: From Bourgeois Emancipation to Sexual Liberation* (1989), pp. 168–72, 208–13, 240–1.
30. Cornelie Usborne, *The Politics of the Body in Weimar Germnay: Women's Reproductive Rights and Duties* (1992), pp. 43–53, 203.

to gain greater recognition, and for a loosening of the divorce laws, Nazi policies towards women and the family, motivated by the requirements of the Nazi state, were no victory for women.[31]

In Germany, both in the 1920s and 1930s, women's career advancement was hindered by the fusion of political culture and long-standing ideology. In the 1920s an increasing number of women entered careers such as teaching and nursing: roughly one third of teachers were women and four fifths of all health workers (mainly nurses). Governments, however, confirmed women's subordinate position in relationship to men. In 1919 Prussian law meant that one third of staff in girls' schools, and one third of science teachers had to be men. In 1922 a court decision put women on a lower pay scale than men. The numbers of women entering traditional male occupations were so small that few women were affected when the Nazis banned women from legal posts. In the 1920s social work expanded and offered employment to more working-class women than in the past and to middle-class women fallen on hard times who could no longer undertake unpaid work. The senior positions in social work, however, remained under male control, and according to Christoph Sachße, social work changed from being a vehicle of female emancipation to a male-dominated field with posts for women at a low municipal level.[32] While National Socialists would have preferred women not to have entered universities they did not ban women, and their propaganda against women's higher education was ineffectual. Very soon after they came to power, moreover, the build-up for war required university-trained specialists, whether women or men.[33] The inherent contradictions of National Socialism meant that although, ideologically, women's place was seen as being in the home, the material needs of war preparations meant that women were actually needed in the labour force.

Conclusions

Although the political culture of the fascist regimes appears on the surface to have reinforced existing attitudes and practices and made careers for women harder and more uncomfortable, the contradictions of the regimes were so much greater than in Britain, France, Australia and the USA that

31. Ute Frevert, *Women in German History*, pp. 187–9, 230–6.
32. Christoph Sachße, 'Social mothers: the bourgeois women's movement and German welfare-state formation, 1890–1929', in Seth Koven and Sonya Michel, eds, *Mothers of a New World*, pp. 136–58.
33. Jacques Pauwels, *Women, Nazis and the Universities* (Westport, CT, 1984), pp. 135–7.

the experience for most women employed in the welfare field, with the notable exception of Jewish women in Germany, was not so different.

In all the countries mentioned above women campaigned to raise the standard of living of white working-class women. Campaigners were rarely exclusively concerned with women as mothers or as workers, and their emphasis shifted over time and between countries. Women's position was weakest at times of high unemployment because men's position in the labour market, in terms of access and promotion, was privileged over that of women. This was justified by reference to a domestic ideology premised on a home-based, unpaid role for women. Women campaigned around policies based on a concept of women's rights, but when governments adopted policies which women had promoted, a concept of women's rights did not underpin the policies.

Governments actively put hurdles in the way of women's contribution to policy making and to their autonomy in careers. Women's policy-making role and advancement in welfare careers did not go hand in hand. Women could be making progress in one while forced to retreat in another. It was difficult for women to move from obtaining the parliamentary vote to exercising parliamentary or governmental power. However much women displayed an interest in national and international affairs, it was far harder to achieve a policy-making role than in local politics. For meaningful power and equality in occupations it is important that government strategy, and the ideology underpinning it, are in accordance with feminists' goals. If not, public relations gestures towards women will not be in their overall interests.

CHAPTER EIGHT

Woman Power in the Second World War

Introduction

Women's contribution to the war effort in Britain – in munitions industries, working on the land, serving in the auxiliary forces (WRNS, WAAF, WAACs and ATS), taking children from the evacuated cities into their homes, or contributing to women's voluntary organisations – has always been acknowledged as vital and far-reaching. From March 1941 all women aged between 19 and 40 had to register at labour exchanges and, as with male workers, could only change employment with the agreement of the Ministry of Labour. From December 1941 single women aged between 20 and 30 (in 1943 the age was reduced to 19) could be called up for war work. Women with children aged under 14 were exempted from war work and it was possible for women with other domestic responsibilties to wheedle their way out of it. This extraordinary government control over women's lives helped to harness the economic life of the nation to strategies for winning the war. The government monitored the labour needs of industry and the armed forces, and tried to find new sources of labour, in order to match up supply and demand. Women's labour was, throughout the war, dignified with the term 'woman power'.

The unprecedented control over women's lives took place just as day-to-day living became more stressful. Women had to juggle paid and unpaid work when the latter grew more time-consuming. Rationing made shopping and cooking more difficult; married women in paid work with young children required nurseries, which were not provided in adequate numbers. Those living in cities and subjected to enemy air attacks had to cope with added danger, uncertainty, inconvenience and tiredness.

Government policies helped to turn organised women's sense of grievance into a campaign against institutionalised sexism. This, in turn, meant that women campaigners focused more on the issues which united them than on those which had divided them over the past couple of decades. Alison Oram has pointed to the contradictory nature of the war for women. Britain's defence of democracy in other countries inspired British women to fight for greater political participation for themselves; the rhetoric of equality of sacrifice encouraged them to fight against blatantly discriminatory wartime measures. The policy of evacuating cities meant that women took on further responsibilities in the family, and this helped to politicise women's role in the family.[1]

This chapter examines the opportunities for women to make policy and the limitations they experienced. Harold Smith has argued that in the initial stages of the war women exercised more influence than in the later stages. At first, women formed the Woman Power Committee (WPC) and Women's Publicity and Planning Association (WPPA), and harried the government successfully in order to gain equal compensation for civilian women and men suffering war-related injuries. Their influence then subsided.[2] Yet, even in the early days of the war, it is hard to see women, despite their activities, and important role in implementing policy, actually drawing up policies. The relationship between government and women's groups was largely a one-way process. War, by diverting women's time and disrupting their lives, enhanced the role of some women's organisations while constraining others.

Women's groups organised and planned together, and lobbied government. They played a crucial role in implementing government policy on the home front. While the relationship between government and women's groups was closer than ever before, they remained at one remove from the heart of power. In the 1920s and 1930s various women-dominated organisations had campaigned unsuccessfully for a range of social policies. Was not this the moment to have their ideas translated into policy? Yet, it was not to be: thousands of women spent the war implementing government policies with no quid pro quo during, or at the end of, the war.

Women's groups, such as the Women's Voluntary Service (WVS), whose role was especially important to the government, had no particular interest in furthering the power relations of women in general vis-à-vis government,

---

1. Alison Oram, ' "Bombs don't discriminate!" Women's political activism in the Second World War', in Christine Gledhill and Gillian Swanson, *Nationalising Femininity: Culture, Sexuality and British Cinema in the Second World War* (Manchester, 1996), pp. 53–65.
2. Harold Smith, 'The effect of the war on the status of women', in Harold Smith, ed., *War and Social Change* (Manchester, 1986), pp. 223–5.

although senior members certainly wrestled with government for control over WVS activities. Women's organisations which struggled for women to play a bigger role in policy making were more dispensable to governments. Moreover, while it was nothing new for government to work through voluntary organisations, it now tended to work through new bodies, such as the WVS, rather than longer-established organisations which aimed to promote women's interests.[3]

The close relationship between women's organisations and government was crucial to the war on the home front. Women voluntarily organised themselves and took initiatives, mainly over issues affecting women and children. They critically assessed their own performance as the war continued and, recognising the limitations of voluntary and untrained women, attempted to operate more effectively in meeting wartime needs by improving their coordination and knowledge, and by putting pressure on government to use professionally trained women. A number of women also implemented government policy in a trained and paid capacity, working, for example, in industry as welfare supervisors.

Despite the close relations between women's organisations and women MPs, and between organised women and the government, there were few women in influential positions, and this lack of real power had a knock-on effect on women's longer-term impact on social policies. Women demonstrated a strong interest in reconstruction policies for the post-war world, and attempted to influence policies, but with little success. This interest in the post-war world was not confined to Britain. British professional women and European refugee women established close links as they discussed possibilities for the future, thus linking, as in the past, domestic and foreign affairs. Women's concern over the welfare of European women and children was also demonstrated in the Aid to Russia campaign, when they worked with governmental blessing and support, and in the campaign to raise the blockade against occupied Europe when their ire was directed at government policy.

Women's organisations and the war effort

In 1938 Sir Samuel Hoare, the Home Secretary, asked Stella Isaacs, Lady Reading (1894–1971), to form a women's organisation, funded by central

---

3. Vera Douie, *The Lesser Half: A Survey of the Laws, Regulations and Practices Introduced During The Present War Which Embody Discrimination Against Women* (1943), p. 26; H.M.D. Parker, *Manpower: A Study of War-time Policy and Administration* (1957), p. 395.

and local government, and attached to local authorities, to work voluntarily to solve problems arising from the war. Stella Reading took up the challenge and set up the WVS, which by 1942 boasted over 1 million women volunteers. The WVS, more than any other women's group, was used by the government to implement its policies on the home front. The WVS was crucial to evacuation plans – indeed, on 1 September 1939 17,000 members helped organise the evacuation of the cities – and it worked in a variety of capacities with civilians, in particular 'refugees' from home and abroad, and with the armed forces. It organised feeding for those bombed out of their homes, but more especially for the civil defence services. Its work ranged from making black-out curtains for hospitals to judging drama competitions. The WVS worked with local authorities and the Home Office over evacuation; and with the Ministry of Health over transport and information on lost or separated relatives of refugees from Holland, Belgium and France. It worked with the Ministry of Labour on welfare, opening creches and day nurseries for children of married women working in the factories, and setting up emergency canteens inside factories.[4]

The main work of the WVS was in connection with the evacuation of cities. The WVS helped to move children, and in some cases their mothers, from cities to rural areas where it was hoped that they would not be subjected to enemy bombs or gas attacks. The cities were first evacuated during September 1939, although by the beginning of 1940 80 per cent of evacuees had returned home. Further evacuations took place during the blitz in late 1940, and again in 1944 when the Germans dropped V1 and V2 rockets. People with private means, roughly 2 million, arranged their own moves. So the WVS, who were unpaid, had time to spare and were therefore predominantly middle-class, helped organise the transfer of mainly working-class children and women. Many WVS women from rural areas had little knowledge and even less understanding of the lives of those in the cities. While the WVS contributed to the evacuation of the cities, many in the WVS spread alarmist and judgemental stories about poor inner-city children. Pride and prejudice greeted many of the children.[5]

Members of the WVS immediately perceived evacuation not only as a means of protecting the vulnerable from the enemy, but also as a means of bringing about social change. Lady Reading spoke in October 1939 of evacuation being the 'biggest social experiment since the Exodus'. Another WVS member wrote that better social conditions in the peace might depend

---

4. WVS, *Bulletin* (December 1940, February 1941, July 1941).
5. John Macnicol, 'The evacuation of schoolchildren', in Harold Smith, ed., *War and Social Change*, pp. 6–7, 27.

on finding a solution to war problems on the home front. Perhaps it was to encourage those dealing with evacuees that readers of the WVS *Bulletin* were told 'enuresis and impetigo may have a real historical value'.[6]

The work undertaken by the WVS was novel in the extent of its contribution to life on the home front, it was, nevertheless, traditional women's work: organising creches, nurseries and feeding, and undertaking clerical work, as well as often running the new Citizens' Advice Bureaux. Much of the work, moreover, could be better described as 'public-spirited' rather than war-related work. There was, for instance, the 'Housewives Section' of the WVS for those women who could only volunteer to help neighbours in the same street. Looking at WVS activities raises questions about what could be described as 'war work', and the problematic nature of the relationships it created. While helping to forge links between women and the government, it did not of itself create greater social solidarity. There is evidence that class distinctions persisted. The WVS *Bulletin*, for example, reported in a patronising tone that a cleaning lady 'presented rather a problem when she came into a WVS office some weeks ago, stating that she wished to take up voluntary work'. They gave her some cleaning to do.[7]

Initially, at least, the WVS displayed an authoritarian and unrealistic approach towards evacuees and their parents. In December 1939 the WVS did not want children to be 'allowed' to return home for Christmas or to be visited by their parents, not because of a concern over their safety but to ensure that the children remained in their billets.[8]

The WVS also played a crucial part in a small wartime imperial project on its own doorstep. After Italy entered the war, Gibraltarian civilians – roughly 5,359 women, 1,690 men and 392 children – were shipped to Britain. Only those contributing to the war effort remained on the Rock, and plenty of accommodation was thereby released for use by the armed forces. Once the Gibraltarians had arrived in Britain the British government faced two linked problems: how to accommodate and how to occupy them. Out of these problems developed an imperial social experiment, in which the WVS was to play a key role: an attempt was made through 'welfare work' to inculcate in the evacuees British 'habits and outlook'. The presence of the Gibraltarians in Britain, and the voluntary welfare work, reinforced tensions between the British government and the Gibraltarians, between the government and the WVS, and between the WVS and the evacuees. It also brought to the surface tensions between the indigenous

---

6. Women in Council, *Newsletter* (October 1939); WVS, *Bulletin* (December 1939).
7. WVS, *Bulletin* (July 1941, April 1942, October 1943).
8. WVS, *Bulletin* (December 1939).

population and the evacuees, and between the former and the bureaucracy of wartime government. Tensions revolved around class differences (the evacuees were poorer Gibraltarians as the better-off had made their own arrangements for leaving the Rock), and cultural differences (although the evacuees carried British passports the majority were Spanish-speaking).

Ministers as well as backbenchers displayed irritation, and viewed the Gibraltarians with a sense of 'otherness'. A lonely plea from Eleanor Rathbone for the Gibraltarians to be moved out of London for their own safety was not considered administratively feasible, and her defence of the men who did not work because of prejudice against them, not through their own unwillingness, received short shrift. Clear cultural differences existed over food, but the authorities did not regard as genuine complaints which the Gibraltarian women expressed in letters home. It was thought that they grumbled in order to arouse the men's sympathy and to squeeze more money out of them, as well as to make them feel guilty because the women suspected that the men were enjoying themselves with other women on the Rock. Florence Horsbrugh, the Conservative Parliamentary Secretary to the Minister of Health with responsibility for the Gibraltarians, publicly criticised them for a whole range of failings. Ernest Brown, Minister of Health, remarked on their 'entirely different habits', and commented that there was no more difficult job in the war than dealing with them. 'Dealing with them' included trying to teach them about community life, and strengthening ties between the two countries.[9]

Although independent of the government, the work of the WVS with the evacuees was often government-inspired and government-related. The WVS tried to make the evacuees more aware of the 'Mother Country'. It organised a range of activities, such as Girl Guide and Boy Scout troops, first aid lectures, language classes, war savings groups, summer outings, libraries, sport, cinema shows, dancing, and various crafts. They also attempted to start a WVS group among them to 'foster a spirit of service . . . completely lacking at present'. The WVS recognised that their efforts were not on the whole welcome, commenting that the women would rather be left alone to live their lives without interference or organised activities. The greatest hostility towards the WVS was when its work was overtly for the government, as on one occasion when the WVS was distributing means-tested clothes and the evacuees apparently responded with abuse and threats.[10]

---

9. HC Deb. vol. 371 col. 946 8 May 1941; vol. 377 col. 1876 19 February 1942 Eleanor Rathbone; vol. 408 col. 1353 27 February 1945 Florence Horsbrugh; vol. 372 col. 1094 2 June 1941 Ernest Brown. PRO CO 91/516/6 and CO 91/516/12.

10. PRO CO 91/516/12 and CO 91/515/8 Report on welfare work started in Gibraltarian centres by WVS 21 March 1941; CO 91/515/9 4 December 1941.

Ministers and civil servants did not always enjoy an easy relationship with the WVS. Members of the government's committee on Gibraltarians were appointed by name in order to keep certain women off the committee. Within Whitehall it was thought necessary to 'tread warily' with the WVS because of their independence, so although the evacuees saw the WVS as simply the arm of government, the government itself saw the relationship as more complex. At times praise was lavished on the WVS, at other times the civil service criticised the WVS for 'spoon-feeding' Gibralterians, and reinforcing their lack of initiative.[11]

The extent to which the WVS exercised independence is hard to gauge. Most of those in government circles perceived Lady Reading as highly independent, although others saw the WVS as little more than the stooge of government. The WVS's autonomy fluctuated. Its very existence was the result of government policy, but the WVS was able to use a fair degree of independence in operating evacuation on the ground; it then took the initiative in developing a range of activities, and the manner in which it implemented policies reflected its individual members. When it adopted an authoritarian attitude towards evacuees, for instance, in trying to prevent children returning home, it was ignored the length and breadth of the country. Close coordination with local authorities became increasingly important as the mass of regulations grew and procedures were formalised, which inevitably reduced the scope of the WVS for independent initiatives.[12]

Other women's organisations had a less direct and intimate relationship with government than the WVS, although some of them were involved in war-related work. The Women's Institute (WI) was not officially involved with evacuation but it did organise creches, communal meals, and entertainment and welfare work for the armed forces, and it preserved fruits. It also worked closely with government departments. In 1942 it had links with ten departments, including the Board of Education over school meals in rural areas; the Ministry of Health over diphtheria immunisation and VD campaigns; the Ministry of Supply over the collection of medicinal herbs, and the Treasury, over national savings. The WI and other voluntary organisations, such as the Townswomen's Guild and Girl Guides, occasionally pooled their resources for the war effort.[13]

Women's groups propped up and implemented government plans, so that the government was, in effect, 'purchasing' for free the services and skills of

---

11. PRO CO 91/515/10; CO 91/516/12 Acheson to Shuckburgh 8 January 1941.
12. Fawcett Library WF/A1 WGPW Executive Committee (15 June 1943). WGPW (December 1939). WVS, *Bulletin* (August 1945).
13. WI February 1941; WI, *Annual Report* 1943.

women's voluntary organisations. Many women did not feel, however, that government was making full use of their skills.

Professional and political women

Women put pressure on the government to make more use of professional women. The women saw their interests and those of the country as complementary. Government, however, found it easier to use women in a voluntary capacity in the WVS, which required no rethinking of, or disruption to, its employment practices. Whereas government did learn a number of lessons from the First World War, there was no example of incorporating women into high-level posts to follow. In the spring of 1940 women's organisations were perturbed at the failure of government and big business to make more use of professional women 'when idleness is a national waste'. Women in the professions and in women's organisations saw the war as an opportunity for an enhanced role for themselves. The war increased their collective sense of worth, even though government showed little interest in making use of their skills, in contrast to the way in which it briskly exploited untrained and unpaid women. The British Federation of Business and Professional Women (BFBPW) repeatedly expressed its concern at the way women's worth was not being recognised and at the limited contribution of women to the war effort, which it contrasted unfavourably with the number of Soviet women in positions of real authority. In March 1942 the BFBPW criticised the failure of the government to appoint more women as divisional and assistant divisional food officers, posts in which it was thought that women could apply to the nation their knowledge of food gained in the home.[14]

With no encouragement from government, and with war on the horizon, women had paid for themselves to be trained as supervisors in industry, but they then had difficulty in finding work. Only later, in 1941, did the government take overall responsibility for the training of welfare supervisors. The Ministry of Labour, but not the supply departments, had been converted to the idea that welfare work was a useful part of industrial relations strategy. The Women's Consultative Committee (see below) criticised the supply departments for their lack of interest in welfare and personnel management. Even the Ministry of Labour's interest was short-lived;

---

14. Women in Council, *Newsletter* (March 1940). BFBPW, *Women at Work* (February 1941, December 1941, March 1942, Winter 1944).

industrial welfare work never became part of the longer-term strategy of the Ministry.

Government did, however, make more use of trained social workers than in the past, and this policy was not later reversed. A number of government departments employed social workers during the war. From mid-1940 social workers found work in regional welfare offices of the Ministry of Health dealing with evacuation. The Ministry encouraged local authorities to employ experienced social workers to develop welfare provision for evacuees and for those made homeless through bombing raids.[15] The high proportion of male probation officers meant that the service was greatly depleted by enlistment, which gave a few women the opportunity to take up responsible work which would have otherwise been denied them. Only in the male-dominated probation service was a war bonus paid, and then the bonus was less for women than for men. Almoners were in greater demand than previously and their numbers doubled to 650. With major population movements, hospital admissions involved more administration. In 1942 the Ministry of Health asked the Institute of Almoners for its views on the future of the health services. Although the Institute replied that it was important for almoners to be able to place patients in the context of their home and social setting, no mention was made of almoners in the 1944 White Paper on the future of the health services.[16]

Nurses, the largest group of health service workers, do not appear to have been asked, or to have offered, their views on future services. Relations between government and nurses did, nevertheless, become much closer than in the past, and as a result of government intervention in hospital services nursing started to become more homogeneous. The Emergency Medical Service provided the much-needed coordination of wartime hospital services; it began to break down the resourcing differences between hospitals which, in turn, helped to standardise working conditions for nurses; and in April 1941 the government introduced a national pay scale for nurses.[17]

Women doctors also developed a closer relationship with government, and one that was more cordial than during the First World War. Before war broke out the Medical Women's Federation (MWF) and War Office agreed on the role women doctors would play in the armed forces: women were to receive the same rates of pay as men doctors and the same allowances

15. Women in Council, *Newsletter* (March 1940, February 1941, June 1941); Vera Douie, *The Lesser Half*, p. 59. Peggy Inman, *Labour in the Munitions Industries* (1957), p. 261; E. Younghusband, *The Newest Profession: A Short History of Social Work* (1981), p. 23.

16. R.G. Walton, *Women in Social Work* (1975), pp. 168–9, 174, 177.

17. Robert Dingwall, Anne Marie Rafferty and Charles Webster, *An Introduction to the Social History of Nursing* (1988), pp. 103–5.

as single men doctors. The Federation's request for women to be commissioned was rejected by the War Office which instead granted women 'relative rank'. Women, through the MWF and the British Medical Association (BMA) continued to press for commissions (which in 1950 the War Office finally conceded). A number of women played an important role in organising the delivery of medical services. Dr Letitia Fairfield was appointed to the Royal Army Medical Corps as the senior woman Medical Officer with the relative rank of Lieutenant-Colonel; Dr Dorothy Fenwick was appointed senior woman Medical Officer to the RAF medical service, with the relative rank of Squadron Leader, and Dr Genevieve Rewcastle was appointed (the sole woman) to the medical department of the Royal Navy, with the relative rank of Surgeon-Lieutenant. Women doctors served with the armed forces, treating women and men, in all war zones, and although they were not meant to be posted to the front line, in practice it was not always possible to make this distinction. The MWF pressed successfully for women to serve on a range of medical boards and panels of consultants, but it did not succeed in getting a woman doctor appointed to the Ministry of Labour's Whitehall staff. It did, however, attend conferences at the Ministry of Labour, and its negotiations must have been assisted by the presence of Dr Janet Campbell, who for many years had held a senior post at the Ministry of Health (until forced to retire on marriage), on the MWF's team. The MWF lobbied government over issues ranging from nursery schools, the employment of women in the Foreign and Diplomatic Service, equal pay and the birth rate. Hence, women doctors not only contributed to medical services in wartime (as they had done a generation earlier), but also played a more wide-ranging role in pressing for social policy changes which affected women's overall wellbeing.[18]

In September 1943 Eleanor Rathbone commented that men still resented women in authority.[19] A few women did wield authority but they were spread too thinly to make a collective impact. Of the 14 wartime women MPs – eight Conservative, four Labour, one Liberal and one Independent – one Labour and one Conservative joined the government. Ellen Wilkinson was briefly Parliamentary Secretary at the Ministry of Pensions and then Parliamentary Secretary at the Ministry of Home Security. She was responsible for the high-profile air raid shelter policy. Initially she and her department were unpopular with Londoners for their tardy response to the need for deep shelters. She was also involved in the decision taken in 1941 for young

18. Wellcome Institute for the History of Medicine, Contemporary Medical Archives. Medical Women's Federation Annual Reports 1940–45.
19. BFBPW, *Women at Work* (September 1943).

unmarried women to undertake work of national importance or auxiliary civil defence work. In August 1942 everyone aged between 20 and 45, not doing alternative war work, was liable for firewatching duties. This was unprecedented in Europe and was greeted with criticism by those who did not wish to do it. Wilkinson was sympathetic to firewatching exemptions for women either with young children or working very long hours, but she had no patience with the large number of other women who tried to evade it.[20]

Between 1939 and 1945 Florence Horsburgh was Parliamentary Secretary at the Ministry of Health. From 1939 she was involved in planning the evacuation of the cities, and in policies for the health and welfare of air raid victims. There is no evidence, however, that she participated in discussions over the future of health services. In 1944 Horsbrugh undertook a successful tour of Canada and the USA on behalf of the government delivering speeches and meeting public health experts.[21]

In the spring of 1945 Churchill sent both Horsbrugh and Wilkinson as part of the British delegation to a conference in San Francisco where the UN charter was drafted, even though neither had responsibilities for foreign affairs or a related brief. They made it plain to foreign journalists that they were attending as political figures in their own right who, as members of the government could speak with authority, and were not there as women. Indeed, Wilkinson tartly told reporters that she thought it 'absurd' that women should present a united front. The two women were notable more for their contrasting styles than for any similarities.[22]

A number of women MPs sat on advisory committees. Jennie Adamson, Labour MP, 1938–46, sat on the War Service Grants Advisory Committee; Lady Davidson, Conservative MP, 1937–59, sat on the Select Committee on National Expenditure along with Ellen Wilkinson until she was appointed to a government post. Megan Lloyd George, a Liberal, chaired the Salvage and Waste Committee on which all the women MPs sat. Eleanor Rathbone, who undertook a great deal of work for refugees, sat with Lady Reading on the Foreign Office's Advisory Council on Aliens.[23]

The government appointed a few women to senior posts who were able to influence the way in which policies developed. There were two women

---

20. Ellen Wilkinson was also Parliamentary Secretary at Pensions for five months in 1940; she left the government in May 1945. In the caretaker government at the end of the war Horsbrugh was Parliamentary Secretary at Food, and Thelma Cazelet-Keir was Parliamentary Secretary at the Ministry of Education.

21. Charles Webster, *The Health Services since the War, Vol. 1 Problems of Health Care: The National Health Service before 1957* (1988), the official history of the NHS, makes no reference to Horsbrugh. Churchill College Cambridge, Florence Horsbrugh papers 6/10.

22. Churchill College, Cambridge Florence Horsbrugh papers 1/4.

23. Peggy Scott, *British Women in War* (1941), pp. 260, 265, 269–70, 274.

in the Ministry of Labour at an advisory level, with the possibility of influencing policy. Caroline Haslett, 1895–1957, had long promoted women's interests. She was a suffragette and qualified engineer. In 1919 she became secretary of the newly formed Women's Engineering Society and later editor of its journal. She then founded the Electrical Association for Women and edited its journal. Her work aimed to improve women's education and to open up careers in engineering. She also tried to make women more aware of the possibilities of using electricity in the home, in the belief that it would lighten housework. In 1940 she became an advisor to the Ministry of Labour on the training of women. At the same time Verena Holmes was appointed technical officer to the Ministry of Labour attached to the training department. In 1941 the Ministry of Labour established a Women's Consultative Committee to offer advice, no more, on recruitment and registration of women. Bevin's Parliamentary Secretary offered to chair the committee on the grounds that he would be able to resist the women's charms, and Bevin agreed: such attitudes do not suggest that they intended to take the women seriously. The nine women members, representing a range of women's groups, met twice a month with the Parliamentary Secretary to the Minister in the chair; Haslett attended the meetings in her capacity as advisor to the Minister. She also undertook propaganda work for the Ministry, broadcasting a series of talks in which she encouraged women to undertake war work, and another series in which she explained how the register of women for war work operated. (Employment exchanges actually interviewed women and decided whose domestic responsibilities justified exemption from war work.)

The experience of Verena Holmes when she tried to change pay policy illustrates the difficulties women faced in influencing policies, even when they were working within Whitehall. Here was a woman who did not mince her words, criticised a policy the men had drawn up and suggested an alternative to the 'crazy structure' which they had built. In 1941 she repeatedly criticised, on the grounds of inefficiency and injustice, the unequal wages payed in munitions industries – which in practice meant women being paid less then men – based on an agreement reached in 1940 between the Engineering Employers' Federation (EEF) and the trade unions. She argued that 'women munition workers had about as much say in agreements on their wages as Czecho-Slovakia had in the Munich agreement', because they had no independent organisation or powerful representation. Thus, their wages were settled by two powerful bodies, each considering male interests. 'The poor wages, the anomolies and much unfairness are the results.' She explained to her male colleagues why women were not to blame for their weak position: women were only just coming into munition work when the agreement was drawn up; few of them had a past or future in engineering; the majority could not afford the trade union subscriptions, and they feared victimisation. Yet, 'Women in industry are fast becoming essential to our national effort. They are entitled to a fair return for their labours, but to whom can they turn to obtain it?' When a colleague complained that her criticisms were only destructive she responded with an immediate policy for a minimum wage, a medium-term one for women's rates to rise to those of men, and a long-term policy for family allowances.[24]

The most sympathetic reaction to Holmes came from a colleague who adopted the fatalistic approach that it was too late to overturn an agreement even though it was flawed. Far more hostile was the Deputy Secretary, whose response demonstrates the interlocking male networks and shared assumptions which spread from industry to the heart of government policy making, and which systematically operated to the disadvantage of women. When women briefly broke into this network they were resented. 'I have discovered recently a very uneasy feeling in trade union circles on the subject of the developments in the Ministry on the subject of women in industry. The appointment of the Women's Advisory Committee has brought this to a head and I think that the underlying cause of the uneasiness is that it is felt that some of the members are not friendly to trade unions, that they resent the position of trade unions as negotiating bodies for women, and that they represent the feminist movement. It would be most unfortunate if the Ministry becomes the battleground of women v men.' Finally, he dismissed Holmes as having 'insufficient regard for the facts', and commenting that 'For men their work is a life matter.' His reaction shows why individual women in Whitehall were not able to overturn policies which were drawn up by men and from the point of view of men's interests.[25]

Within the civil service women, nevertheless, had some scope for influencing policy. The number of women in the administrative grade indicates that women were now able to forge careers in the civil service, in contrast to the situation during the First World War when this was not possible except for Inspectors, or others in 'technical' posts. Whereas in the First World War Whitehall had been willing to incorporate only men into responsible posts for the duration, in the Second World War women were also incorporated. In July 1944 there were 14 women in grades above that of Principal and 100 women in the grade of Principal. Women took on new and enhanced responsibilities in a number of departments. In December 1939 E.S. Fraser was put in charge of one of the Ministry of Labour's 12 divisional areas. The Board of Trade appointed Mrs Newman, a London

---

24. PRO LAB 8/378 for all correspondence and quotations in this, and following, paragraph.
25. PRO LAB 8/378.

County Council alderman, to sit alongside eight men on the Prices Regulation Committee which met weekly throughout the war. In 1941 when the Board of Trade introduced clothes rationing it sought the opinion of a businesswoman, a housewife and a woman buyer. The Ministry of Food had at least two women out of the ten consumer members on each of the 1,500 local Food Control Committees. By 1942 18 of the 249 assistant divisional food officers were women. From 1941 to 1944 Sybil Campbell, a barrister, was Assistant Divisional Food Officer (Enforcement) in the London division of the Ministry of Food, with hundreds of enforcement officers working under her to catch black marketeers. The Ministry of Food used women not only for implementing its rationing policy but also in its educative work on how to eke out limited resources. Hundreds of women sent in details of how they managed with short supplies. The Food Advice Division initially operated under Helen Tass of King's College until her death in 1942, when Edith Walker of the WI took over. The Ministry of Food invited women to demonstrate local dishes and pick up tips from each other. Stafford Cripps, Minister of Aircraft Production, appointed Ann Shaw to serve on the Production Committee. At the Ministry of Supply 30 women calculated the war materials required for the invasion of the Continent while at the War Office Masika Lancaster made scale models on which the prefabricated landing stages used in the invasion of Normandy were based. The Ministry of Information used various women who travelled around numerous countries presenting Britain's position on the war.[26]

Evelyn Sharp and Alix Kilroy were among the women who had joined the administrative grade of the civil service in the mid-1920s and were now in senior posts. Evelyn Sharp, promoted to Assistant Secretary in the Ministry of Health, organised temporary hospitals and extra hospital beds. Alix Kilroy, at the Board of Trade, initially dealt with Regional Controllers. In 1942 she was promoted Principal Assistant Secretary in charge of a large department with responsibility for non-textile factories and for furniture rationing. All her senior staff were men. For the first time in her career she felt that she met prejudice from an Assistant Secretary who thought he had been asked to undertake work which was beneath him. At the beginning of 1943 Kilroy was put in charge of a newly formed Reconstruction Department to work out plans for peace-time policies in the home market.[27]

Although the numbers of women civil servants had grown over the past generation, the numbers were still paltry; women were not satisfied; they

26. Vera Douie, *Daughters of Britain* (1949), pp. 137–9.
27. Alix Meynell, *Public Servant, Private Woman: An Autobiography* (1988), pp. 208–11, 217.

called for more women in senior civil service posts but to no avail.[28] While women were used extensively to implement government policy, and to offer advice on various aspects of the war on the home front, which inevitably intimately affected women, women were not so evident at the policy-making level. None of the ministers involved with planning long-term reform were known for having an interest in gender equality. None of the Labour Party ministers, in keeping with the Party policy-making machine, took an especial interest in women's welfare.

It was not simply a question of the small number of women at the policy-making level but also of their attitudes. The presence of women in senior posts did not necessarily mean that other women's interests were served or the views of women's organisations reflected in advice to ministers; this was demonstrated by Mary Smieton, an Assistant Secretary at the Ministry of Labour, who in league with Zoe Puxley, an Assistant Secretary at the Ministry of Health, tried to block the wartime expansion of children's nurseries, believing that mothers should be at home with their children.[29]

It was certainly not automatic, moreover, for women to be incorporated into government, even when issues screamed out for an input from women. The committee set up in 1942 to look into women's 'welfare' (actually their morals) in the services at first did not contain a single woman; there was such an outcry that it was reconstituted with Violet Markham in the chair; other members included Thelma Cazelet-Keir and Edith Summerskill. This was not the only occasion when women were used to pursue questions of other women's morality. Summerskill also sat on a committee on women's conscription which decided that a convicted prostitute should be exempted from service. As in the First World War, organised women displayed a heightened concern over the morality and personal safety of other women. A wide range of women's organisations saw this need being met in part by the appointment of more women police, but the issue of women police was firmly distanced from feminism. Perhaps because of official hostility to suffragettes who became women patrols in the First World War, the Woman Power Committee firmly denied that the cause of women police was a feminist issue.[30]

In June 1940 most women MPs, with the exception of Horsbrugh and Wilkinson, who were in the government, and some Labour MPs, who joined later, collaborated with leading women in other fields to form the

---

28. Women in Council, *Newsletter* (May 1941).
29. Penny Summerfield, *Women Workers in the Second World War* (Beckenham, 1984), p. 68.
30. Edith Summerskill, *A Woman's World* (1967), p. 76; LSE WPC (1 August 1940).

Woman Power Committee (WPC) in an attempt to counter the absence of women at the heart of government and, initially, to put pressure on the government over the numbers of unemployed women. Such formal cross-party cooperation between women was only possible because party politics had been suspended for the duration and men, with two women, from all the parties worked together in government. Even so, there was lingering suspicion from some women that the committee would promote middle-class women's interests at the expense of those of working-class women.

The WPC sprang from women's position of weakness in the war, not their collective strength. The two most powerful women in Parliament, those with government posts, did not belong to the WPC. The origins of the WPC lay in pressure from women's organisations on women MPs to urge the government to make better use of women's labour. The WPC was a response by women MPs to feminist pressure groups. The BFBPW was particularly concerned that trained women could not find work. The women MPs duly went to the Treasury with a 'national not a feminist plea', and when the Supply Board refused to appoint a woman, Caroline Haslett suggested that the women form their own committee. The WPC met fortnightly at Nancy Astor's London home when Parliament was in session. Irene Ward, a Conservative backbencher since 1931, chaired the meetings. (She was defeated in 1945 but returned to Parliament in 1950, when she devoted herself to the campaign for equal pay. Throughout her long parliamentary career she campaigned for better, and equal, treatment of women.)

The WPC firmly set itself against undertaking any welfare or philanthropic work. It also agreed not to touch anything which fell within the province of the trade unions. It urged Ernest Bevin, Minister of Labour and National Service, to appoint a Woman Power Board and a woman minister, but instead he appointed General Appleyard as liaison officer with the Committee. The WPC immediately began lobbying government over a range of issues which grew in scope over the years, but revolved around the care and safety of mothers and children under five, including nursery schools, evacuation, equal injury allowance, women police, and dependants' allowances for women in the services. The WPC enjoyed close relations with government, and the cordial nature of meetings with government ministers was frequently commented on, but they rarely produced results for the women. In 1941 the WPC complained about the large number of committees with few or no women; two years later it was not surprised that the Ministry of Labour was organising an industrial health conference with no input from women. In March 1943 the WPC met with Clement Attlee, the Deputy Prime Minister, and this raised hopes that opening up a direct link with a member of the War Cabinet would prove to be useful; there is no evidence that the hopes were realised.[31]

Women MPs often coordinated their approach, as, for instance, in March 1941, when they agreed the different points they would make in a debate on the recruitment and use of women's labour. Irene Ward pointed out, 'Today, for the first time when we are officially discussing matters relating to women, we have got the women members of Parliament of all parties united in a common policy.' Women spoke in all the women's labour, known as woman power, debates. In the first woman power debate in March 1941 most of the women spoke. They dominated the debate, engaging in spats with male MPs. In subsequent debates, on 5 March 1942 and the debate on women in national service on 3 August 1943, men played a larger part. In March 1941 Irene Ward opined that 'Women should be given a share in the planning of policy', and complained that women had no executive or administrative job of real responsibility. She told the House, 'We do not want people to be regarded in the war as men or women, but, as is our right, as citizens, proud to defend the liberties of this country and of the democracies of the world.' Thelma Cazalet-Keir remarked, '. . . what a long way we still have to go before co-operative equality in high places has been established between men and women'. Summerskill voiced the concern of many women on 5 March 1942 when she complained that 'the war is being prosecuted by both sexes but directed only by one', and she wondered 'what the country would say if the whole question of man-power were dealt with by women'. Ward demanded more cooperation between women and men 'in all aspects of our national effort. . .'.[32]

Getting their voices heard and pushing women's issues to the fore was one thing, dispelling ignorance and prejudice was more difficult. Sir George Broadbridge commented in the 1942 woman power debate that 'Women are not mechanically minded like men, and it would not surprise me if the response of women for munitions work was not on a large scale.' A year later in the woman power debate Sir Henry Morris-Jones announced, 'I am a great believer in women in the home . . . the home is the paramount place intended for women. . . .'[33]

Even though women had formed the WPC because of their concern over women in the workforce, in practice their time was largely devoted to issues affecting women outside the workplace, and their children. Trade

31. LSE WPC 28 June 1940, 7 Jan 1941, 27 May 1941, 2 March 1943, July 1941.
32. HC Deb. 20 March 1941 vol. 370 col. 325, 327 Ward, Cazalet col. 351; HC Deb. 5 March 1942 vol. 378 col. 848 Summerskill, Ward col. 827.
33. HC Deb. 5 March 1942 vol. 378 col. 843 Sir George Broadbridge, 3 August 1943 vol. 391 col. 2175 Sir Henry Morris-Jones.

union hostility to the WPC meant that it tried to keep off trade unionists' patch. The WPC's concern over the problem of split responsibilities for children between the Ministry of Health and Board of Education led them to try, unsuccessfully, to persuade ministers to set up a Department of Child Welfare.[34] (The American one may have been their inspiration.) Thus, although, at first glance, the WPC was concerned with different issues from the bulk of women in the labour movement, who saw the WPC as a voice for middle-class women, in practice their concerns were similar, with women in the labour movement campaigning for the government to supply milk, control rents and provide better council housing.

The WPC issued regular reports on the use of women's labour, investigated complaints and forwarded them to the relevant departments. Its work also received publicity in 1943 when Ethel Wood wrote *Mainly for Men*, which highlighted and detailed women's unequal treatment in the labour market, and the work of the WPC to counter this inequality. The WPC rarely looked to issues beyond Britain's shores, although in 1943 it did raise the issues of children in occupied Europe, and it put pressure on the government to provide refuge for Jews and other groups being exterminated by the Nazis.[35]

The Women's Publicity and Planning Association (WPPA) began life as a means of publicising abroad what British women were doing. It soon switched to bringing women's activities to the attention of the British government and to demanding changes, in particular more women in public life and equal citizenship for women and men. It is a further example of the way in which a range of women's organisations came together during the war to work and campaign together. The WPPA was formed after a meeting on 12 December 1939, called by Margery Corbett Ashby and Rebecca Sief, and attended by representatives of numerous women's organisations, including the Women's Engineering Association, Medical Women's International Association, Women's Cooperative Guild (WCG), Women's Parliamentary Association, Women's Peace Crusade, National Council of Women (NCW), WVS, Women's International League for Peace and Freedom (WILPF), National Union of Women Teachers, Townswomen's Guild, and the WI as well as a Foreign Office and three Ministry of Information representatives. Initially, it seemed that the Ministry of Information would use the WPPA as a means of bridging the gap between Whitehall and the country, as well as Britain and the Empire. Such high hopes soon turned

---

34. LSE WPC 21 May 1941.
35. LSE WPC 2 February, 16 February 1943.

sour; the women wrote articles for the Ministry of Information's use, but as the latter failed to inform the WPPA what, if any, material it used, the WPPA decided to abandon this channel of publicity and instead to publish its own journal with women's articles. In the summer of 1940 after the government refused WPPA paper for its publication, Corbett Ashby arranged for the WPPA to take over the *Women's International News*, the paper of the International Alliance of Women for Suffrage and Equal Citizenship, for the duration. From then on the WPPA's activities were directed primarily at the British government as it campaigned for equal compensation for war injuries and equal pay. It employed Dorothy Evans as a national organiser for an equal citizenship campaign and published her works on the subject. It also commissioned and published Vera Douie's *The Lesser Half*.[36]

Women for Westminster grew out of a WPPA committee, following a meeting with Edith Summerskill. It aimed to encourage more women to stand for Parliament and to sustain the wartime cross-party cooperation of women MPs. It was not a great success. In 1944 it had 2,703 members in 33 branches. It failed to mobilise women in large numbers as it had hoped to do; and this is instructive: the key lobbying groups were not mass movements and although the women were well placed, they were not well placed enough. Whereas most contemporaries and historians have seen the war as an explanation for social and policy change during the 1940s, Women for Westminster saw the war as the reason why they were not more successful in helping to bring about change. While the war did mobilise people and ideas, it also consumed much of women's energies, so that lectures and classes which Women for Westminster arranged for women were not as well attended as it had hoped. Women were hard-pressed to find spare time during the war; whether they were paid or voluntary workers, their days were consumed – even more than in peacetime – by immediate needs, such as working, shopping and queuing. Those living in bombed areas would have been even more tired than those in safer areas, and many wanted to enjoy themselves in their free moments, rather than engage in heavy discussion. (Women did not have time on their hands as troops would periodically have done in the tedium between actions.) Women for Westminster aimed at self-education, and also joined with other women's groups in lobbying Parliament. Indeed, there was often an overlap in membership between the various women's groups.[37]

---

36. Fawcett Library WPPA 5/WPP/A1–A8.
37. LSE R (Coll.)Misc. f. 335 VI 8. 2nd Annual report 1943–44.

Policy issues

The pursuit of gender equality loomed large in many women's wartime campaigns. Until her death in 1944 Dorothy Evans of the Six Point Group, backed by Vera Brittain and Edith Summerskill, tried to get an anti-discrimination Bill, the Equal Citizenship (Blanket) Bill, introduced, which would remove in one fell swoop all legal discrimination against women, whether in the family or the labour market. None of the parties would touch it. Many women united around the twin questions of equal pay for women and equal compensation for civilians injured as a result of the war. While women failed to secure equal pay, they were more successful in compensation for war injuries.

A number of women MPs, most notably, Jennie Adamson, Edith Summerskill, Mavis Tate, Irene Ward and Ellen Wilkinson, and women's groups had expressed their outrage in 1939 when differential rates of civilian compensation were introduced. Women sent deputations to the Ministry of Pensions, organised demonstrations and wrote letters to the press. Government held firm for fear of equal compensation opening the floodgates to equal pay. Women repeatedly raised the issue in Parliament and on 1 May 1941 nine out of ten women MPs voted against the government and in favour of equal compensation. (Nancy Astor did not vote.) The following October numerous women's groups, including the Fawcett Society, the Open Door Council and the Six Point Group, banded together to form the Equal Compensation Campaign Committee (ECCC), with Mavis Tate in the chair. The committee included representatives of the BFBPW, WPC, NCW and numerous other women's groups. It focused on persuading MPs to support equal compensation. Tate organised the lobbying of her fellow Conservatives, winning over substantial numbers of backbenchers. The 1942 Labour Party conference backed equal compensation and, by the autumn of 1942, roughly 200 MPs from across the political spectrum supported a reversal in government policy. Fearful of a back-bench revolt the government began to temper its outright opposition, but voices within the government continued to urge a firm stand against equality for fear of creating a domino effect and bringing down the principle of unequal pay. On 25 November 1942 all the women backbenchers voted against the government on the issue. Faced with crumbling support for its policy, the government set up a select committee to look into the question of equal compensation, taking the precaution of explicitly banning it from considering equal pay. Mavis Tate sat on the committee. In 1943 the government implemented the committee's recommendation for equal treatment. This was to be the high water mark of women's collective success in shifting policy. The women managed to gain enough cross-party back-bench support to create unease in the government over an issue which was based on a very hard to defend principle.[38]

From now on the focus shifted to equal pay, and from 1944 to 1947 Tate chaired the Equal Pay Campaign Committee (EPCC). The goal of equal pay for equal work proved more elusive than equal compensation for civilian war injuries. Women industrial workers received 50 to 70 per cent of men's wages for the same work, a differential which employers and male trade unionists were eager to maintain. Women's groups, women trade unionists and women MPs all pressed unsuccessfully for equal pay. The response to Verena Holmes within the Ministry of Labour has already been discussed. Until 1943 the WPC refused to take up the question, even when pressed to do so by the National Association of Women Civil Servants and the Council of Women Civil Servants, because it did not want a confrontation with trade unions and it did not think it would have any chance of success in the House of Commons. During 1943 the WPC had overcome opposition to equal compensation, so it could turn its attention to equal pay, and there were indications that the House might not be as hostile as feared. At the beginning of 1944 the EPCC began demanding equal pay for civil servants. The first opportunity for obtaining equal pay came with the Education Bill, when Thelma Cazelet-Keir put down an amendment in committee for equal pay for women and men teachers which just squeaked through in the face of government opposition. This was the only occasion when Churchill's government was defeated. The government then adopted the same tactic as that used in 1936 over the question of equal pay: it put down the amendment again as a vote of confidence. The amendment was defeated; only two women dared to vote against the government, Edith Summerskill and Agnes Hardie.

Why was the government so opposed to equal pay for teachers? There was strong hostility among male trade unionists to equal pay in industry, a fact which ensured that Ernest Bevin, previously a trade union leader and now Minister of Labour, also opposed equal pay in industry. Government worries that male trade unionists would strike against women being granted equal pay outweighed their concerns over women striking for equal pay. A further consideration for government was that a number of male teachers also opposed equal pay, although their hostility never posed the same threat as male workers in industries essential to the prosecution of the war.

---

38. Harold Smith, 'The problem of "equal pay for equal work" in Great Britain during World War II', *Journal of Modern History* 53 1981, pp. 661–2; Brian Harrison, 'Women in a men's house: the women MPs, 1919–45', *Historical Journal* 29 (1986), p. 635.

Government, nevertheless, feared that equal pay for teachers would have a domino effect: if women teachers were granted equal pay, it would be harder for government to withstand pressure from civil servants for equal pay. R.A. Butler, the President of the Board of Education, also claimed – rather disingenuously for a minister who supported greater state intervention in other fields – that if he stipulated that there should be equal pay he would be interfering in the independent pay negotiating machinery between teachers and local education authorities (LEAs), and thus destroy its independence.[39]

Fearful that the issue would not go away, in 1944 the government fobbed off the campaigners with a Royal Commission on the social, economic and financial implications of equal pay, which was forbidden to express its views on whether equal pay should be introduced. It was to be merely a 'factual' enquiry so that it could not possibly recommend equal pay, and its very existence meant that a decision was postponed until after the war. There was strong hostility at the heart of government to a select committee on equal pay. The government was still smarting from the select committee on equal compensation for civilian war injuries which was 'an awful warning of what would happen. That committee's proceedings made very little pretence at impartiality. The women members had already made up their minds and were not prepared to listen to any arguments which conflicted with their views.'[40] By the same token, government was not going to listen to any views which conflicted with its own on equal pay.

At the very moment when women were praised by others, and congratulating themselves on their contribution to the war effort, the NCW criticised women's lack of responsibility as citizens, which they blamed on unequal pay. The NCW argued that unequal pay was symptomatic of women's inferior position in society, which created irresponsibility and lack of respect among women, anti-social behaviour, apathy and greater absenteeism. Further, there was no chance of the Great Powers achieving their goals of freedom, equality and justice between nations when they did not exist within nations.[41] Such criticism of women and the nation may appear rather out of place, although it does not seem that any members of the Royal Commission were swayed in their beliefs by the evidence received. As so often, members used information to back up already formed opinions.

39. Harold Smith, 'The problem of "equal pay for equal work"', pp. 652–70; HC Debates 28 March 1944, 29 March 1944 and 30 March 1944 cols. 1356–1380.
40. Harold Smith, 'The problem of "equal pay for equal work"' (1981), pp. 652–72; PRO PREMIER 4 16/14. See especially JAB to Sir Richard Hopkins 27 April 1944.
41. Memorandum by the NCW to the Royal Commission on Equal Pay. 1944.

Social reconstruction

Women's organisations not only took up immediate social policy issues but they also looked to long-term policy questions. A number of women's organisations, notably the WPC, Women for Westminster, the Women's Group on Public Welfare (WGPW), the NCW, and the WPPA, drew up plans for, and lobbied government over, social reconstruction. The broad issues with which they were concerned: education – especially nursery education – housing and health, continued the pre-war priorities of women's campaigning. Organisations, such as the WI, which were not primarily lobbying groups also took an interest in post-war planning. The WI held conferences around the country to stimulate thought among its members over the future, and it submitted evidence to various committees, such as the Committee on Land Utilization in Rural Areas, chaired by Lord Justice Scott. Housing and education were the WI's two key interests.[42]

In September 1939 the National Council for Social Services had called a conference which led to the establishment of the Women's Group on Problems arising from Evacuation, in 1940 renamed the Women's Group on Public Welfare. The WGPW saw itself as a two-way channel of information between the 'citizen housewife' and statutory authorities. It grew out of a concern with the effects of evacuation, and therefore focused on women and children, thus continuing the pre-war concern of women's organisations with women as mothers, rather than as paid workers. Its members were mainly drawn from women's organisations concerned with child welfare, social services, education and health, trade unions and business, politics and religion, together with advisors from several government departments. It had some immediate input into government policies. It helped to secure a recognised training for helpers in nurseries, and adequate supervision for children in agricultural work. It worked with government departments, for instance in Make-Do-And-Mend campaigns. It collected information for the enquiry into the post-war organisation of domestic employment. Early in 1940, the WGPW, concerned about voluntary workers' ill-informed and unsuitable work, set up a clearing house for coordinating information.[43]

In 1943 the group made a national impact with the publication of *Our Towns: A Close-Up*. The enquiry, on which the book was based, had been urged by the WI in order to investigate the causes of 'the low standard of

---

42. WI, *Annual Report* 1943, 1944.
43. WGPW, *Report 1939–45*, p. 9; WGPW, 16 January 1940.

customs and living of a small section of women and children evacuated from towns'. The WGPW regarded the problem, and its solution, as a mixture of the structural and personal. It called for better education for all children, and the teaching of children from all social classes together so that they would grow up with a common conception of rights and duties. It also demanded action on poverty, such as better wages, children's allowances, price control of basic commodities, a national medical service, and greater control of commercial exploitation. These were far-reaching demands from a group which had been set up with an essentially conservative and judgemental outlook. The group thought social integration should be promoted through the mixing of children from different classes, housing people from different classes together and reducing poverty: their first two demands were certainly not attempted by the coalition or post-war government. The enquiry perceived class differences as the root of the problem, and solutions were therefore proposed to reduce these differences. The WGPW aimed to integrate the working class into what it saw as the middle-class norm. Problems, the enquiry believed, had been created by the separation of the classes and by poverty. There is a more explicit class analysis here than in the reports of women in the 1930s, which used a gender analysis of poverty, but in both decades the reports focused on the social and environmental difficulties of working-class mothers.

In contrast to the WGPW, the WPC was quite slow to take up questions of reconstruction. For a long time it postponed discussion of post-war issues and instead focused on immediate problems. By 1943 the WPC wanted women to be involved at a senior level in reconstruction planning. In March 1943 it sent a deputation to Attlee to complain about the lack of senior women involved with reconstruction. Women's organisations bemoaned the lack of women involved in planning for post-war housing.[44]

Women were scattered around reconstruction committees, and were therefore only able to present opinions in isolation on subjects on which organised women had definite views. Eva Taylor, Professor of Geography at the University of London, and Mrs Lionel Hichens were the only women to serve on Lord Reith's consultative panel on reconstruction. Mrs Youatt sat on the Agriculture Education Committee, chaired by Lord Justice Luxmore. Lady Denman and Mrs Lionel Hichens sat on a committee under Lord Justice Scott to consider conditions which should govern building and other constructional developments in country areas. Mary Agnes Hamilton, a temporary Under-Secretary and ex-Labour MP, sat on the Committee on

---

44. LSE WPC 10 March 1942; 2 February 1943; 2 March 1943; Women in Council, *Newsletter* (June 1942).

Reconstruction Problems under Arthur Greenwood, Minister without Portfolio. Hamilton also served on the (Beveridge) Committee on Social Insurance and Allied Services, along with Muriel Ritson, a civil servant from the Department of Health for Scotland.[45]

The Beveridge Committee very soon became a one-man show, so the limited presence of women on the Committee was not a particular disadvantage. In fact, Hamilton, unlike her colleagues, was able to influence Beveridge. Women's groups, women MPs and women members of the Committee all gave Beveridge their opinions. There was no single 'woman's view'. The NCW demanded a planned economy, an extended and universal public health service, and dependants' allowances. The Married Women's Association presented the Beveridge Committee with a seven-point charter and a draft Bill for earnings to be split between husband and wife, an unprecedented level of intervention in financial relations between wife and husband when they were not in dispute. The long-standing tension remained unresolved between those women who believed equality meant treating women and men actually the same, and those who believed that social provision should treat women and men differently in order to achieve equality.

Women's organisations greeted the Beveridge Report with varying degrees of warmth on its publication in December 1942. Most women's groups welcomed the report, although generally they disliked the different treatment of married and unmarried women, and the assumption that married women would only be at home. The Women's Freedom League (WFL) attacked the assumption embodied in the report that married women's entitlement came via their husbands. In the autumn of 1943 it held a conference to debate the report and the following year a deputation of 12 women's organisations met the Minister of Reconstruction, to no avail. The WPC also expressed a number of specific criticisms: married women who continued in employment would lose insurance rights and full benefits; married women would be encouraged to gain exemption; married women would lose their right to an individual pension on the husband's retirement; guardianship benefit was restricted to married mothers, and men paid a higher rate of contributions for the same benefits. Such criticisms did not reflect the mainly uncritical reception of the report by large sections of the population, whether women or men. The minority of critics appeared carping and divided, and stood no chance, therefore, of winning over ministers.[46]

---

45. Women in Council, *Newsletter* (February 1942).
46. WPC 4 May 1943, 15 May 1945. For this and the previous paragraph I am very dependent on Jose Harris, *Beveridge* (Oxford, 1997 edn), pp. 391–8, 417.

The 1944 Education Act did make one important advance for women by removing the marriage bar, but not for the reasons advocated by women's organisations. The Board of Education was initially loath to remove the marriage bar, but a teaching shortage and the personal predilections of Chuter Ede, the Parliamentary Secretary at the Board of Education, swung the argument. Chuter Ede made his antipathy to women clear when he asserted that he was not influenced by 'negative and feminist' reasons but by 'positive and educational' ones. He claimed, without of course being able to provide any evidence or explanation, that 'acute difficulties are not infrequently caused on staffs when a Head Mistress in her fifties who had led a life of repression has to deal with young and good looking assistants'. With the anticipated raising of the school leaving age he thought it better to have staff better able to deal with problems of adolescents than a 'sex-starved spinster'.[47] There was a yawning gulf between these ignorant comments which formed the basis of policy which directly affected women, and the detailed planning of civil servants and ministers which was behind the key clauses of the Education Act for post-war education. While the wartime planning of the new education system – with its provisions for children to receive a free education in primary and separate secondary schools, for streamlining the work of local education authorities and for the closer integration of voluntary schools with the state – came from within the Board of Education, numerous women's and women-dominated organisations did make representations to the Board throughout the war about post-war education and teaching needs. There were two notable recurrent themes, one was the need to provide high-quality nursery education, and the other was the need to ensure an adequate supply of teachers at the end of the war. Both policies fitted in with Board thinking and were taken up.

The 1945 Family Allowances Act created a false image of Whitehall prioritising the needs of mothers. While the government introduced family allowances for the second and subsequent child in order to avoid a minimum wage and to encourage labour mobility, they appeared to be a response to the long campaign headed by Eleanor Rathbone, which had, however, been primarily concerned with family poverty, particularly of mothers and their children. The extent to which government thinking was adrift from that of Eleanor Rathbone and other supporters of family allowances was made clear when the government assumed that the allowances would be paid to the father. Rathbone was furious and led the successful campaign to

---

47. Quoted in Harold Smith, 'The womanpower problem in Britain during the Second World War', *Historical Journal* 27 (1984), p. 942.

have the payments made to mothers.[48] Rathbone wanted payments made to mothers for both practical and symbolic reasons: 'This Bill gives the mother, through her children her share, although it is only a very little share so far . . . looking after children is the mother's job. Why in Heaven's name, not recognise that and stimulate the mother to do her job well by State recognition. . . . If the money is given to the mother, and if they know that the law regards it as the child's property, or the mother's property to be spent for the child, that will help them to realise that the State recognises the status of mothers.'[49]

The Family Allowances Act was the piece of welfare legislation most obviously affecting women, and the one which Beveridge claimed to be the most distinct departure from the past. Beveridge wrote of family allowances that they were 'assigned to individual citizens rearing citizens of the future, in order to make sure that they had the means for the task'.[50] Payments of 5s 0d a week for second and subsequent children were not to be sneezed at in August 1946 when family allowances were first paid.

Would social policies have been substantially different if women had played a more central role in policy making? All sorts of groups, including women's ones, were discussing and forwarding proposals for the future. If women had enjoyed a high-profile input to reconstruction planning this might have affected the standing of professional women, but it does not mean that plans would automatically have looked any different. Although feminists have since criticised Beveridge's proposals, at the time he received mixed messages from women's organisations; there was not a 'woman's line' on social insurance.

There were, however, two areas, housing and education, where policies would have been different if the views expressed by women's organisations had been reflected in policy. A common theme of women was that housing should mix social classes; and housing, employment and transport needs should be considered as a whole, not as separate issues.[51] Most significant, however, would have been the priority accorded nursery education if government had listened to women's voices. NCW plans, for instance, envisaged nursery education receiving the same importance as other stages of education. The NCW called for nursery education to be available to all children whose parents desired it for them. 'Such education, far from weakening parental

---

48. John Macnicol, *The Movement for Family Allowances* (1980), pp. 169–202.

49. HC Deb. vol. 411 col. 1420 11 June 1945; vol. 408 col. 2279 8 March 1945.

50. William Beveridge, 'Epilogue', in Eleanor Rathbone, *Family Allowances* (1949), p. 270.

51. Women in Council, *Newsletter* (February 1942).

responsibility, throws a new light upon it, and is found actually to raise the standard of home life by enabling parents, through contact with the school, to understand their children better, and by relief afforded to the mother, to enjoy them more fully.'[52] Government failed to appreciate the educational and social value of nursery education. Instead, nursery education was seen as a means of aiding war production by freeing up mothers for the war effort, which was a temporary not permanent argument in favour of nursery education.[53]

While women's organisations took up the issue of reconstruction at home and abroad, in September 1942 Dorothy Fells urged them to encompass a wider group of women in their thinking about the post-war world. She argued that women in the past had displayed too much negligence and complacency, and she urged those active in women's groups to reach out to others who were ignorant of the workings of national and local government and 'pitifully ignorant of both the privileges and responsibilities of citizenship'. The BFBPW felt that government took advantage of women's alleged apathy and failure to make their views known to their MPs. Later, in 1944, the BFBPW emphasised the importance of women taking more interest in world affairs.[54] These claims were echoed three years later about German, not British, women when the claim was made that British women were good, active citizens and an example to the Germans in this respect. (See Chapter Nine.)

Those organisations most actively involved with government were also the ones which were least concerned to change gender relations and, as voluntary organisations, were least concerned to increase the power of the state. They had little time to devote to post-war planning, although they did have views on issues which had long-term implications. Those organisations which were pressing for change were primarily interested in seeing an increased or altered responsibility for the state, and they too were not necessarily interested in exploiting the role of women in voluntary organisations. The leaders of women's voluntary organisations were well connected with Whitehall and Westminster, but that is not the same as being able to take policy decisions. Beveridge and the Conservatives emphasised the importance of voluntary work in welfare provision. The Labour Party prioritised a powerful and dynamic state, and it was to be Labour's vision which dominated the post-war years.

---

52. Women in Council, *Newsletter* (September 1942).
53. See for example HC Deb. vol. 406 col. 1967 31 March 1944 Willink.
54. *Women at Work* (December 1941, June 1944).

Post-war planning across Europe

Although planning for post-war Europe was an integral part of women's planning for the future in Britain, the latter has received little attention from historians and the former none at all. The WGPW soon turned its attention to coordinating plans for the future of continental Europe. European women refugees were in contact with the WGPW and the British and continental women aimed to learn from each other and plan together. The presence of continental refugee women in Britain for an extended period was a golden opportunity not to be missed by British women. Here was a chance for an exchange of ideas. The factor linking them was their gender, yet the women saw themselves training and preparing for the future not because they were women, but because they were all potential citizens of a democratic Europe. They did not see their work as part of a feminist project but of a democratic European one.

In January 1942 the first AGM of the International Women's Service Groups in Great Britain, a collection of business and professional women, took place. The initiative for this organisation had come in November 1940 from the non-British women. It is understandable that professional women catapulted into a foreign country, with their own country overrun by Nazis, would want to get together and to feel that they were doing something, not only for the war effort, but also for the future of their country as well. The members of the organisation were concerned above all with working during the war and with training themselves, the better to rebuild their countries after the war. They saw their goal as part of a long-term strategy for equality and citizenship. In 1941 there were 546 members. They joined together to find employment and training, but also for social and cultural activities. Although low-key, they did hit one newspaper headline as the 'New Army of mercy', in an article by Alison Settle on the training of women to rebuild Europe.[55]

By the autumn of 1942 a liaison committee of Women's International Organisations was preparing for the future by running conferences and courses in social work training. The WGPW was acting as a coordinating committee, collecting information on reconstruction plans.[56] The international aspects of post-war reconstruction were by now firmly on the WGPW agenda, and this reflected a widespread interest among women's groups both at home and abroad (the NCW for instance had a reconstruction

---

55. Fawcett Library Women's Group on Public Welfare January 1942.
56. Fawcett Library WGPW 18 November 1942.

committee which looked at reconstruction across Europe). The BFBPW also set up two committees to look into the lives of professional and business women in Britain and abroad after the war.[57]

By the autumn of 1943 women were expressing the view that they should be included in all aspects of reconstruction, not just unofficial ones. Women wanted to hold official positions in international organisations, such as the United Nations Relief and Rehabilitation Administration (UNRRA). Here, too, was a role for the pacifist WILPF in wartime; it could help build towards the peace. In September 1943 it convened a conference on the post-war world. One speaker stressed that it was not for British women to interfere in other countries' affairs, but rather to show what they were doing to solve their problems, and to learn from other European women. (The idea of showing European women the British way of doing things was taken up after the war when a limited number of German women who had not been in Britain during the war but spoke English were brought over and shown various British institutions at work.) Similarly, the WGPW was primarily concerned with the exchange of information between British women's organisations and women from abroad.[58]

Many of the women involved in discussing, and drawing up plans for, the post-war world linked national and international developments. Perhaps the physical closeness of women from different countries meant that the common problems they faced were more obvious, and living through a war drove home to them the fact that their fates depended not only on their own government, but on other governments too. Two wartime welfare campaigns, the campaign to raise the blockade of occupied Europe, and the Aid to Russia campaign, both highlighted the relevance of the British government's international policies for women and children, and British women's long-standing active concern for the welfare of continental women and children.

The campaign to raise the blockade

The allies' economic blockade prevented goods, including foodstuffs, from entering the Axis countries and their occupied territories. The campaign to raise the blockade of enemy-occupied Europe on humanitarian grounds, of which Vera Brittain, Peggy Duff and Edith Pye were the linchpins, was an

---

57. Fawcett Library WGPW 12 October 1942; BFBPW, *Women at Work* (March 1943).
58. Fawcett Library WGPW 11 September 1943, 3 October 1943.

almost complete failure. It ran contrary to wartime strategy, and although its leaders succeeded in establishing a network of support around the country, it failed to fire people's imagination. The well-known pacifism of both Vera Brittain and Edith Pye may well have contributed to the campaign's weakness, for their presence made it easy for critics to portray the campaign as unpatriotic. The fact that there were those within Whitehall, particularly in the Foreign Office, who were secretly wheeling and dealing for a relaxation of the blockade because they wanted to please Britain's allies, did not detract from the public image of the campaigners as a bunch of 'conchies' set against the government. The belief that the First World War campaign to lift the blockade had given succour to the enemy strengthened the resolve of those ministers, in particular, Winston Churchill, the Prime Minister, and Hugh Dalton, Minister of Economic Warfare, who both adamantly believed that the blockade made good strategic sense, however much it irritated Uncle Sam.

The campaign to raise the blockade grew out of the Peace Pledge Union (PPU) whose support had plummeted since the outbreak of war. The PPU established a Food Relief Campaign with Vera Brittain as chair, and in May 1942 George Bell, Bishop of Chichester, took up Vera Brittain's suggestion and launched the National Famine Relief Committee. Edith Pye acted as national organiser. The Committee focused on the needs of women and children in occupied Europe:[59] it was hoped that since women and children were non-combatants, their plight would arouse sympathy, and, there was a tradition, personified by Edith Pye, of helping the enemy's starving children.

Maggie Black infers that the campaigners worked to dispel the 'indifference' of the British, but this is rather to miss the point. First, the campaign was hampered not only by its association with pacifism but also by the difficulty of obtaining hard facts about standards of living on the Continent. The information it did collect, moreover, was insufficient to move the government, not because of indifference but because hard-nosed and unpleasant decisions had to be taken. The strength of the humanitarian case was overwhelmed by the government's strategy for winning the war. In May 1940 Hugh Dalton had warned a secret session of the House of Commons that there might well be pressure to let food through the blockade, supported by German propaganda, 'misguided' American humanitarianism, and the self-interest of producers outside Europe. He argued against any relaxation on the grounds that some foodstuffs could be used to make explosives, the war would be prolonged, and casualties would increase. The economic warfare policy complemented naval, military and air action.

---

59. Maggie Black, *A Cause for Our Times: Oxfam The First 50 Years* (Oxford, 1992), p. 9.

Dalton, like Churchill, was single-minded in his determination to win the war. He correctly believed that shortages during the First World War had helped to stir up revolution in Germany, and he now hoped that shortages would provoke hostility towards the regime among the peoples of Germany and occupied Europe. This policy depended on a successful blockade. Small concessions were made, but none that would have jeopardised the overall strategy. Churchill announced that food stocks would be held in trust for occupied Europe and released when Germany had been driven out: food and freedom would go together. One further concession was made to Greece, the country suffering most from food shortages. On 16 April 1942 it was announced that regular shipments of relief would be allowed through the blockade.[60]

The part played by the blockade in winning the war is hard to gauge. Those campaigning against it warned that it would cause immense bitterness towards Britain after the war, but of this I have found no evidence. It is possible that it may have fuelled discontent and therefore aided resistance movements. Its greatest significance lay in what it threatened to do; fear of shortages meant that the Germans systematically pillaged the countries they occupied, which could have done nothing to endear them to local populations. The prospect of shortages, moreover, may have encouraged Hitler to turn his attention eastward and attack the Soviet Union, thereby providing Britain with a new ally and a lightening conductor for the German onslaught.[61]

Dalton and Churchill had a constant struggle to keep at bay those critics within the Cabinet, supported by the Foreign Office, who believed that the allied governments in exile should be humoured by lifting the blockade, but the supporters of the blockade won the day. When Churchill chose to make a humanitarian gesture it was one which fitted in with, rather than contradicted, high strategy, and worked to the benefit, not of an occupied ally, but an unoccupied one, the Soviet Union.

The British Red Cross Aid to Russia Fund

In the autumn of 1941 the Red Cross launched a welfare campaign to help the Soviet Union. This caught the public's imagination and aroused far more sympathy and support than any other aid to allies. It was headed by

---

60. Maggie Black, *A Cause For Our Times*, pp. 7, 9, 10; Hugh Dalton, *The Fateful Years: Memoirs, 1931–1945* (1957), p. 350; Ben Pimlott, *Hugh Dalton* (1985), pp. 281, 289.
61. Ben Pimlott, *Hugh Dalton*, p. 293.

Clementine Churchill, who was also President of the Young Women's Christian Association wartime fund. The combination of Clementine Churchill and the Red Cross provided the dream ticket for popular support. Just as her husband embodied Britain's unswerving, dogged and unyielding determination to win the war, so Clementine personified the concern and admiration felt by the British for the Russians and symbolised the importance the British government attached to good Anglo–Soviet relations. The campaign gave civilians, including children, a feeling that they were positively contributing to the war effort beyond Britain's shores, and enabled them, to express in a practical fashion their respect and support for the Soviet Union. Groups of adults at work and children at school regularly collected for the Russians; flag days and Anglo–Soviet weeks were held. The WI collected and cured rabbit skins and made them up into coats and hats for Russian women.[62]

The campaign's real value did not lie in the amount of relief provided for the Soviet Union, for this was paltry set against the need. For the government the campaign's importance lay in promoting good Anglo–Soviet relations for the duration, and Whitehall, and Churchill himself, were keen to support it. By personalising the campaign, the human element in Anglo–Soviet relations was focused on, and this meant that the very real and intractable problems of Anglo–Soviet relations could be skirted around. Clementine Churchill claimed that her visit to Russia in 1945 was the beginning of friendly relations, though in fact it was the climax. While she was unfavourably contrasting the Germans with the Russians, who were 'heroic' and 'brave', with a 'veneration for the cultural inheritance', and referring to the 'great warrior leader of Russia, Marshall Stalin', such sentiments were already becoming dated. She even wrote of the Aid to Russia campaign as signalling friendship and comradeship, the latter an unusual term for a Conservative to use! By the end of the war over £7 million had been raised; nearly £5.5 million was spent through charities on surgical and medical items and clothes. The government also gave a grant of £2.5 million for clothing. A great deal of the money was wasted, especially at the beginning when, for instance, the Russians did not provide adequate specifications for British manufacturers, and needles were sent which did not fit Russian syringes.[63] Such bunglings not only undermined the aid Britain

---

62. WI, *Annual Report* 1943.
63. Mary Soames, *Clementine Churchill* (Harmondsworth,1979), pp. 437–537; Martin Gilbert, *Winston S. Churchill vol. VIII 1941–1945* (1986), pp. 101, 122, 382, 1254–5, 1267; Clementine Churchill, *My Visit to Russia* (1945), pp. 9–28; Joan Beaumont, *Comrades in Arms: British Aid to Russia, 1941–45* (1980); The British Red Cross *Quarterly Review* (July 1944).

could provide to Russia, but it put British merchant seamen to unnecessary risk; the Russian convoy was notoriously dangerous. Here then was a welfare campaign which, unusually, combined popular sentiment and government strategy, and provided Clementine Churchill with a high-profile, albeit traditional, role akin to that of Eleanor Roosevelt, the US President's wife.

Beyond Britain

Did women manage to exert a greater influence elsewhere in wartime? Given the unprecedented influence of an elite group of women during the New Deal, the most obvious place to look for women's influence is Roosevelt's wartime America. As pointed out in Chapter Seven, however, Susan Ware has argued that women's influence had peaked in 1936 and, by the time America entered the war in 1941, women's influence was fast fading. There was no flow of women into government as in the early years of the New Deal and indeed positive steps were taken to keep women out. Men threatened to resign from the War Management Commission if they were joined by women, and, as a result, women were confined to the Women's Advisory Committee with no research staff, and their advice was usually ignored. Examples can be found of women wielding influence, but they were isolated; the formidable network of women in the early years of Roosevelt's presidency had virtually disappeared.[64]

Throughout the war Eleanor Roosevelt tried to encourage voluntary organisations in their work with refugees and children. From 1943, when 50 countries founded UNRRA to offer not only short-term relief but also long-term self-sustaining policies, Eleanor Roosevelt concentrated her efforts on its work. The President apparently found Eleanor Roosevelt's focus on domestic issues irritating when he was preoccupied with the war, and enormous hostility built up towards her not only from Republicans but also from Democrats advising the President. Even so, Roosevelt used Eleanor during the war for goodwill missions in 1942 to Britain, in 1943 to the armed forces in the Southwest Pacific and in 1944 to the Caribbean. Although criticised at the time for travelling in army planes and for wearing a Red Cross uniform, she made a positive contribution to improvements in Red Cross facilities and she publicised her trip to Britain in order to bring the realities of war home to an isolationist American public.

Eleanor Roosevelt was often isolated in her war work: she failed to arouse Cabinet wives to help the young women pouring into Washington

---

64. Susan Ware, *Beyond Suffrage: Women in the New Deal* (Cambridge, Mass, 1981), pp. 127–8.

DC for war work. Despite the success of NYA programmes, with which Eleanor Roosevelt was associated, they were shut down in 1943 because of increased hostility towards them. Although most biographies of Eleanor Roosevelt are little more than hagiography, there are criticisms of her war work. Lois Scharf, for instance, argues that Roosevelt shifted from radical social-reforming critic with the President's ear to that of a comforting mother-figure. Yet, there was no possibility of Eleanor Roosevelt influencing an extension of federal social reforms. While her work expanded as a result of the war, her scope for executing change diminished.[65]

In 1943 two women entered the Australian Federal Parliament in Canberra for the first time, Dorothy Tangney for the Australian Labor Party (ALP), entered the Senate and Enid Lyons of the United Australia Party (UAP) entered the House of Representatives. Lyons was the widow of a former Prime Minister. She highlighted issues around the family, but complained that when she spoke on other issues the media ignored her. On occasion she managed to tilt her party's policies, as for instance in 1946, when she persuaded it to promise to extend child endowment to the first child; she also lobbied successfully for the Party to stop discriminating against women in allowances paid to those who had been demobbed. (In 1949 she became the first woman to sit in the Cabinet as Vice-President of the Executive Council and Minister without Portfolio. She resigned in 1951 due to ill-health.) Dorothy Tangney, who was unmarried, promoted the role of women in the family. She also supported equal pay and equal opportunities in the workplace. She had little success with policies explicitly promoting women's interests, such as increased pensions at the same level as the basic wage for widows with children, or pensions for unmarried women with family responsibilities, but she was able to add her weight to government policies over extending federal powers in social security, housing, education and a national health scheme. She was a member of the Joint Committee on Social Security, set up in 1943 by the Labor government, whose report formed the basis of an extension of government welfare. Thus, she contributed to strengthening government policies in the welfare field, but not in changing their direction.[66] Elsewhere, formal political channels still remained closed to women.

65. Eleanor Roosevelt, *The Autobiography of Eleanor Roosevelt* (1962), p. 178; Hida Black, *Casting Her Own Shadow: Eleanor Roosevelt and the Shaping of Postwar Liberalism* (New York, 1996), p. 47; Tamara K. Hareven, *Eleanor Roosevelt: An American Conscience* (Chicago, 1968), pp. 155–60, 217–20; Lois Scharf, *Eleanor Roosevelt, First Lady of American Liberalism* (Boston, Mass, 1987), p. 128.
66. Marian Sawer and Marian Simms, *A Woman's Place: Women and Politics in Australia* (St Leonards, NSW, 1993), pp. 112–27.

At first women were presented as equal partners in the French Resistance and women such as Lucie Aubrac were portrayed as leaders and heroines. A generation later the focus switched to the specific activities of more 'ordinary' women. Women acted as couriers, took members of the underground into their homes and ran risks, but there were few women leaders. The daily routine of women as mothers, lovers and housewives provided convenient 'cover' for them to act as go-betweens or gun-runners. The role of women was a supportive one; men took the decisions. The memoirs of Lucie Aubrac demonstrated the guile and bravery of women, but give no sense of Aubrac as part of the Resistance's policy-making process in Lyon.

In the early days of the war there were no clearly assigned roles for women and men in the Resistance but these swiftly developed and it was usually only in groups with communist connections that women played a combative role, and even then it was unusual. Towards the end of the war, when partisan units were integrated into regular units, women were completely excluded from combat, turning instead to a traditional supportive role.[67]

In Italy, as in France, women were heavily involved in the Resistance from September 1943, when they acted as couriers, and housed and fed members of the underground. They toured police stations and German military posts to locate prisoners, plead for them and supply them with basic necessities. Initially, when women formed women's defence groups in Milan they were loosely under the control of the Committee of National Liberation. The twin aims of this body were aiding the resistance and working for women's emancipation, but the latter aim was soon swallowed up in the immediate day-to-day demands of resistance. According to de Grazia, the women's involvement in the Resistance grew out of a commitment to their family and community; their role in the Resistance was an extension of their caring role in the family and not an attack on gendered social roles.[68]

In Germany the *Frauenschaft*, the Nazi women's organisation, was merely a cipher for decisions taken elsewhere. Even when it pushed for policies which would have been in the Nazi state's interest and in the interests of women – for instance, over equal pay – it was ignored. Given the difficulty encountered in trying to recruit women for war work, it would have helped the German war effort if this concession had been made. Instead, the Nazi war machine managed to mobilise relatively few women, and this passive

---

67. Laure Adler, *Les Femmes Politiques* (Paris, 1993), pp. 129–30; Lucie Aubrac, *Ils Partiront Dans L'Ivresse* (Paris, 1984); Paula Schwartz, '*Partisanes* and gender politics in Vichy France', *French Historical Studies* 16 (1989).
68. Victoria de Grazia, *How Fascism Ruled Women: Italy 1922–45* (Berkeley, 1992), pp. 283–6.

resistance, not to the regime, but to low-paid work, has been cited as one way in which the Nazi state's powers were limited.[69] This is very different, however, from saying that women exercised any power or authority in government.

Thus, beyond Britain the war gave women only limited, or no, opportunity to manoeuvre into positions of power. Political constraints and the difficulties of political mobilisation in wartime meant that, despite women's access to the formal structures of power, the construction of a gendered welfare state continued apace.

Conclusions

In terms of their numbers and the positions they occupied, women were far better placed in the Second World War than in the First World War to make a contribution to the process of governance. Women carved out a role in various, and often overlapping, ways. There were women, albeit very few, offering advice on the committees which mushroomed in every nook and cranny of government. The majority of women were involved in implementing, with some degree of autonomy, policies already thrashed out. Very few women were actually involved in the planning of general domestic strategies. Women campaigned to change or modify government policies, but in almost every case government put up a brick wall against women's attempts to break down institutionalised gender inequalities.

Contemporary perceptions of the extent to which war enhanced women's autonomy in the public sphere varied between individuals and groups, and over time. Expressed opinions also depended on the intended audience. During the war, when Vera Douie was campaigning on behalf of the WPPA, she wrote about the limitations imposed on women's contribution to governance. By 1949 she was writing of the great contribution made by women to the war effort.[70] Government made a great deal of use of women, and many women were happy to be used in this way. Those women who not only wanted their horizons widened, but also to determine those horizons were less satisfied: there was a difference between implementing policy and actually making it.

---

69. Leila Rupp, '"I don't call that *Volksgemeinschaft*": women, class and war in Nazi Germany', in Carol Berkin and Clara Lovett, eds, *Women, War and Revolution* (New York, 1980).
70. Vera Douie, *The Lesser Half*, pp. 26–9; *Daughters of Britain*, pp. 136–41.

CHAPTER NINE

Post-war Reconstruction

Introduction

The continuation of rationing, progressive tax policy, food subsidies and rent controls after the war helped to maintain working-class living standards. Full employment and regional planning meant that the old depressed areas of the 1930s joined in the economic recovery.[1] Any gains for women were a reflection of general improvements in society; women did not make gains vis-à-vis men, and thus women's relative disadvantages remained. This chapter shows why, at a time when politicians were rebuilding Britain, the opportunity for a gendered reshaping of the social and political fabric of society was lost. Women's organisations, although interested in a range of changes, were not able to exert any real influence over the rock-solid Labour government majority. The Labour governments of 1945 to 1951 downplayed women's needs and assumed that working-class women would benefit from improvements in working-class men's employment, and from the welfare and housing programmes.[2] Whereas Labour was dismissive of women's specific needs, the Conservative Party recognised that a loosening of the government's austerity policy and the introduction of equal pay would help women in their private and public roles; the former sat neatly with Conservative Party thinking and both suited the Party's electoral strategy.

The priority accorded group and community identity by broad swathes of women after the war meant that while class was an important source

---

1. Kevin Jefferys, *The Labour Party Since 1945* (Basingstoke, 1993), p. 16.
2. Martin Francis, *Ideas and Policies under Labour, 1945–51 Building a New Britain* (Manchester, 1997), pp. 204, 209–10.

of identity, locality and gender together created a sense of community, manifested in the strength and activities of organisations such as the Townswomen's Guild (TG) and Women's Institute (WI). Women's organisations which emphasised self-education and individual fulfilment within a public and group setting enjoyed enormous popularity. This was not an era of solely private, family and consumer-oriented life for women, who joined political parties with alacrity and groups such as the WI and TG in their droves. Briefly, during 1946–7, many middle-class housewives joined the British Housewives' League to campaign against the government's policy of austerity, which caused women continuing shopping problems because of long queues and rationing.

Precisely because women's organisations were so closely connected with meanings of citizenship, public responsibility and adult education, governments used them as part of a strategy for maintaining international peace and shoring up Germany against the encroachments of the Soviet Union's communism. It was here, in the symbolic meanings of active citizenship, that women left their mark on the period, not in the direct part they played in government policy making. Of course, not all women became involved in women's organisations or in the re-education of Germans, but those women who did do so helped to create the atmosphere of the time.

Westminster and Whitehall

In the 1945 general election 24 women were elected as MPs: 21 Labour; one Conservative, Lady Davidson; one Liberal, Megan Lloyd George, and one Independent, Eleanor Rathbone. At least two women MPs curtailed their careers to suit their husbands. Nancy Astor did not stand for election in 1945 because her husband did not wish it. Astor had passed her peak, so her husband's opposition was a blessing in disguise for her. More controversial was Jennie Lee's decision to hold back her career in order to advance that of her husband, Aneurin Bevan. Lee wrote that she would have liked to have stood for election to the Labour Party's governing body, the NEC, but did not do so because her election would have meant one less place for friends whose support her husband needed.[3]

Clement Attlee, the Prime Minister, appointed a few women to government posts: Ellen Wilkinson as Minister of Education; Edith Summerskill as Parliamentary Secretary at the Ministry of Food; Jennie Adamson as Parliamentary

---

3. Jennie Lee, *My Life With Nye* (1980), p. 168.

Secretary at the Ministry of Pensions, and Barbara Castle, PPS to Stafford Cripps at the Board of Trade. In 1950 Margaret Herbison, Labour MP, 1945–70, became Joint Parliamentary Under-Secretary at the Scottish Office. Later, Herbison was Minister of Pensions and National Insurance, 1964–6, and Minister of Social Security, 1966–7. According to Castle, Cripps asked her to advise him on complaints from women about clothes rationing and other problems relating to the shortage of raw materials. When Cripps moved to the Treasury, Castle remained at the Board of Trade as PPS to Harold Wilson. Leah Manning later claimed that Castle's appointment as a PPS as soon as she entered Parliament caused resentment, demonstrated in Jean Mann's comments about Castle in her *Woman at Westminster*.[4]

From the moment Castle entered Parliament she was somewhat of a rebel and she attracted attention, which inevitably created strong enemies and friends. Building a professional relationship with Wilson proved useful to Castle's long-term career; in 1964 when Wilson became Prime Minister, he appointed Castle Minister of Overseas Development with a place in his Cabinet. She was subsequently Minister of Transport, 1965–8, Secretary of State for Employment and Productivity, 1968–70, and Secretary of State for Social Services, 1974–6. Castle's most notable parliamentary effort for women between 1945 and 1951 came on 13 December 1950 when she moved an amendment to the Criminal Law Amendment Bill in order to extend the protection of the law to prostitutes. Its effects included bringing traffic in prostitution within the scope of the law. Previously, it had been a criminal offence to procure a girl or woman under 21 for sex with a third party except if the woman was a prostitute or of known immoral character. It had been a criminal offence to induce a girl or woman to leave her usual place of abode and inhabit a brothel, except if her usual place of abode was a brothel; and it had been a criminal offence to procure a woman or girl to have sex by false pretences or by false representation except if she was already a prostitute or of known immoral character. The exceptions were now removed.[5]

Edith Summerskill as Parliamentary Secretary to the Minister of Food, 1945–50, and as Minister of National Insurance, 1950–51, was closely involved in policies affecting women. Both Summerskill and Castle dealt with questions which affected women on a day-to-day basis. Shortages and rationing (of food in particular) caused problems for women. Women ministers could not, however, dislodge Labour's gender-blind policies which worked

---

4. Barbara Castle, *Fighting All the Way* (1993), pp. 135–6; Leah Manning, *A Life for Education: An Autobiography* (1970), p. 202; Jean Mann, *Woman in Parliament* (1962).
5. HC Deb. vol. 482 13 December 1950.

to women's daily disadvantage, and soon to Labour's electoral disadvantage. Ina Zweiniger-Bargielowska has shown how the Conservative Party exploited the Labour governments' insensitivity to women's dissatisfaction with food rationing and controls, and how this contributed in large measure to Labour's 1951 general election defeat.[6] Ellen Wilkinson, as Minister of Education, saw the implementation of the 1944 Education Act, although she did not display any particular interest in girls' and women's education. There is evidence that the atmosphere of Whitehall may well have constrained women Ministers from speaking up for women's interests. Summerskill later wrote that senior civil servants did not give her, as a woman Minister, the respect which they accorded her male colleagues; she cited the prejudice of the Permanent Secretary to the Treasury, Sir Edward Bridges.[7]

There were by now senior women civil servants who had entered Whitehall in the 1920s. In 1946 Alix Kilroy became an Under-Secretary and in 1949 she was awarded a DBE, which was, strictly speaking, too high an honour for an Under-Secretary, but the appropriate honour – the Order of the Bath – was not open to women. Kilroy was then seconded to the Monopolies Commission. She unsuccessfully tried to negotiate for equal pay and for those seconded to receive some financial recompense because it was recognised that secondments were a disadvantageous career move. When she returned to the Board of Trade in 1952 she had been an Under-Secretary for six years. She was at first offered a dead-end post, which she turned down, and then a mainstream one, which she accepted. In the nine months following her return, two vacancies came up for Second Secretaries. The first was filled by a man junior to Kilroy and the second by someone brought in from another department. In 1955 Kilroy retired, annoyed at not gaining further promotion: earlier in the year she had been passed over for a post which went to a man junior to her in age and seniority who had worked under her in the past.[8] How far Kilroy's failure to reach the top reflected widespread prejudice against senior women, individual prejudice against her, or men who were more competent than her, is impossible to prove. That only one woman, Kilroy's old friend, Evelyn Sharp, made it to the top of the civil service by the mid-twentieth century, suggests that the failure lay with a prejudiced civil service.

After the war Evelyn Sharp became Deputy Secretary to the Ministry of Town and Country Planning, and from 1955 to 1966 she was Permanent

---

6. Ina Zweiniger-Bargielowska, 'Rationing, austerity and the Conservative Party recovery after 1945', *Historical Journal* 37 (1994), pp. 173–97.
7. Edith Summerskill, *A Woman's World* (1967), pp. 145, 107.
8. Alix Meynell, *Public Servant, Private Woman: An Autobiography* (1988), pp. 246, 252, 254, 261, 265–6.

Secretary at the Ministry of Housing and Local Government. Sharp was a formidable and respected civil servant, who had a reputation for getting things done. While it was a notable personal achievement for Sharp to have risen so high in the civil service, the fact that she was the lone woman was a notable failure on the part of the civil service as an organisation. More women were entering the administrative grade of the civil service, but their climb to the top was slow and uneven. In 1950, 93.4 per cent of permanent posts (2,522) in the administrative grade were held by men while women occupied only the remaining 6.6 per cent of permanent administrative grade posts (179).[9]

Women did make some gains from the post-war Labour governments, 1945–51, but only when women's interests fitted in with the overarching project of the government. Women worked in key areas of the expanding welfare state as teachers, nurses and social workers, but the importance of their contribution was not recognised either in their promotion prospects or in equal pay.

Full employment

The full employment of the 1940s and the substantial increase in real wages, up 20 per cent between 1938 and 1949, meant that most women and their families were able to enjoy a higher standard of living than in the past. Husbands brought home more, and steadier, wages, while women who went out to work enjoyed more choice in the type of work they undertook, and higher wages than in the past. Even so, their wages remained lower than men's wages.

William Crofts has explored the contradictory nature of the Labour government's employment policy towards women. On the one hand the government wanted women to stay at home, rebuilding the family and repopulating the country; on the other hand, and the priority from 1947, the government needed women in the workforce to meet the apparently insatiable demand for labour. The needs of the economy won, and in 1947 the government launched a campaign to entice women aged between 35 and 50 into key export industries. Despite women's wages averaging just under half those of men, the shortage of nursery school places for children, and long queues, more women did take up paid work; the cost of living was

---

9. Figures taken from E.M. Kemp-Jones, *The Employment of Women in the Civil Service: The Report of a Departmental Committee* (1971), p. 39.

creeping up and some women were glad to get away from being full-time housewives.[10]

Neither middle-class nor working-class women found much difficulty in finding work after the war. Teachers, nurses and social workers were in desperately short supply and women made a major contribution to building the new welfare state in all three occupations. The urgent demand for teachers after the war and the emergency training scheme (ETS) opened up opportunities for women and men to enter a profession which they might not otherwise have considered, and it therefore helped to create some social mobility. War casualties, the run-down of teacher training during the war, the increased demands of implementing the provisions of the 1944 Education Act and the post-war baby boom, which peaked in 1947, meant that the teaching profession was in need of a large injection of new blood. Under the ETS there were means-tested grants for students, and no tuition or boarding costs. The scheme offered intensive training for one year – instead of the normal two years for non-graduates – during which trainee teachers undertook three teaching practices as well as theoretical study at a teacher-training college, many of them quickly adapted from military use.

The ETS scheme was controversial; fears were raised about the 'dilution' of the profession, and the speed of the training, yet, without the ETS, class sizes would have been even larger than the usual 40–50 children and it would not have been possible to raise the school leaving age to 15. The scheme brought into the profession women and men who had undertaken national service and were therefore older (21 was the minimum age), with a wider experience of life than the normal recruits to teaching. The maturity of the students, the intensive training and the doors which the scheme opened for those who might not previously have thought of entering teaching were all bonuses for the profession. The scheme failed to attract as many recruits as were needed, however, and despite the scheme's efforts to recruit women for primary schools, it actually attracted more men.[11] Although new opportunities opened for women to enter teaching, the scheme did not (and was not intended to) improve women teachers' career prospects vis-à-vis male colleagues. The marriage bar no longer operated but unequal pay for women and men continued.

The demand for trained social workers continued after the war, with many more local authorities employing women in child care, but the shortage

---

10. William Crofts, 'The Attlee Government's pursuit of women', *History Today* 36 (1986), pp. 29–35.
11. See Martin Loveday, *Into the Breach: The Emergency Training Scheme for Teachers* (1949), pp. vii–viii, 4–13.

of trained social workers meant local authorities continued to employ un-qualified workers. The Labour government had no interest in overhauling social work training, and social work remained a low-status subject in the universities. The gender division continued, with men holding posts in which they could exercise their authority, in areas such as the National Society for the Prevention of Cruelty to Children, probation and mental welfare, and administrative positions such as wardens of community centres, settlement wardens and youth workers. They also normally worked with boys and men.[12] The demand for labour and the continuing, if slow, expansion of opportunities for educated women, meant that social work had to compete along with a number of other employment openings for women. The growth in the number of married women in the labour force has been one of the most striking changes in the post-war labour market, but the change was gradual. Many women continued to give up work on marriage or when they started a family. Senior social work posts were disproportionately dom-inated by men so that, as with teaching, the growing demand for women did not right the gender imbalance at the top.

The largest group of NHS workers, and one that was overwhelmingly female, had no input into the shape or nature of the service. There is no evidence that the Royal College of Nursing attempted to influence plans for the NHS; in striking contrast, the male-dominated BMA played a vocifer-ous and high-profile part in policy making for the new NHS and ministers struggled to do deals in order to ensure the BMA's cooperation. The influ-ence of nurses in the running of the service was barely discernable. Accord-ing to Dingwall, Rafferty and Webster, the Ministry of Health had established a small nursing division to oversee the direction of nursing labour, staffed by civil servants with five nursing advisors from the Chief Medical Officer's staff. A further 12 nursing officers were based in the regions, concerned mainly with public health. The chief nursing officer had the rank of a Principal, so only reported to ministers via senior civil servants; unlike the Chief Medical Officer, she did not enjoy direct access to ministers. It does not seem that nursing officers' views carried much weight within the Minis-try. The failure to have nurses' interests taken into account was reflected in the fact that neither the 1946 NHS Act nor the 1949 Nurses Act tackled the twin problems of a nursing shortage, and the poor pay and conditions of nurses. Under the 1946 Act a central Health Services Advisory Council was set up with a number of standing advisory committees, including ones for nursing, maternity and midwifery and one for mental health and mental health nursing. The nursing committee had a narrow majority of

---

12. R.G. Walton, *Women in Social Work* (1975), pp. 203, 208, 196.

nurses on it, and on occasion its recommendations did feed into Ministry policies.[13]

While nursing remained far more marginal in the policy process than medicine, within medicine women did make headway after the war. One of the most significant changes for women doctors was the introduction of mixed medical schools. This move towards coeducation, which had been so fiercely resisted before the war by London medical schools, resulted from the recommendations of the 1944 interdepartmental committee, chaired by Sir William Goodenough, into the organisation of medical schools and, in particular, clinical training and research. The report criticised discrimination against women in hospital appointments as unjust and contrary to the public interest, and called for open competition for all hospital appointments. In practice, it proved easier to implement the recommendation to open medical schools to women than to stamp out discrimination against women in appointments. The Medical Women's Federation continued to promote the interests of its members as well as wider women's issues. It called for women in all branches of medicine, for more specialist training and for more women GPs.

Blackford asserts that the relatively low number of middle-class married women in the paid workforce in the 1940s and 1950s helps to explain why middle-class feminists focused on issues affecting women in the home.[14] In fact, the issue which mobilised middle-class women more than any other was the question of equal pay for equal work. Even those women who may not have been in the paid workforce, such as members of the WI, supported the campaign.

In the early post-war years many women operated to a large extent outside the confines of party. The formal cross-party links between women MPs did not survive the war; the Labour Party discouraged even informal links. Women were united, nevertheless, in their pursuit of a number of goals, of which equal pay was by far the most important.

As in earlier periods, government policies were not fashioned with women's interests specifically in mind. Policies which benefited women were only ever introduced when they formed part of broad government strategy and not until the mid-1950s did equal pay come into this category. Women who banded together over equal pay were marginal to power: two Conservatives, from 1944 Mavis Tate, and then from 1947 Thelma Cazalet-Keir,

13.   Robert Dingwall, Anne Marie Rafferty and Charles Webster, *An Introduction to the Social History of Nursing* (1988), pp. 108–9.
14.   Catherine Blackford, 'The best of both worlds'?: Women's employment in post-war Britain, in Jim Fyrth, ed., *Labour's High Noon: The Government and the Economy, 1945–51* (1993), p. 218.

chaired the Equal Pay Campaign Committee (EPCC). Although women MPs supported the Committee it held no sway over senior members of the Labour government, who dismissed it as a reflection of middle-class women's demands, and thus of no relevance to Labour's broad project of reducing class inequalities. At Labour Conferences attempts were made to gag women who complained at Labour's failure to introduce equal pay.

The high-profile campaign for equal pay attracted women from across the political spectrum, as well as women organised in non-party women's organisations. The campaigners produced leaflets, organised meetings and in 1949 Jill Craigie produced the film *To Be A Woman*. Women based their claim for equal pay on economic grounds and on principle. Mavis Tate pointed out that, if Britain was to compete internationally and increase productivity, the best person for a job should be attracted to do it. She argued that, while marriage was the supreme career for women, it should not be undertaken as the easiest means of obtaining security and leisure; and she drew attention to the fact that, although married men enjoyed a tax allowance to support their responsibilities, there were many women with dependants who enjoyed no tax allowance.[15] Margaret Cole, 1893–1980, a socialist writer and member of the Fabian Women's Group, also called for equal pay on the grounds of women's need for the money, of social justice, and of the widespread support of the public.[16]

Such pleas fell on deaf ears. First, as Blackford has shown, support for equal pay was stronger at the grass roots than at the head of the labour movement. The Labour Party Conference voted for equal pay, while the NEC and the TUC supported it in principle but backed the Labour government's claim that it could not afford to implement the Royal Commission on Equal Pay's recommendations for equal pay in the public services. (The women members of the Commission, Janet Vaughan, Anne Loughlin, a trade unionist, and Lucy Nettleford, had also called for equal pay in industry, although their male colleagues opposed this on the grounds that women's work was not of equal value to men's work.) The government claimed that equal pay would lead to men demanding an increase in family allowances, and that, with more money in their purses, women would spend more and this would fuel inflation. Florence Hancock, 1893–1974, a leading trade unionist, urged Labour Party women to accept the government line.[17] Martin Pugh emphasises the limited nature of the campaign, with middle-class women asserting middle-class women's interests, but this of

---

15. Mavis Tate, *Equal Work Deserves Equal Pay*, Equal Pay Campaign Committee (1945?).
16. Margaret Cole, *The Rate For The Job* (1946).
17. Catherine Blackford, 'The best of both worlds?', pp. 222–3.

itself was not a weakness, especially as support was cross-party. It was not the class background of the EPCC which was a weakness, but the rock-solid Labour government majority, which operated within a political culture hostile to the specific interests of women, whatever their circumstances. In 1954 the Conservative government accepted equal pay for civil servants. A need to recruit more women into the civil service and the eventual success of the EPCC have both been put forward as reasons for this policy, but the most convincing explanation is that the Conservatives introduced it as a party political tactic in order to steady the female vote in the forthcoming 1955 general election.[18] In women's most prominent campaign, success was gradual and partial. In other areas, too, governments only ever met women's demands and needs in a slow and limited fashion.

Social policies

Most of the 1940s social welfare legislation was drawn up exclusively by men, and much of it has since been criticised for this, as well as for its gender bias. The 1945–51 Labour governments attempted to pursue policies which were underpinned by a concern with equality in general terms, and a fairer distribution of resources. On occasion, these policies did not work to women's advantage, even though women's specific needs were not prioritised.

One symbolic statement of women's greater equality with men came in the 1948 Nationality Act, with a clause, for which women's organisations had campaigned for many years, ensuring that if a woman married a foreigner she did not lose her British nationality. After the war, women coordinated their efforts with women in Australia and Canada, an essential move because the issue was dealt with in a commonwealth context. The Nationality Act demonstrated that the government was willing to make a change in married women's nationality, but there is no evidence that it would have done so if this had not formed part of wider legislation. In 1943 the wartime coalition would not consider making the change as part of narrower legislation, although there is evidence of changing attitudes within Whitehall at that time, for Osbert Peake, Parliamentary Secretary at the Home Office, stated that the Home Secretary would look out for a suitable occasion to seek a way around the difficulty. The new nationality legislation,

---

18. Martin Pugh, *Women and the Women's Movement in Britain 1914–1959* (1992); Harold L. Smith, 'The politics of Conservative reform: the equal pay for equal work issue, 1945–1955', *Historical Journal* 53 (1992), pp. 401–15.

passed in 1948, provided the required occasion.[19] The government would only make the change in the context of nationality within the empire.[20]

While the overarching context for the Nationality Act was an imperial one, the immediate post-war context also helped to shape the convoluted and judgemental thinking about women's citizenship. Those women who had married a foreigner and thus lost their British nationality under the old legislation were considered for British nationality if they were of 'good character' and had shown no evidence of 'disloyalty'. In Whitehall, attempts were made to help British women married to Austrian and Italian men, who, it was thought, should be helped as they were 'involuntary partners' in the Axis, and there was more pro-British feeling in these countries. This view was balanced by the assumption that British women in Germany had probably had a worse time and suffered greater antagonism and should also be helped.[21] As well as the plight of British-born women who wanted to regain their nationality, there was also the question of what to do about British troops in Germany marrying local women. The Home Office prioritised marriage and the family unit over diplomatic considerations. In the late 1940s German brides of British soldiers were granted visas to enter Britain when other Germans were still denied entry.[22]

As well as the security which full employment brought with it, the 1946 National Insurance Act, soon to be followed by the 1948 National Assistance Act, offered a further (albeit thin) layer of financial security. A major problem with benefits under both Acts was that they were too low; people living on national assistance could not afford to get their shoes mended.

The main controversy over the national insurance legislation revolves around the gendered nature of its provision. It assumed that married women were, and would continue to be, financially dependent on their husbands and that any paid work they undertook was temporary and not crucial to their financial security. Married women in the workforce paid a lower national insurance contribution than other workers and received lower benefits; married women in paid work could even opt out of the scheme altogether. If married women gave up paid work, they received a down payment and then lost any rights to benefit based on their previous contributions. The relationship between a married woman and the state was mediated through the husband; this lack of a direct relationship reflected the fact that men's, not women's, needs and rights still underpinned policy.

---

19. Fawcett Library Nationality of Married Women box.
20. PRO HO 213/410 Nationality Bill 1948.
21. PRO HO 213/398 28 August 1946; 11 October 1946.
22. PRO HO 213/709 18 August 1948.

Women's organisations, such as the National Council of Women (NCW), criticised the differential treatment of women and men, and called – unsuccessfully – for both to make the same contributions and to receive the same benefits. Barbara Castle had attempted to get various amendments adopted, including one for single women to receive pensions at the age of 55, for which the Spinsters' Pension Movement campaigned, and one for the inclusion in the insurance scheme of married women at work. Castle had to wait 30 years until she was Secretary of State for Social Security in order to abolish the married women's opt-out clause.[23] When policy was not framed from the point of view of men and their rights, it prioritised the needs of their children. Thus, widows lost their benefits if they earned over 30s 0d a week. Summerskill explained that the intention had been to 'discourage widows with children from taking full-time employment because the children had already been deprived of one parent and it was felt that they should have the guidance and care of the other parent for some time'.[24]

Sheila Blackburn has defended the Act against the criticism that it unfairly treated women by arguing that feminists at the time promoted the image of women as mothers, and that even those women who criticised the Beveridge Report, on which the legislation was based, accepted that most women aspired to motherhood. She points to the overall inadequacy of levels of benefits; national insurance benefits could only be claimed for one year, and strikers could not claim benefits at all. So, it was not only dependent women who had to claim national assistance but the long-term unemployed, the chronically sick, the elderly and young workers.[25] This is true, of course, although it has to be remembered that all the evidence points to women having to shoulder a greater burden than men when poverty hits a family.

Women's needs were addressed, in part, by the 1946 NHS Act. The financial worries associated with medical treatment disappeared, and this was especially important for those – the bulk of married women, young workers and children – who had not been covered by the previous National Health Insurance scheme. At first the free GP and hospital treatment appeared impressive and the absence of the promised network of health centres providing an integrated preventative service was hardly noticed. Mothers, as those most intimately concerned with children's health, benefited not only from NHS facilities but also from the expanding School Medical

23. Barbara Castle, *Fighting All the Way*, p. 134.
24. HC Deb. vol. 473 col. 989 4 April 1950 Summerskill.
25. Sheila Blackburn, 'How useful are feminist theories of the welfare state?', *Women's History Review* 4 (1995).

Service. Services for mothers remained uncoordinated and inadequate, but it was some time before feminist critiques emerged of NHS services for women.

Family planning services formed no part of the NHS. The campaign for family planning information to be made more widely available was at a low ebb, and Bevan, the Minister of Health – like so many of his colleagues, pursuing a gender-blind policy – ignored calls for family planning centres. So, the NHS was not set up with the specific and distinctive needs of women in mind. Women were using contraceptives much more effectively than in the past, indicating that family planning was important to them. The war had afforded opportunities not just for sex but also for the freer dissemination of knowledge about contraception. Knowledge gained during the war meant that when the birth rate went up after the war, as a result of the armed forces returning home, it was – to a greater extent than in the past – within women's control. The poverty and frequent pregnancies of many women were becoming an example for their daughters to avoid rather than a continuing reality. One of the main factors in the improved standard of health for women over the course of the twentieth century was women's increased control over their fertility. Women's campaigns for free and easily accessible contraceptives for married women were disregarded when the NHS was set up; the NHS did not, therefore, play as central a role in improving women's health in the post-war years as it might have done if women's views had figured at the planning stages.

The implementation of the 1944 Education Act benefited the overwhelming bulk of children, both girls and boys, by ensuring that they all received a primary and secondary education. There was, however, gender inequality in school provision, with more grammar school places for boys than girls; and the school curriculum made assumptions about the need for girls to study domestic science because of their future role as mothers.

Women's organisations had taken a particular interest in nursery education. Wartime developments had offered them hope, for although the government made clear that nurseries opened during the war were for the duration only, the 1943 White Paper on educational reconstruction stated that nursery schools were the most suitable form of provision for the under-fives. The 1944 Education Act, which required local education authorities (LEAs) to provide nursery schools or classes for the under-fives, was welcomed by campaigners for nursery education, but uncertainty was later injected over the interpretation of the law. LEAs assumed that the legislation did not require all children under five to be provided with a nursery place, and they got away with this assumption because little notice was taken of the clause. It was 'secondary education for all' which fired the public's imagination, and educationalists were far more interested in developing child-centred methods in the new primary schools, than worrying about the crucial educational and social needs of younger children.

In 1945 the Ministry of Health, never keen on nurseries, began shutting them down; the Ministry's grant to local authorities for nurseries was cut and they were left to local authorities to finance; in 1946 the Ministry slashed its 100 per cent grant for new nursery schools. The closure of nurseries at the end of the war and in the immediate post-war years was dramatic. When married women had been required in wartime industries, the needs of the Ministry of Labour had outweighed the Ministry of Health's hostility to nursery schools. After the war, although there was still a need for women's paid labour, the balance of power within Whitehall had shifted. The educational and social needs of children had never been the driving force behind the growth in wartime nurseries, so in this sense there was no reversal in the influence of the Nursery School Association (NSA) or women's organisations in their calls for the needs of young children and their mothers to be met.[26] Neither the struggling women's organisations – the Women's Cooperative Guild (WCG), the Women's Freedom League (WFL), and the Six Point Group – nor the flourishing ones (the TG and the WI) were able to stamp their mark on government policy.

A community of women

While the importance of 'community' has often been portrayed as a typically working-class value, in the early post-war years, women banded together within a class, gender and spatial identity; in part this reflected less a conscious effort to create these particular groupings than the fact that organisations identified along these cleavages already existed. Why women chose to join them in increasing numbers, however, is not so clear.

For women who joined women's organisations their 'public' roles interlocked with their leisure ones, rather than their labour market roles. After the war younger women were not too absorbed in domesticity and consumerism to take an active part in women's public activities, as the swelling ranks of the TG and WI prove. Both groups laid great emphasis on personal development within a collective setting. Both ran a range of educational activities and provided training in management skills for the development

---

26. For nursery education see Nanette Whitbread, *The Evolution of the Nursery/Infant School. A History of Infant and Nursery Education in Britain, 1800–1970* (1972), pp. 104–11; Denise Riley, '"The Free Mothers: pronatalism and working women in industry at the end of the last war in Britain', *History Workshop 11* (1981).

of the organisations. The Ministry of Education provided the TG with an annual grant for its adult education.

Both the TG and the WI grew significantly in the decade following the war (the TG tripled in size and the WI went from just over 300,000 members in 1945 to nearly 500,000 members in 1954) and younger members who joined were keen to take an active part in the running of the two organisations. After the war the TG underwent a palace revolution, when the decision-making process was decentralised and the old guard resigned. Caroline Merz suggests that the TG appealed to women after the war because they missed the companionship and organised activity of the war; the TG offered a forum for them to express their independence and ability to cooperate, and it was a respite from, and support in, coping with the austerity of the early post-war years.[27]

There were a range of issues, of intense interest to women because they impinged on their day-to-day lives, on which the post-war Labour government was developing policies. The WI and TG continued to press their views on various government departments, as they had done during the war. The WI sat on a number of government committees where it could air its views, and provide information. It thus provided a public forum in which women could both express their views and interests on political issues, and pursue their collective leisure interests. After the war the WI continued to play an advisory role to the Ministry of Health, and it was also represented on the Ministry of Education's Advisory Council. In 1946 it submitted evidence to the Ministry of Health on rural housing needs. In the same year it unsuccessfully pressed for changes in the National Insurance Bill so that married women would not have been financially dependent on their husbands. Throughout 1946 the WI busied itself collecting and presenting its views on a range of subjects from the opening hours of shops to electricity charges. In the late 1940s the WI pursued a wide range of interests and continued to press its opinions on government.[28] While expressing views is not the same as having them acted upon, and there are examples of government ignoring the WI's input – for instance, over the National Insurance Bill – the fact that women also came together in the WI to socialise meant that its attractiveness to women was not undermined when it failed to secure changes in government policies.

While women joined the WI and TG through local networks, not through their paid work, certain issues of paid work did arouse members' interest, in

---

27. Caroline Merz, *After the Vote: The Story of the National Union of Townswomen's Guilds in the Year of its Diamond Jubilee* (1988), p. 32.
28. WI, *Annual Report*, 1946, 1947, 1948, 1949, 1950.

particular that of equal pay for equal work. The concern shown for this issue by women's organisations has been lost on those historians who have noticed the emphases in women's magazines and the media portrayal of women more than their actual activities. Indeed, the NCW complained that the press failed to provide much coverage of women's campaigns, including demonstrations for equal pay. This lack of media interest in the issue of equal pay made it easier for governments to shunt the issue off into a political siding.

A further misleading image of women's lack of commitment to political issues was created by women's organisations, such as the WI and TG, themselves. Although flourishing, taking up a whole range of political issues, and being involved with government departments, the WI in particular claimed to be apolitical; what it actually meant was that the organisation did not support a political party. Within the TG some Guilds studied party politics, despite some members' misgivings, on the grounds that they had fought for democracy, and the democratic method in Britain was through Parliament and the party system: if an appreciable number of women refused to shoulder their responsibilities there would be apathy and the path made easy for dictatorship and fascism. *The Townswoman* called on women to join political parties and to work for them.[29]

In 1951 the Festival of Britain provided women's organisations with the opportunity to display their craft, musical and drama skills to a wide audience. The women arranged a variety of events, including exhibitions and performances.[30] The sense of a cultural community which was central to women's organisations was also at the heart of the Festival, so that the local group culture became an explicit part of the celebration of British culture as a whole.

The wide range of interests displayed by the TG and WI can also be detected in the concerns shown by other women's groups represented through the NCW, such as cruelty to children, housing, the law and prostitution, children and the cinema, married women in industry and, above all, equal pay.[31]

Anglo–German relations

One new area into which both the TG and WI branched was that of closer contact with German women. Indeed, the Control Commission for Germany

---

29. *The Townswoman*, 9 and 13 June 1946.
30. For example see NUTG *Annual Report*, 1951.
31. National Council of Women *Annual Report*, 1948.

(CCG), which was engaged in a halting policy of German re-education, focusing on women, held up the WI as a model of democratic citizenship which German women should imitate. The WI was not particularly enthusiastic about Anglo–German cooperation, for though it cherished its international links, these tended to be with countries of the empire.[32] The WI responded to the Foreign Office's call for help in the re-education process, although it may have been keen to do so because there was a certain cachet in being asked to assist such an august body. In 1946 and 1948, at the Foreign Office's request, the WI sent members to Germany to give talks to German women. In 1949 two WI members toured Schleswig Holstein and Hanover, meeting members of the *Landfrauenverein* and, in the autumn, running two sessions at the trizonal conference of *Landfrauenverein*. Another WI member toured Westphalia. Also, at the Foreign Office's request, the WI organised educational tours to Britain for members of the *Landfrauenverein*.[33]

The TG, in contrast to the WI, took the initiative in establishing links with German women. At home it constantly stressed the theme of education for citizenship, and its stated aims were 'to encourage the education of women in order that they, as citizens, might make their best contribution to the common good, and to provide a common meeting ground for women irrespective of creed or party, for their wider education, including social intercourse'. Such aims made the TG a particularly appropriate channel for Foreign Office work with German women.

Late in 1945 the TG met with CCG officials to discuss ways in which German women might have their interest in the responsibilities of citizenship aroused. Six months later, one WI representative, Helena Deneke, and one TG representative, Betty Norris, were chosen to undertake a survey for the CCG of women in Germany. Their visit lasted five weeks and a version of their report to the CCG was published. They stressed the important role women would have to play in rebuilding a democratic Germany, but they also drew attention to the appalling physical conditions and material deprivation which fell most heavily on women. Only when living conditions improved, the two women argued, could a democracy be firmly established. They believed that, despite the distractions of day-to-day living, German women were interested in playing an active role as citizens, and international contacts would help them to do this. British women's organisations could act as a model for German ones. During the course of 1947 the TG

32. WI, *Annual Report*, 1946, p. 10.
33. WI, *Annual Report*, 1946, p. 10; WI, *Annual Report*, 1948, p. 10; WI, *Annual Report*, 1949, p. 15; WI, *Annual Report*, 1950, p. 16.

also briefed British women, such as Lady Doris Blacker, Violet Markham and Jean Rowntree, before they went out to Germany, on the way TG members educated themselves in democracy and the possible application of TG methods to the German situation. TG women also went to Germany on speaking tours. Members of the TG sent reading material, such as weekly magazines, as well as material for make-and-mend groups. Some Guilds formed links with German women's organisations; it was hoped that this would encourage the German women to run their groups on democratic lines.[34]

The TG also organised visits of German women to the UK. The Guild's links with Germany were viewed in terms of what the Germans could gain from the British. So, for instance, the isolation of German women after 1933 was emphasised, along with their desire to establish contact with the intellectual life of other countries. There was a constant emphasis on what German women were learning from the British, but no suggestion that British women might have something to gain from links with German women.[35] By 1948 many TG members were in contact with individual German women. By the beginning of the 1950s the enthusiasm for new initiatives had dried up, but some of the original schemes were built on, so that exchanges were organised not only between TG members and German women, but also between their children.

Other women's organisations, such as the NCW, were also enthusiastic about links with German women, and believed that assisting Germany to become a liberal democracy was of the utmost importance. The NCW organised the first official visit for two German women to the UK, arranging for them to study and visit local government, women police and juvenile courts, adult education, maternity and child welfare centres, the Salvation Army, WVS, Society of Friends and blitzed areas of the UK. The Germans did not return with an idealised vision of the lot of English women. One of them, Dr Agnes von Zahn-Harnack commented, 'We have learned that British women are fighting for their position in the professions and that they have to struggle, against many difficulties in their own homes.' Future visits proved more difficult to arrange because of the problem of accommodation, but once the Bristol branch of the NCW had run a successful visit at the end of 1947, others were quick to follow. Only three years after the war ended, German women were being treated as honoured guests. A group

---

34. TG, *Annual Report*, 1946; TG, *Annual Report*, 1947; TG, *The Townswoman*, March 1947, February 1949; H. Deneke and B. Norris, *The Women of Germany* (National Council of Social Services, January 1947).
35. TG, *The Townswoman*, July 1947, September 1947.

visiting Norwich were given an official reception by the Lord Mayor of Norwich and the best seats at a cathedral service.[36]

The educative value of British policy may be in doubt, but there were positive aspects to the programmes, in particular the forging of international links between women, and the visits of German women to other countries in the years immediately following the end of hostilities. The German women did gain from their visits, but not for the reasons the British intended. The British assumed that if they showed the Germans the British way of doing things, the German women would learn about a system superior to their own. The official feedback which the British received from German women who visited Britain would have reinforced this assumption. Not surprisingly, the formal thanks the women gave the British did not necessarily reflect with their private views.

In October 1947, Frau Frieda Ross – who had been married to the last SPD Mayor of Hamburg before the Nazis took over in 1933, was herself to become a SPD councillor after the war, and was on the governing body of the Hamburger *Frauenring* – visited Bristol for a month at the invitation of the NCW. Nine other women from various parts of the British zone of Germany were also on the trip. After her visit she wrote in a formal report to the CCG, 'All of us found very nice hostesses, for we were staying in private homes. . . . It was very good for us to see how an English family gets through with its rations.' They attended lectures at the university on the English education system which were followed by 'interesting visits to schools and youth clubs'. She went on to outline the activities for the rest of the month, studying local government, health services, various other aspects of social welfare and women's organisations. She drew her report to a close with the observation 'Not once did [we] meet resentment or hate against the Germans, but everybody was well disposed towards us. . . .' The women were grateful for 'being allowed back into the community of nations'.

In fact, Frau Ross had a much more ambivalent attitude towards the visit. For a start, she did not like her first hostess. Second, she was not impressed by the English education system. What the British were showing off as the new way ahead, she had taken for granted before 1933 in Hamburg. Third, she was much preoccupied with the different standards of living in Germany and Britain.[37] She saved her bus fares every day in order to have enough money to take a present home to Germany. She did not feel the British could begin to understand the awful conditions in which the

---

36. NCW, *Women in Council*, October 1946, January 1947, April 1948, June 1947, October 1948.

37. Frau Frieda Ross to Rudolf Ross, 10 October 1947, 16 October 1947.

Germans were living, and at times she did feel ill at ease. In her letters home she wrote of feeling both the 'accused' and a 'beggar'. Yet, the visit was a real break from the struggles of life in Hamburg. Frau Ross was glad to be away on what felt like a holiday. Tucked away in the general report of the women is some indication of the real merits of the visits for the women. On the train through Holland: 'What an event was it to us to be guests in a dining car, where real meals consisting of three courses were served. . . . What experience to travel in a train that had electric light as the night drew on! . . . Of course, you cannot imagine what the look of any English shop window means to us Germans. Even though most of the goods were rationed and therefore not obtainable for us we enjoyed the colourful displays in the windows. . . .' The success of the visits lay less in what the Germans learnt from the British, than in the brief escape from the living conditions in Germany which the scheme afforded a small number of women.[38]

The working-class WCG, like the TG, was especially concerned to promote Anglo–German ties. During the war the Guild was in contact with women in the Free German Movement and in 1944, before such activities received official Foreign Office blessing, the WCG ran a course of lectures for women refugees living in the UK. In 1945 the Guild successfully lobbied the government to allow the women to return home quickly; it was assumed that the WCG would stay in contact with the German and Austrian women, and provide them with support. There was a genuine interest among WCG women in conditions in Germany; they were sympathetic to the plight of German and Austrian women, and, despite rationing and shortages in the UK, sent them food and clothes parcels. Some Guild families 'adopted' a German family, to whom they sent parcels. Frau Riedl, who was organising the WCG in Germany, wrote in a report for 1948 'Good relations are maintained with the Guilds in Switzerland, Sweden, Holland, Belgium and Norway. But the greatest help and encouragement was received from the English Guild. . . . About 2,500 lbs. of used clothing were sent from the English Guilds for distribution to needy cooperative families here. In many other ways English Guildswomen have encouraged and helped us forward. . . .' As well as a concern for the basic necessities of existence, the Guild also saw it as its 'duty to support democratic forces in all countries'. Like the other women's organisations already mentioned, the Guild was involved in Anglo–German exchanges. By 1946 there were

---

38. PRO FO 1049/1245 Visit to Bristol by F. Ross, Hamburg and Report; Frau Frieda Ross to Rudolf Ross, her husband, and to her children, 6, 10, 12 and 16 October 1947. These letters are in the possession of Frau Margaret Ross, Hamburg. I am extremely grateful to her for allowing me to quote from them.

already small women's cooperative groups in Hamburg, Lübeck and Kiel and in November 1946 Emmy Riedl went over to Germany to establish others. As well as women's organisations forging links with German women, others continued the tradition of relief work on the Continent.[39]

Welfare work on the Continent

The experience and motives of women undertaking relief work was varied. Some of the women who worked on the Continent had experience of relief work going back to the First World War and its aftermath. Others had undertaken relief work during the recent war, while women with experience as civil servants or as voluntary workers in women's organisations were also involved. Women worked on the Continent in non-governmental organisations (NGOs), such as the Friends Ambulance Unit, the Girl Guides, Young Women's Christian Association (YWCA) and Save the Children Fund (SCF). SCF continued its earlier work of aiding Europeans in the aftermath of war. It sent relief teams to distribute food and clothing to children in northern and southeast Europe. As well as raising its own money, it was responsible for money raised by the 'Save Europe Now' campaign for, or by, children. In 1946 all five liaison officers in Europe were women. Most welfare work on the Continent was now coordinated by the United Nations Relief and Rehabilitation Administration (UNRRA), in contrast to the post-First World War situation when a series of small *ad hoc* NGO projects were undertaken. Even so, women's grass-root initiatives for relief and welfare work on the Continent emerged independently of grand international organisations such as UNRRA, which was forged by high-level civil servants and politicians operating on the international stage. International organisations were keen to incorporate women, working on the ground in a welfare or administrative capacity, rather than in strategic planning. Very few women held senior posts. The Director-General of UNRRA had ten staff immediately under him, one of whom, Mary Craig McGeachy, was a British woman. Two British representatives, including Kathleen Halpin, OBE, sat on the Committee of Welfare.

A number of factors worked in favour of women's employment in welfare and relief work with UNRRA. UNRRA was a large organisation, set

---

39. WCG, *Women's Cooperative Guild Head Office Bulletin*, November 1945; December 1945; May 1946; October 1946; April 1948; July 1948; January 1949; December 1949; PRO FO 1030/94.

up in a rush and requiring many employees at a time of labour shortages. It was hastily created and had no male culture of custom and practice excluding women. In Britain members of women's services, but not men's services, could be released for work with UNRRA. The nature of the work fitted in with traditional views of women's role in wartime. UNRRA picked out the needs of children and of women, especially mothers in displaced persons, (DP) camps, as requiring attention and for this work women were thought to be particularly appropriate. When UNRAA looked for people with welfare work experience, particularly with children, it inevitably alighted on women.[40]

On paper UNRRA's first priority was to maintain and strengthen family units. For orphans, fostering was thought to be the best solution. Second, UNRRA wanted to establish maternity and infant welfare centres. Where mothers and young women were likely to remain in a temporary community, training courses in child care were to be organised for them. This, it was hoped, would provide personnel for services in the temporary community and also qualify them for services in their own community after they returned. 'Opportunities should be created to awaken and satisfy their natural homemaking instincts.'[41] How far the stated aims were matched by reality is hard to judge.

Audrey Duchesne-Cripps was a welfare officer in a DP camp where she was responsible for youth activities, education, nursery schools, cultural activities and vocational training, as well as requisitioning supplies and improving accommodation. A good deal of Duchesne-Cripps's time was devoted to the needs of unmarried mothers in the camp. Their position was particularly vulnerable because it was often more difficult for them to return home to Poland in the face of disapproving families, and it was also very difficult for them to obtain a place on an emigration scheme. Duchesne-Cripps clearly felt a yawning gulf between herself and the men in the camp, whom she criticised for their 'backward' attitude towards the women, which she put down to their peasant roots. She did, however, sympathise with the women. She

---

40. George Woodbridge, *UNRRA: The History of the United Nations Relief and Rehabilitation Administration* (New York, 1950), p. 236; PRO FO 371/51357; Malcolm Proudfoot, *European Refugees, 1939–1952* (1957), p. 105; UNRRA documents of the sub-committee on welfare (Europe) 1–9, 1944–45; UNRRA document of the sub-committee on welfare for Europe 22 March 1945.

41. UNRRA documents of the sub-committee on welfare (Europe) 1–9, 1944–45 sub-committee on welfare for Europe, 'Social welfare services for mothers, children and young people up to 18 years of age', 8 August 1944, 22 March 1945. 'Special needs of women and girls during repatriation and rehabilitation. A report for the welfare division of the European Regional Office of UNRRA by an International Working Party of social workers, psychiatric social workers, doctors and psychiatrists', June 1945.

noted that the men did not want women on official committees; they would let older women hump heavy loads and perform difficult manual tasks while they sat idly by; and as men were able to find work more easily than the women, women often had to sleep with the men in order to raise their standard of living. She also found the women more altruistic, claiming that the men would not volunteer to do anything which benefited the whole camp, only what was beneficial to themselves.[42]

Doreen Warriner publicised her work and that of UNRRA, and defended the organisation against what she perceived to be American anti-UNRRA propaganda. She demonstrated both a personal commitment, working between 1944 and 1946 as Chief of the Food Supply depot of the UNRRA mission to Yugoslavia, and a broader political commitment to international relief and the building of a new economic order in Eastern Europe. In a Fabian Society tract published in 1946 she defended UNRRA against criticism, fighting a losing battle against it being shut down. She felt that the middle and upper classes of Belgrade complained that UNRRA did not bring them enough supplies because they disliked a system of rationing. Their complaints were fuelled by rumours put about by Americans that UNRRA supplies were going to Russia and to Communists. Warriner argued that UNRRA supplies were of enormous help in aiding recovery and that it was mainly UNRRA food supplies which saved the country from starvation. Until mid-1946 the bulk of supplies were relief goods such as food, clothing and medical supplies. The reconstruction work of UNRRA, providing industrial and agricultural equipment, had hardly begun.

There were already proposals to end UNRRA's work at the end of 1946, against which Warriner railed on the grounds that, if UNRRA closed down, there would be no effective international reconstruction agency. She bitterly criticised the Americans for wanting supplies to cease to the Russian zones of Europe. UNRRA was having to stop work, she argued, because it was too genuinely international: it had directed supplies to those countries which needed them most, not to countries where British and American interests were greatest. She asked the Labour Party to arrange mutual study and friendship exchanges, and she called on the government to take steps to set up an organisation which could continue the work of UNRRA, and to develop trade with Yugoslavia. One of her pleas was answered to some extent by the setting up of the International Relief Organisation. She later defended the new Eastern Europe. In 1950 she wrote that Eastern Europe had a sense of social responsibility, and that the singlemindedness of the

---

42. Audrey Duchesne-Cripps, The Mental Outlook of the Displaced Persons as seen through Welfare Work in Displaced Persons' Camps (Cambridge, 1955).

communist ethos gave it a certain prestige. It was setting new standards, and people did not feel regimented so much as perpetually activated.[43]

The women who chose to undertake relief work on the Continent did so for a variety of reasons, but all of them who have left a record of their experiences gave a sense of having personally benefited from the experience. This is in contrast to those women engaged in re-education work with German women, who at no point give a sense that they were gaining anything from the experience. Some women, such as Ruth Dalton and Francesca Wilson, expressed a desire to escape from Britain after six years of war, and to undertake work where they could feel a sense of personal achievement. A number of the women later expressed a particular affinity with the women they met abroad. Wilson felt that, as a woman, she had something to offer, and wrote that women were better suited to the work than men; welfare work was not a clear-cut job, but messy, temporary and clamorous, and women were less likely to succumb to the temptations of life in a conquered country. Not surprisingly, given her long experience of welfare work on the Continent, she was conscious of a tradition of women's relief work there. For Doreen Warriner her work in Eastern Europe was an extension of her professional interest in Eastern Europe, and of her political activities.

While the welfare work of women after the First World War was a direct challenge to governments, this aspect was rare after the Second World War. International efforts to reconstruct Europe after the war were, in part, depoliticised by the welfare work of UNRRA, whereas the post-First World War welfare work was an explicit challenge to the victorious, powerful nations. In the 1940s the women appear to have felt a strong empathy with the women with whom they worked in DP camps. Whereas after the First World War the bond was often that of a common middle class, after the Second World War the empathy was more closely based on a feeling of women's shared interests, and for middle-class relief workers this overcame the gulf which existed between British women working with DPs from an East European peasant background.[44]

Relief was now on a broader scale, with international support and a more formal organisation than after the First World War. Yet, the main relief work organised by UNRRA took place in DP camps rather than in the wider community, which was also suffering insecurity, poverty, overcrowding and shortages. The British, however, were not unaware of, and some not unsympathetic to, the needs of the wider German community.

---

43. Doreen Warriner, *Yugoslavia Rebuilds* (1946), pp. 9, 21–4; Doreen Warriner, *Revolution in Eastern Europe* (1950), p. vii.
44. F. Wilson, *Aftermath* (West Drayton, 1947), p. 172.

The 'Save Europe Now' campaign, launched in the autumn of 1945 was spearheaded by Victor Gollancz, the Jewish publisher, and he, more than anyone, exposed the abysmal housing, low standard of living and starvation rations of Germans. His aims were to prevent further expulsions of Germans from Eastern Europe and to avert starvation.[45] His message reached a cross-section of British society as he wrote about conditions in Germany for both the tabloids and quality papers.

Eleanor Rathbone provided a prominent British woman's voice on what was perceived to be primarily a 'woman's problem'. In October 1945 she moved a motion in the House of Commons, with all-party support, expressing concern about conditions in Europe. Rathbone tried to get the food allocations to Germans increased. On 20 August she had already spoken about the food situation and urged that more generous resources should be made available to UNRRA. On 16 November she again spoke on the subject in the House of Commons.[46]

Comparisons

Amid the devastation of Germany at the end of the war, there were superficial signs of changes in gender relations: women greatly outnumbered men, many of whom were either dead or still incarcerated in prisoner of war camps; women had to be independent of men and resourceful to survive. Constraints on women's continued independence, however, quickly emerged. The day-to-day struggle for existence took up most of women's energies and meant that it was virtually impossible for a critique of gender relations to emerge or for new patterns to establish themselves. This was partly due to the fact that the occupying powers banned women's groups which were formed immediately the war ended, and also because, when men did return home old patterns of gender relations rapidly re-emerged. There was no conscious challenge to gender relations, they merely shifted briefly by default, and the shift back again was, on the whole, regarded as unproblematic.

Just over one quarter of a million German women were in paid work at the end of the war, a lower percentage than before the war. Paid work offered women few attractions as there was almost nothing in the shops and markets, and time was better spent looking after the family. Those jobs

---

45. Ruth Edwards, *Victor Gollancz: A Biography* (1987), p. 411.
46. Mary Stocks, *Eleanor Rathbone: A Biography* (1949), pp. 319–20.

which were available were on the whole unattractive, and, with the exception of the rubble workers, the icon of immediate post-war German woman, they were in traditional 'female' occupations. Welfare policy privileged the traditional family with a clear sexual division of labour. Housing allocation prioritised 'traditional' families; women's benefits were linked to their roles as wives and mothers; school hours were predicated on the assumption that mothers were at home, and in the 1950s the family was perceived, as in the USA, as the bulwark against communism. In the German Democratic Republic (GDR) – East Germany – women played a more public role in the labour market and social policies operated to support women in paid work, but women in the GDR were no closer to the hub of policy making than their counterparts in the Federal Republic of Germany (FRG), West Germany. There were actually fewer women in the Bundestag (Parliament) than during the 1920s Weimar Republic. In 1949, 7 per cent of Bundestag members were women, a figure which, until the late 1980s, remained fairly constant.[47]

The end of the war appeared auspicious for Italian women: they were granted the vote and the 1947 constitution enshrined the principle of equality of all citizens and the removal of barriers to that equality. Although the paperwork was in place, the implementation of this principle remained a long way off. In 1946 20 women were elected to the Constituent Assembly, charged with drawing up a new constitution; in 1948 8 per cent of parliamentary deputies were women, but this figure fell to 6 per cent in 1953 and continued to fall thereafter. Women had been granted the vote by an unelected resistance government when there was no properly constituted Parliament and when much of Italy was still under the domination of the Nazis. There was little debate and no major campaign around women's enfranchisement, which has subsequently been seen as a weakness, as the vote was regarded as a gift rather than a right actively won by women. Women's enfranchisement was not the result of a commitment to women's rights or gender equality so much as a party political move by the Communists and Christian Democrats to try to secure women's support; the Christian Democrats made a point of emphasising women's duty to vote to defend the family and destroy communism.[48]

---

47. For German women see Ute Frevert, *Women in German History: From Bourgeois Emancipation to Sexual Liberation* (Oxford, 1989), pp. 256–65; Ilona Ostner, 'Slow motion: women, work and the family in Germany', in Jane Lewis, ed., *Women and Social Policies in Europe: Work, Family and the State* (Aldershot, 1993), pp. 96–106.

48. For those who do not read Italian see the review essay by Perry Willson, 'Women, war and the vote: gender and politics in Italy, 1940–46', *Women's History Review* 7 (1998), pp. 617–23.

There were two huge problems for women attempting to join together to campaign over issues of common concern. First, there was the north–south divide and, in part related to this, there was a Catholic, Christian, right wing versus left-wing Communist split in politics. In the south, custom and tradition meant that women were in practice excluded from politics. In the north, women could more easily organise and campaign, but in areas dominated by the Catholic Church, women's life was seen as revolving around their families; this virtually excluded an independent role in the public sphere. On the other side of the political spectrum, women's role was not seen as substantially different. Although the Communists encouraged women to organise and take an active part in the UDI (closely aligned with the Communist Party), the view of women's central place being in the family was not challenged. So, even when and where women did organise, as in the Turin bread riots after the war, there was little chance of them developing a gendered critique of society, or of gaining a role in policy making. Their power in the workplace, moreover, actually contracted after the war as the number of women in the paid workforce decreased.[49]

In France the immediate post-war years began hopefully as women expected that their role in the resistance movements would strengthen their position in society. In 1945, 33 women out of 545 delegates were elected to the first National Constituent Assembly, a higher proportion than women in the British Parliament. By the time the second National Constituent Assembly was elected in 1946 the number of women had fallen to 30. In the first National Assembly elected in 1946 there were 39 women out of 618 deputes. The Assembly elected two women Vice-Presidents and a woman Secretary. In the same year, 1946, women achieved 21 seats out of 31 in the Senate. Two out of the four Vice-Presidents were women. In June 1946 Andrée Viennot became the first post-war member of a government as Under-Secretary of State for Youth and Sport. The increased political activity of women then nose-dived. After 1946 the number of women in the National Assembly fell and their influence was minimal. As in Italy, so in France, the new constitution enshrined equal rights, but social policies, drawn up without any input from women, placed them at a disadvantage. One's role in the labour market determined one's social rights and this inevitably disadvantaged women, who had far lower participation rates in the paid labour force. The 1939 *Code de Famille* continued in operation,

---

49. See, for instance, Franca Bimbi, 'Gender, "Gift relationship" and the welfare state cultures in Italy', in Jane Lewis, ed., *Women and Social Policies in Europe*; Judith Adler Hellman, *Journeys Among Women* (Cambridge, 1987), pp. 32–9, 60–1, 114–17, 142–3, 168–9.

which underlined the link between a woman's rights and her role as a mother.[50]

The picture in the USA, as in Britain, was a mixed one. On the one hand, the family was portrayed as a bulwark against communism, and women's most important role within the family was that of wife and mother. The traditional picture of post-war American woman, as white, middle-class and living in the suburbs surrounded by a growing array of white goods, made possible by a husband bringing in a salary which could support this upward and outward mobility is a partial one. Black women had no such ease of lifestyle. Many women, moreover, did pursue more than domestic bliss as they joined voluntary groups, and supported state and voluntary welfare at home and the work of the United Nations abroad.[51]

In the 1940s women's organisations tried to get women into positions of power, largely unsuccessfully, by drawing up lists of possible women for posts and pressing their case. More successful was India Edwards, head of the Women's Division of the Democratic National Committee, who campaigned for Truman in 1948 and enjoyed the President's confidence. She made out strong cases for particular women to be appointed when Truman was filling senior posts. Truman did appoint a few women to high office: Eugenie Anderson became the first woman diplomatic appointment at ambassadorial level; Georgia Neese Clark became Treasurer of the USA, Anna Rosenberg an Assistant Secretary of Defense and Frieda Hennock joined the Federal Communications Commission. Truman, however, refused to nominate a woman to the Supreme Court or to have a woman in his Cabinet. In 1952, when Eisenhower became President, women members of the Republican Party pressed for women to be appointed to the Cabinet. Eisenhower appointed one woman, Oveta Culp Hobby, as Secretary of Health, Education and Welfare. The President rewarded Katherine Howard who had campaigned for him with a senior post in the Civil Defense Administration and he appointed the first woman to the Whitehouse staff. Overall, women gained very few posts under either Truman or Eisenhower.[52]

In Australia the experiences of women varied according to their ethnic background, with newly arrived immigrant women more likely to take up

50. Laure Adler, *Les Femmes Politiques* (Paris, 1993), pp. 139–44; Linda Hantrais, 'Women, Work and Welfare in France', in Jane Lewis, ed., *Women and Social Policies in Europe*, pp. 116–20.

51. Rosalind Rosenberg, *Divided Lives: American Women in the Twentieth Century* (Harmondsworth, 1993), pp. 141–52; Susan Lynn, 'Gender and post World War II progressive politics: a bridge to social activism in the 1960s USA', *Gender and History* 4 (1992), pp. 215–18.

52. Susan M. Hartmann, *From Margin to Mainstream: American Women and Politics Since 1960* (Philadelphia, 1989), pp. 13–14.

paid employment than longer-established ones. The latter, if they did work, were more likely than the newcomers to hold professional, clerical or sales posts. Many women lost their jobs at the end of the war as government gave Service personnel priority in the labour market, and where women and men did continue to work alongside each other, women received roughly 75 per cent of the male rate. The 1940s social security system, as in so many other countries, operated on the assumption that women were dependent on male breadwinners, and were entitled to benefits accordingly. While women's influence over social policy developments were strictly circumscribed, middle-class women took the initiative in establishing nursery schools for their children, along the lines of those provided for the children of women workers in the war. Women politicians fared badly, with the political parties unenthusiastic about selecting women candidates, especially for the lower house. Women MPs were typically Anglo-Celtic, middle-aged with grown-up children and husbands who supported them financially. The parties rewarded a few long-serving women party activists with seats in the upper house.[53]

As in the past, Australian women's organisations displayed an interest in women's groups abroad and this was boosted by first-hand accounts as women who had been abroad during the war returned home. Interest in Europeans took a new turn, however, as women in various organisations displayed an especial concern with the type of Europeans who might wish to emigrate to Australia, wanting only those who could 'integrate' into Australian society.

Conclusions

During the Second World War, politically active women had devoted much energy to fighting women's inequality in the public sphere. They continued to express concern over the welfare of women, but the false dawn of the early post-war years – with full employment and a more inclusive state welfare system – temporarily blinded many to the continuing pattern of gendered poverty and inequalities within families. The domestic ideology was still adhered to by most women but, whereas before the Second World War, politically active women had tried to improve the conditions in which

---

53. Cora Baldock and Bettina Cass, *Women, Social Welfare and the State* (1983); Marian Sawer and Marian Simms, *A Woman's Place: Women and Politics in Australia* (St Leonards, NSW, 1993), p. 127.

women performed their domestic role, in the post-war years these efforts dwindled. Although it is always hard to prove a negative, there is little to suggest that, had women continued their earlier campaigning priorities, success would have come any more easily.

There were strong continuities from the war to early post-war years. In many countries women were absent from the centre of power where governmental policy decisions were taken, despite their organisation and pressure. In Britain an enormous gulf existed between the interests and activities of women's groups and the path to power. Government continued to use women's organisations, so giving the false impression that women's views were important. Governments' concept of social welfare remained partial and far narrower than that of many women. There were occasions when women's long-standing policies were taken up and used by governments, such as family allowances and the formal coordination of relief work on the Continent after the war. In this, as in other areas of welfare, women's voices were marginal and women's interests only partially served.

If women are to dislodge engrained culture they need to be in positions to take decisions over major government policies. It is important for women to break down isolation, to attack existing cultures in terms of attitudes and beliefs, as well as to reform structures; to do this women need to be part of an effective network within (not parallel with) the policy-making process. Hierarchies impede the distribution of power, and for this reason hinder the incorporation of groups which are underrepresented. Pioneers need to encourage others to follow in their path, and help to create the structures in which any particular individual is dispensable. The mere presence of women will not in itself advance other women.

If women, or any other group, are being used by governments, they must ensure that there is something in it quite explicitly for them, and that they extract a quid pro quo for their cooperation. Participation is not the same as power. Overall improvements should not distract from patterns of inequality. If governments occasionally latch onto policies advocated by some women, this will not create a less gendered society. Unless feminist projects are at the centre of government strategy, policies affecting women will not work to their advantage.

SELECT BIBLIOGRAPHY

Unpublished sources are cited in the notes.
The following is a select list of published works.

Contemporary published sources

Vera Douie, *The Lesser Half: A Survey of the Laws, Regulations and Practices Introduced During the Present War Which Embody Discrimination Against Women* (1943).
Vera Douie, *Daughters of Britain* (1949).
Hansard: House of Commons debates.
Winifred Holtby, *Women* (1934).
Margaret Llewelyn Davies, ed., *Maternity: Letters From Working-Women* (1978). First published 1915.
Margaret McMillan, *The Nursery School* (1930).
Hilda Martindale, *Women Servants of the State, 1870–1938: A History of Women in the Civil Service* (1938).
Margery Spring Rice, ed., *Working-Class Wives* (1981). First published 1939.

Reports and publications of: National Council of Women, Open Door Council, Townswomen's Guild, Women's Co-operative Guild, Women's Group on Public Welfare, Women's Institute, Women's Voluntary Service, Women in Council.

Autobiographies and biographies

Margaret Bondfield, *A Life's Work* (1950).
Barbara Castle, *Fighting All The Way* (1993).
Thelma Cazalet-Keir, *From The Wings* (1967).
Mary Agnes Hamilton, *Mary Macarthur: A Biographical Sketch* (1925).
Helen Jones, ed., *Duty and Citizenship: The Correspondence and Political Papers of Violet Markham, 1896–1953* (1994).
Jennie Lee, *The Great Journey: A Volume of Autobiography, 1904–45* (1963).
Jennie Lee, *My Life With Nye* (1980).

Jill Liddington, *The Life and Times of a Respectable Rebel: Selina Cooper, 1864–1946* (1984).

Jean Mann, *Woman in Parliament* (1962).

Leah Manning, *A Life for Education: An Autobiography* (1970).

Alix Meynell, *Public Servant, Private Woman: An Autobiography* (1988).

Edith Picton-Turbervill, *Life is Good: An Autobiography* (1939).

Eleanor Roosevelt, *The Autobiography of Eleanor Roosevelt* (1962).

Mary Soames, *Clementine Churchill* (Harmondsworth, 1979).

Carolyn Steedman, *Childhood, Culture and Class in Britain: Margaret McMillan, 1860–1931* (1990).

Mary Stocks, *Eleanor Rathbone: A Biography* (1949).

Edith Summerskill, *A Woman's World* (1967).

Christopher Sykes, *Nancy: The Life of Nancy Astor* (1979). First published 1972.

Lis Whitelaw, *The Life and Times of Cicely Hamilton* (1990).

Historical studies

Books

Johanna Alberti, *Beyond Suffrage: Feminists in War and Peace, 1914–1928* (1989).

Olive Banks, *The Politics of British Feminism, 1918–1970* (Aldershot, 1993).

Robert Dingwall, Anne Marie Rafferty and Charles Webster, *An Introduction to the Social History of Nursing* (1988).

Ute Frevert, *Women in German History: From Bourgeois Emancipation to Sexual Liberation* (Oxford, 1989).

Pamela Graves, *Labour Women: Women in British Working-Class Politics, 1918–1939* (Cambridge, 1994).

Victoria de Grazia, *How Fascism Ruled Women: Italy, 1922–45* (Berkeley, 1992).

Patricia Grimshaw, Marilyn Lake, Ann McGrath and Marian Quartly, *Creating a Nation, 1788–1990* (Ringwood, Victoria, 1994).

Felicity Hunt, *Gender and Policy in English Education: Schooling for Girls, 1902–1944* (Hemel Hempstead, 1991).

Susan Kingsley Kent, *Making Peace: The Reconstruction of Gender in Interwar Britain* (Princeton, New Jersey, 1993).

Seth Koven and Sonya Michel (eds), *Mothers of a New World: Maternalist Politics and the Origins of Welfare States* (1993).

Cheryl Law, *Suffrage and Power: The Women's Movement, 1918–1928* (1997).

John Macnicol, *The Movement for Family Allowances, 1918–45* (1980).

Alison Oram, *Women Teachers and Feminist Politics, 1900–1939* (1996).

Susan Pedersen, *Family, Dependence, and the Origins of the Welfare State: Britain and France, 1914–1945* (Cambridge, 1993).

Martin Pugh, *Women and the Women's Movement in Britain, 1914–1959* (1992).

Margaret Randolph Higonnet, Jane Jenson, Sonya Michel and Margaret Collins Weitz, eds, *Behind the Lines: Gender and the Two World Wars* (1987).

Sîan Reynolds, *France between the Wars: Gender and Politics* (1996).

Rosalind Rosenberg, *Divided Lives: American Women in the Twentieth Century* (Harmondsworth, 1993).

Sheila Rowbotham, *A Century of Women* (1997).

Marian Sawer and Marian Simms, *A Woman's Place: Women and Politics in Australia* (St Leonards, NSW, 1993).

Theda Skocpol, *Protecting Soldiers and Mothers: The Political Origins of Social Policy in the USA* (1992).

Harold Smith, ed., *British Feminism in the Twentieth Century* (1990).

Ronald G. Walton, *Women in Social Work* (1975).

Susan Ware, *Beyond Suffrage: Women and the New Deal* (1989).

Angela Woollacott, *On Her Their Lives Depend: Munition Workers in the Great War* (Berkeley and Los Angeles CA, 1994).

Articles

Brian Harrison, 'Women in a man's house: the women MPs, 1919–45', *Historical Journal*, 29, 1986.

Jane Lewis, 'Gender, the family and women's agency in the building of "welfare states": the British case', *Social History*, 19, 1994.

Margaret Mitchell, 'The effect of unemployment on the social condition of women and children in the 1930s', *History Workshop Journal*, 19, 1985.

Susan Pedersen, 'Gender, welfare and citizenship in Britain during the Great War', *American Historical Review*, 95, 1990.

Perry Willson, 'Women, war and the vote: gender and politics in Italy, 1940–1946', *Women's History Review*, 7, 1998.

INDEX